# PRIVATE SHAW *and* PUBLIC SHAW

# SAINT JOAN

*to Shaw from Shaw*
*to replace many stolen copies until*
*this, too, is stolen*
                                    7th Feb. 1934.

G.B.S. gave me first a copy of the acting version of S. Joan. It was borrowed from me by an R.T.C. reader, who lent it to another and he to a third. So it disappeared.

Then G.B.S. sent me another Joan, like this, inscribed "To Pte. Shaw from Public Shaw". This was one of my chief joys at Clouds Hill: but in 1932 it also vanished.

Hence this third copy, with its pessimistic inscription.

                                              T.E.S.

2.34.

(Top) Inscription by G.B.S. in T. E. Lawrence's copy of SAINT JOAN. (Bottom) Explanatory note by T. E. Lawrence added on the verso. (*Courtesy of the Humanities Research Center, University of Texas*)

# PRIVATE SHAW
*and*
# PUBLIC SHAW

*a dual portrait of*
*Lawrence of Arabia and G. B. S.*

*by* STANLEY WEINTRAUB

GEORGE BRAZILLER          *New York, 1963*

*To Rodelle, my collaborator and wife*

"*Fame is the focus of all the misunderstandings which gather about a great name.*"
                                        *Rilke*

# Contents

# Illustrations

# Foreword

In the still-to-be-written definitive biographies of Bernard
Shaw and T. E. Lawrence, there are likely to be chapters in
each in which the other man is co-hero. Had Shaw, for
instance, known that Lawrence had written to Sir Edward
Elgar that knowing G.B.S. was "a great adventure," he
would probably have declared the feeling mutual. This
study attempts the recounting of the dozen years in which
Bernard Shaw and T. E. Lawrence—two of the most fascinating literary personalities of our time—were engaged
in the adventure of their improbable friendship.

Of course, by no means everything in the life that each
"Shaw" lived affected the other. Only enough of those
aspects which are needed to render "Public Shaw" and
Private Shaw comprehensible in their friendship appears in
these pages. Both men led active, many-sided lives before
the story they share opens. In 1922 the younger man was
thirty-four, and already beyond the "Lawrence of Arabia"
phase for which he is best known. In the same year G.B.S.,
at sixty-six, was one of the major public figures of his time,
at the crest of a playwriting career which had begun before
Lawrence was born. Even so, G.B.S. was to outlive the
younger man by a decade and a half, continuing his produc-
tive career into 1950. We are concerned, then, with an area
almost entirely outside the boundaries of many of the controversies connected with the Lawrence of Arabia "myth";

and beyond, by more than a generation, the creation of the "G.B.S." image that so effectively concealed the Shavian inner man.

It is of no consequence here how vital to the winning of the First World War the contribution in Arabia of Lieutenant-Colonel Thomas Edward Lawrence was, nor whether his reports of his military or diplomatic or personal activities then—or recounted later—were fact, hyperbole, or fantasy. Nor is it of consequence here how effective or how influential Lawrence's services were at the Paris Peace Conference of 1919, or as Churchill's aide at the Colonial Office in the early twenties. Other than where background requires, *Private Shaw and Public Shaw* begins when Bernard Shaw and T. E. Lawrence first meet, and concludes when the end of a life prevents us from discovering what might have been the beginning of a new turn in their relationship.

The individuals and institutions making this work possible have been many, and I am grateful for all their help, whatever its scope, whether or not their generosity has found acknowledgment in this brief catalogue of indebtedness. The Pennsylvania State University's Central Fund for Research provided essential financial aid and encouragement. The staff of the University's Pattee Library was generous in its help. I am particularly grateful, too, to the New York Public Library, the Humanities Research Center of the University of Texas, the University of North Carolina Library, the University of Pennsylvania Library, the Library of Congress, the University of Virginia Library, the Houghton and Widener Libraries at Harvard University, the Bodleian Library at Oxford, the Library of the Air Ministry and the British Museum.

Many persons were asked for help, and most of them generously responded with documentary or background information, or other requested assistance, without which this book could not have been completed. Among them have been the late Mr. Richard Aldington, Viscountess Nancy Astor, Professor F. W. Bateson, Mr. Eric Batson, Mr. La-Fayette L. Butler, the late Sir Sydney Cockerell, Mr. Maurice Collis, Mr. Tom English, Mr. E. M. Forster, Mr. David Garnett, Dr. John Gordan, Mr. Robert Graves, Dr. Felix Grendon, Mr. Christopher Hassall, Dr. Archibald Henderson, Mr. David M. Holtzmann, Mr. Walter Hudd, the late Sir Barry Jackson, Mr. William Jackson, the late Augustus John, Mr. Francis Kettaneh, Mr. Bayard L. Kilgour, Jr., Professor Dan H. Laurence, Professor A. W. Lawrence, Captain (Retired) B. H. Liddell Hart, Mr. Lawrence London, Mrs. Marian Maury, Mrs. Georgina Musters, Miss Blanche Patch, Mr. Robert Phelps, Dr. Harry H. Ransom, Mr. Terence Rattigan, Dr. Warren Roberts, Mr. Ben C. Rosset, Mr. Walter L. Royall, Professor E. E. Stokes, Jr., Miss Betsy Stout, Miss Dorothy Walker.

Hundreds of publications and thousands of unpublished manuscripts and documents on both sides of the Atlantic were consulted in preparation of *Private Shaw and Public Shaw*. To cite every reference to them would submerge the reader in a sea of footnotes. Many credits appear in the body of the text, and many others in end-notes. Often citations have been dispensed with where the references are to obvious and easily obtainable publications. A list of these works appears as a bibliography. A reference to "Letters" in the text cites the invaluable *Letters of T. E. Lawrence* (London and New York, 1938), edited by David Garnett. Other references to letters of T. E. Lawrence generally refer to the correspondence with the Shaws bound into two volumes and classified as British Museum Additional Manuscripts 45903 and 45904. The most important of these references are identified in end-notes. Valuable also were other British Museum holdings, including letters by G.B.S. and Charlotte Shaw to Lawrence, and the manuscripts of *The*

*Mint* and *The Odyssey*, the latter two volumes originally given to Charlotte Shaw and transferred by G.B.S. after her death to the British Museum. Many references to statements by friends and acquaintances of Lawrence refer to the first edition of *T. E. Lawrence by His Friends* (London, 1938), a valuable biographical document edited by A. W. Lawrence. Now available, and of great value as source material, is a selection from correspondence T.E. received, *Letters to T. E. Lawrence*, also edited by A. W. Lawrence (London, 1962). The Shavian part of the correspondence, however (there are no letters from Mrs. Shaw), was examined by the author prior to its publication in Professor Lawrence's volume, and references to these letters, which in some cases were first printed in part elsewhere, may refer to the earlier sources, or to the manuscripts.

Where uncredited, suppositions and critical comments are my own. Also my own are the inevitable errors and omissions.

For permission to use copyright material I am grateful to the Society of Authors and the Public Trustee (Estate of George Bernard Shaw), the Trustees of the Estate of Mrs. Bernard Shaw, A. W. Lawrence and the T. E. Lawrence Trustees, and G. P. Putnam's Sons. For use of other material I am indebted to many of the individuals and institutions previously enumerated.

STANLEY WEINTRAUB
*University Park, Pennsylvania*

PRIVATE SHAW *and* PUBLIC SHAW

Portrait of G. B. Shaw, by Augustus John. (*Courtesy of Fitzwilliam Museum, Cambridge, England*)

*"As for me who write, I pray that nothing be looked for in this book but the seeing of a hungry man and the telling of a most weary man; for the rest the sun made me an Arab, but never warped me to Orientalism."*

—Doughty

# ONE

*1922-1923*

It was said of T. E. Shaw that he was always stepping back into the limelight—a limelight in which he was better known as Lawrence of Arabia. No such accusation could have been made of his elderly friend Bernard Shaw, whose G.B.S. image is one of the twentieth century's triumphs of calculated self-advertisement. It was by chance that these two outwardly dissimilar men were drawn together. By 1922, after Lowell Thomas's illustrated lecture "With Allenby in Palestine and Lawrence in Arabia" had played a season at the Royal Opera House in Covent Garden, Queen's Hall and Albert Hall, G.B.S. could not have helped hearing of the young man. The melodramatic travelogue had transformed T. E. Lawrence—a young archeologist just a few years out of Oxford when the First

World War began, and a thirty-year-old colonel when the war ended—into a modern legend.

Only a few sentences of the familiar tale need be repeated here—about Lawrence's stirring up of Arab nationalism as a weapon against the Turks, and the creation of a "second front" in the Turkish rear; the exploitation by press and publicists not so much of the exotic events as of the Lawrence personality, symbolized by the Bedouin garb, the belt adorned by the short, curved sword of a Prince of Mecca. The young man at this time was unsure whether to stride into the limelight or avoid as much of it as he could. He had already abetted the war correspondent's lecture by posing in Arab dress for him in 1917, and thereby found himself from the start an accomplice in creating the popular image of the "uncrowned king of Arabia."

Incongruously, he was then living a quiet life at Oxford and in London as a Research Fellow of All Souls College, working on his memoir of the Arabian war. Lowell Thomas's platform magic (based in large part on information supplied by the subject in 1919) drew Lawrence to the lecture hall to see his fabled self, and he returned again and again, fascinated by the extravagant perspective of himself gained through the excitement of hero-hungry audiences eager for romance after the years of grim wartime hysteria. Even so, he refused to use his war services or postwar fame for quick personal gain, remaining on his All Souls fellowship until persuaded by Winston Churchill early in 1921 to join the Colonial Office as adviser on Arab affairs. Though he had some success, he felt awkward in the role; and not even Churchill's hints of greater power and responsibilities for him in future assignments could appease his desire to quit.

In London on March 25, 1922, Lawrence (still drawing

his £1200 a year Colonial Office salary) met Sydney
Cockerell for a one o'clock luncheon at the Carlton Hotel.
Cockerell, curator of the Fitzwilliam Museum at Cambridge, had common cause with Lawrence—devising a way
to extend financial aid to the venerable Charles Doughty,
to whom and to whose *Travels in Arabia Deserta* both
were devoted. After they had agreed upon a scheme calculated not to injure Doughty's pride, their conversation
turned to other subjects, from politics to typography.
Suddenly Cockerell noticed that it was already 2:40, and
remembered aloud that he had to go on to Adelphi Terrace to Bernard Shaw's flat to remove an Augustus John
portrait of G.B.S. After many appeals to Shaw, including
the reminder that a similar John portrait hung in his country home at Ayot St. Lawrence, Cockerell had been offered
the Adelphi Terrace painting for the Fitzwilliam (where
it now hangs next to the John portrait of Thomas Hardy,
another elderly literary friend Lawrence was to make).

Lawrence was excited by the reference to G.B.S. He
expressed admiration for Shaw's work, but was interrupted
by Cockerell, who suggested that the two of them go to
Adelphi Terrace to cart away the portrait. Lawrence
backed away. He made a point, he confessed, of avoiding
his heroes, for fear that they would turn out to be disap-
pointing in the flesh. It was a Saturday afternoon, Cockerell pointed out; the Shaws by then would have gone
off to Ayot St. Lawrence for their customary long week-
end, which usually lasted until the following Wednesday.
Since this took care of the only objection Lawrence raised,
the pair walked through Trafalgar Square and on to the
Shaws' flat—only to find the great man still at home. The
Shaws were late, but about to leave. Hastily, Cockerell
made the introductions, and great warmth was shown on
both sides. After this further half-hour's delay the Shaws

left for Hertfordshire. The two visitors unhooked the painting and took it down.

Cockerell noticed with disappointment that not only was there a white patch in the background, but the painting was also unsigned. As they carried the portrait between them to a taxi, he suggested that it ought to be first taken to Augustus John's studio in Chelsea for the necessary repairs. Since John had already twice painted Lawrence, there was no reason for the latter to demur. They found the artist at home, and left the painting with him.

Not for some months was Lawrence to concern himself again with G.B.S. Yet no doubt the chance meeting fixed in his mind the idea of approaching Shaw, for he urgently craved as much high-level literary counsel as he could quietly get. He was also planning a new direction for his own life, and he wondered what part in it a book he had written about his Arabian adventure should be allowed to play. It was too much a part of his life to remain in manuscript, unread; yet he did not want to—as he conceived it —vulgarize or capitalize upon his wartime glory by offering it to a commercial publisher. He knew that almost any publisher would have accepted a "Lawrence of Arabia" book. And he knew why. So that it could be read and evaluated, yet not be publicly available, Lawrence, at his own expense had the book set in type from his manuscript at the office of the *Oxford Times*. During the summer of 1922 eight copies were printed, the printing somehow satisfying his need for secrecy incongruously combined with publicity. He began drafting a list of would-be reviewers, whose reviews would not be for the newspapers, nor even for the literary "little magazines," but only for himself. The reviewer was to receive his copy on loan—a unique variation on reviewing custom.

The bound copies were not to be ready until mid-Au-

gust. Before Lawrence delivered any of them, he expected
to have burnt his bridges to both literary and political
careers: his readers' anticipated flattery combined with
advice directing him toward one or the other of those ends
would be futile. Through Sir Hugh Trenchard (a wartime associate) he had obtained assurances that he could
enlist in the Royal Air Force ranks. This taken care of, he
wrote his letter of resignation as adviser to the Colonial
Secretary on July 4.

His departure from the Colonial Office was officially
noted on July 20, having been accepted by Churchill in
the automatic nature of civil servant departures. The next
day, with the delivery to Lawrence of the last eight chapters of *Seven Pillars of Wisdom*, the *Oxford Times* printing was completed. The bill: £175, before binding—the
next task.

It was not until August 17 that Lawrence mailed, from
Sir Herbert Baker's architect's office in London, his long
self-deprecating letter to G.B.S.

> Dear Mr. Shaw,
>
> You will be puzzled at my writing to you: but
> Cockerell some months ago took me round and intro-
> duced me, and you did not talk too formidably.
>
> I want to ask you two questions: the first one, 'Do
> you still read books?', doesn't require an answer. If
> you still go on reading I'm going to put the second
> question: if you don't, then please skip the two
> inside pages of this note and carry over to my signa-
> ture at the end, and burn it all without replying. I
> hate letter-writing as much as I can, and so, prob-
> ably, do you.
>
> My real wish is to ask if you will read, or try to
> read, a book which I have written. It's about the war,
> which will put you off, to start with, and there are
> technical unpleasantnesses about it. For instance it is

very long: about 300,000 words I suspect, though I
have not counted them. I have very little money and
do not wish to publish it: however it had to be
printed, so I got it done on a lino. press, in a newspaper office. That means it's beastly to look at, two
columns on a quarto page, small newspaper type
which hurts your eyes, and dozens of misprints, corrected roughly in ink: for only five copies exist,
and I could not afford a proof. The punctuation is
entirely the compositor's fancy: and he had an odd
fancy, especially on Mondays.

That's the worst to be said on the material side.
So far as concerns myself you must be told, before
you commit yourself to saying 'yes', that I'm not a
writer, and successfully passed the age of 30 without having wanted to write anything. . . .

In my case, I have, I believe, taken refuge in
second-hand words: I mean, I think I've borrowed
expressions and adjectives and ideas from everybody
I have ever read, and cut them down to my own size,
and stitched them together again. My tastes are daily
mailish, so there's enough piffle and romance and
wooliness to make a realist sick. There's a lot of
half-baked thinking, some cheap disgust and com-
plaint . . . : in fact all the sham stuff you have spent
your life trying to prick. If you read my thing, it
will show you that your prefaces have been written in vain, if I'm a fair sample of my generation.
This might make you laugh, if the thing was amus-
ingly written: but it's long winded, and pretentious,
and dull. . . .

You'll wonder, why if all this is true (and I think
it is) I want any decent person still more a person
like yourself to read it. Well, because it's a history,
and I'm ashamed for ever if I am the sole chronicler
of an event, and fail to chronicle it: and yet unless
what I've written can be made better I'll burn it. My

own disgust with it is so great that I can no longer believe it worth trying to improve (or possible to improve). If you read it or part of it and came to the same conclusion, you would give me courage to strike the match: whereas now I distrust my own judgement, and it seems cruel to destroy a thing on which I have worked my hardest for three years. While if you said that parts were rubbish, and other parts not so bad, and parts of it possible, (and distinguished those parts variously) then your standards might enable me to clear up mine, and give me energy enough to tackle the job again. (If you say it is all possible then I will reluctantly get rid of your own books from my shelves.)

All this is very unfair—or would be, if you knew me: but deleting that twenty minutes with Cockerell we are utter strangers, and likely to remain so, and therefore there is no pressure on you to answer this letter at all. I won't be in the least astonished (indeed I'll write another of the same sort to a man called Orage whom I have never met, but whose criticism I enjoy): and my opinion of you will go up. Yours with many apologies

T. E. Lawrence
[*Letters*, No. 161]

Conspicuously omitted from the letter was the news that the reluctantly issued authorization for Lawrence to enlist in the R.A.F. under the alias of John Hume Ross had been signed that day. Hopefully, the Air Force had added the terms that if he should apply for release at any time, he would be discharged immediately, without formality. Nothing of this could Bernard Shaw have learned from the seemingly humble letter he had received. Nor did he know that two others—Edward Garnett and Eric Kennington—

had already seen Lawrence's book. The letter, calculated
to intrigue Shaw, did exactly that. Although interruptions
caused him to alter the date on his letter before he mailed
it, he replied almost immediately in the affirmative—to the
Barton Street address Lawrence had given him. The book
would get published regardless of its flaws, G.B.S. pointed
out, because Lawrence's own fame meant a guaranteed
commercial success to a publisher; the fact that the book
had already coerced itself from the reluctant author was
evidence enough that in time it would be published. But
Shaw was deep in a busy schedule of Fabian Summer
School and Labor Research Department Summer School
activities, following which he had to go to Ireland to ac-
company Charlotte home. It wouldn't waste his time to
read it after mid-September, Shaw wrote, because it would
be a book he would be likely to want to read on publication anyway: his taking time to read it, though, might
delay the book's publication unnecessarily. More impor-
tantly, he added in closing, Lawrence had no need to be
timidly ceremonious with either of the Shaws. As a "priv-
ileged soul," he was commanded to regard them as old
friends.

Lawrence, still in London awaiting his opportunity to
enlist, replied by return mail that he would send a copy
of the book since "you say it will not waste your September
time," but insisted that he had no intention of publishing
it, even though Shaw (without having seen the book) had
helpfully suggested using his good offices with his own
publisher, Constable. Lawrence omitted mention that a
major alteration in his way of life was imminent, yet
three days later (August 30) he presented himself for
enlistment. The only vague clue in the letter to G.B.S.
—addressed from Barton Street, as usual—was the admoni-
tion that Shaw get the address "just right." This meant

that the "Colonel" had to be expunged. [*Letters*, No. 165]
Not for several months did G.B.S. know that it should
have been replaced by A/C 2 No. 352087.

"Ross" first reported to the R.A.F.'s London recruiting
depot, and was escorted by a sergeant-major to Chief Recruiting Officer Johns, who was unobtrusively signaled that
the applicant was a suspicious character. (Sometimes crim-
inals wanted by the police used the armed services as a
place temporarily to lose their identity, and the depot had
a file of Scotland Yard photographs to check.) "Ross"
had no papers of identity, and was told that regulations
required a birth certificate, attestation to his sound moral
character, and a reference from his last employer. He gave
a date of birth and offered to get the other credentials.
When Johns checked with the birth records office in
Somerset House he discovered, not to his surprise, that
there was no birth certificate. When "Ross" returned with
his references it was easily seen that they were forgeries,
and the sergeant-major escorted him to the door.

Soon the persistent would-be recruit was back, accompanied by an R.A.F. messenger, who bore the order au-
thorizing the enlistment; for when "Ross" could not effect
his own enlistment, Lawrence used his connections in
Whitehall. Even then his troubles were not over. The medical examiners, seeing his back laced with scars of flogging,
refused to pass him, even when ordered first by the local
commanding officer, and then by the Air Ministry. An
outside doctor was summoned. He signed, and J. H. Ross
was posted to training at Uxbridge. By then even the
R.A.F. personnel involved in processing Ross's enlistment
had a good idea that here was someone with friends in
high places. Private fears of reprisals may have caused
depot personnel to keep the tantalizing information largely
to themselves. Johns, however, telephoned his suspicions

to the flight lieutenant who was to receive Ross at Uxbridge.

Later, Lawrence dramatically telescoped and romanticized the events surrounding his enlistment into the first chapter of *The Mint*.

### I: RECRUITING OFFICE

GOD, this is awful. Hesitating for two hours up and down a filthy street, lips and hands and knees tremulously out of control, my heart pounding in fear of that little door through which I must go to join up. Try sitting a moment in the churchyard? That's caused it. The nearest lavatory, now. Oh yes, of course, under the church. What was Baker's story about the cornice?

A penny; which leaves me fifteen. Buck up, old seat-wiper: I can't tip you and I'm urgent. Won by a short head. My right shoe is burst along the welt and my trousers are growing fringes. One reason that taught me I wasn't a man of action was this routine melting of the bowels before a crisis. However, now we end it. I'm going straight up and in.

\*

All smooth so far. They are gentle-spoken to us, almost sorry. Won't you walk into my parlour? Wait upstairs for medical exam? 'Righto!' This sodden pyramid of clothes upon the floor is sign of a dirtier man than me in front. My go next? Everything off? (Naked we come into the R.A.F.) Ross? 'Yes, that's me.'

Officers, two of them. . . .

'D'you smoke?'

Not much, Sir.

'Well, cut it out. See?'

Six months back, it was, my last cigarette. However, no use giving myself away.

'Nerves like a rabbit.' The scotch-voiced doctor's hard fingers go hammer, hammer over the loud box of my ribs. I must be pretty hollow.

'Turn over: get up: stand under here: make yourself as tall as you can: he'll just do five foot six, Mac: chest—say 34. Expansion—by Jove, 38. That'll do. Now jump: higher: lift your right leg: hold it there: cough: all right: on your toes: arms straight in front of you: open your fingers wide: hold them so: turn round: bend over. Hullo, what the hell's those marks? Punishment?' 'No, Sir, more like persuasion, Sir, I think.' Face, next, chest, getting hot.

'H ... m ... m ... , that would account for the nerves.' His voice sounds softer. 'Don't put them down, Mac. Say *Two parallel scars on ribs*. What were they, boy?'

Superficial wounds, Sir.

'Answer my question.'

A barbed-wire tear, over a fence.

'H ... m ... m ... and how long have you been short of food?'

(O Lord, I never thought he'd spot that. Since April I've been taking off my friends what meals I dared, all that my shame would let me take. I'd haunt the Duke of York steps at lunch-time, so as to turn back with someone to his club for the food whose necessity nearly choked me. Put a good face on it; better.)

Gone a bit short the last three months, Sir. How my throat burns!

'More like six' . . . came back in a growl. The worst of telling lies naked is that the red shows all the way down. A long pause, me shivering in disgrace. He stares so gravely, and my eyes are watering. (Oh, it hurts: I wish I hadn't taken this job on.)

At last, 'All right: get back into your clothes. You aren't as good as we want but after a few weeks at the Depot you'll pull up all right.' 'Thank you very much, Sir.' 'Best of luck, boy,' from Mac. Grunt from the kinder-spoken one. Here's the vegetable market again, not changed. I'm still shaking everyway, but anyhow I've done it. Isn't there a Fuller's down that street? I've half a mind to blow my shilling on a coffee. Seven years now before I need think of winning a meal.

[*The Mint* (London, 1955), Chapter 11]

After each long training day at Uxbridge, Lawrence would sit in bed, blankets pulled up over drawn-up knees, and write letters to friends or his notes for *The Mint*. The bulkiest item in his early correspondence was the Oxford Text of *Seven Pillars*, which he managed to post to Bernard Shaw, as promised. G.B.S. and Charlotte, back from Ireland, were struck first by the book's size, then by its power. The crude format made it difficult reading. Nevertheless, Shaw picked it up now and then to go through a few pages or a few chapters at a time, while Charlotte, fascinated by the personality it evoked in contrast to the improbable young man who did not seem to fit his own word picture, read with greater eagerness. G.B.S. reported this to Lawrence when he acknowledged receipt of the book, and Lawrence professed to be horrified, feeling that there were things in it unfit for a lady's eyes. Charlotte Shaw, he was to find out, was a most determined lady.

Lawrence, stressing the indelicate nature of parts of his opus, pointed out that it was far worse in that respect than the sum of G.B.S.'s output. Though he still wrote ostensibly from Barton Street, Westminster (under his own name), he replied to a G.B.S. query about the latest erroneous and exotic newspaper stories of his whereabouts that "The papers tell many lies. I have gone West: fourteen miles, from Westminster, to be pedantically accurate."

Neither Uxbridge nor the R.A.F. were mentioned, though he did admit having enlisted in some service which was "a cleaner living than Eastern politics, & I haven't a busman's-wages of my own, so must do something. I'd rather it wasn't published in the Press: & therefore leave gladly their impression that I'm in the East somewhere." [30 Sept. 1922]

Leaving Eastern politics, and politics in general, was easier said than done. Regardless of his feelings in the matter, shedding his Lawrence skin did not disassociate him from politics—it only made his involvements in politics more complicated. The newspaper stories of intrigue in which Lawrence was supposedly involved and which Shaw had questioned had more basis in fact than even the newspaper guessing game and even Lawrence himself (in his denial to G.B.S.) then imagined. The Turks, his old foes, were threatening a small Allied occupation force stationed in the Dardanelles area at a place called Chanak, a fortification overlooking the narrows on the other side of which was the peninsula of Gallipoli. The 1918 armistice in Europe had had little effect upon the Middle East, and by 1922 the Turks under Mustapha Kemal had repudiated the 1920 treaty which was to have brought stability to the area. Greeks and Turks resumed hostilities, which at first went well for the Greeks, who were acting in the interests of the wartime Allies as well as their own in keeping the Turks out of all but the thumbnail portion of Turkish Europe left to the Turks by the 1920 settlement.

Through August and early September the Turks, recovered from early setbacks, routed the Greek army and the considerable Greek population in Asian Turkey and headed for the straits. If they entered the demilitarized zone (including Chanak) to the east of the straits, it would be an act of war. If the Allies resisted, it might have as adverse an effect upon the Mohammedan world as if they acquiesced, a dilemma somewhat akin to the Rhineland question a decade later. Telegrams to the Dominions were sent by Churchill from the Colonial Office, asking if they were willing to associate themselves with armed intervention to maintain the freedom of the straits and compel the Turks to a negotiated peace. The situation was becoming increasingly desperate, for King Constantine of Greece, who had been restored, had abdicated a second time, and France and Italy refused to support the use of force. On Sunday, September 17, Churchill released a communiqué threatening force if the Kemalists entered the neutral zone, and an alarmed public harked back to Churchill, 1915, and an earlier adventure at Gallipoli. The Opposition accused the Colonial Secretary of trying to "dragoon the Empire into war," and the crisis continued into October, although the Churchillian threat had caused Kemal to withdraw his troops.

Meanwhile a note to Edward Marsh, Churchill's confidential secretary, from Lord Trenchard of the Air Ministry, shows that Lawrence had been consulted before the affair blew over. "I understand Mr. Churchill wants to see Lawrence. In order to avoid publicity in this I would like you to let me know at least 48 hours beforehand when you want him. . . . I think Mr. Churchill will agree that it is inadvisable for anything to be put on paper disclosing Lawrence's address."[1]

An armistice was signed on October 11, and substantial portions of Thrace were returned to Turkey at the expense of Greece. Lloyd George's coalition ministry could not survive the episode. When it fell, Bonar Law formed a government, and Lawrence's former superior, Churchill, ceased to be Secretary of State for the Dominions and Colonies.

The episode may have meant the beginning of the end for Lawrence's Air Force career also, for any publicity was too much. He had warned Bernard Shaw to keep his whereabouts from the press, and had been careful not even to tell him where he was, nor in what capacity. He had been circumspect at Uxbridge, too, but secret messages from high places can be very public in a barracks situation. On his first hut inspection by the C.O. (Wing Commander Breese), he was asked about the "not ordinary books" in his locker. "Do you read that sort of thing? What were you in civil life?" "Nothing special," said Lawrence. "Working in an architect's office lately." Inevitably the C.O. asked why Ross had enlisted, eliciting the famous reply, "I had a mental breakdown, Sir." "What! What! Sergeant-Major, take this man's name: gross impertinence." Lawrence pleaded the next day that he had been misunderstood, and his incognito remained preserved. Unquestionably there were some at Uxbridge besides a few of his barracks mates who knew his identity, but one who did not know was the civilian master of the R.A.F. school. He had asked all new recruits to write a confidential autobiographical essay, outlining past education, educational shortcomings and what the writer wished to study. Ross semi-fictionalized past honors in history, including a research fellowship, and the effect of the war as spur to his enlistment. He was weakest, he wrote, in the polishing of greasy new boots. The master, he later told biographer Robert Graves, "was very kind to me afterwards, giving me books to read in school hours, and a quiet place to sit in."

By mid-October Lawrence had already confided in Edward Garnett that he was making rough notes about R.A.F. recruit training, and planning with Eric Kennington the illustrations for *Seven Pillars*. Later Air Vice-Marshal Sir

Oliver Swann was to complain that though he handled—secretly, and with reluctance—all matters of Lawrence's entry and movements, his eventual discovery by the press was "solely due to carelessness at the Colonial Office and to Lawrence's unfortunate love of drawing a veil of mystery about himself." [*Letters*, p.363] Lawrence had assumed (and perhaps encouraged) communication from the Colonial Office by writing Swann just after his enlistment that in case he were wanted by his former employers he would keep the Vice-Marshal aware of his changes in station. It may have been the change in station ordered by Swann, however, that precipitated the troubles for him in earnest. Early in November Swann called the commanding officer at Uxbridge to find out why Ross had not yet been transferred to photographic training at Farnborough. It was hardly the kind of interest expected from an air vice-marshal. Of course Ross was dispatched immediately. He sent Swann a thank-you note for shifting him to "this easy comfort," also informing the air vice-marshal that the careful arrangements made earlier, during the Turkish crisis, for conferring with Churchill personally, never had to be put into use. [*Letters*, No. 176] Ten days later he wrote to Swann again, this time complaining that his air photography training was being delayed, and besides, it "wasn't quite the sort of R.A.F." he wanted to write about, although he was glad to be free of the rough physical training of Uxbridge. In substance, the letter was a plea to be reassigned as an aircraft hand in an active squadron. [*Letters*, No. 179]

Soon afterward newspapermen began asking the Farnborough authorities for interviews with Ross, and were refused. Meanwhile, Lawrence was making the most of his plentiful spare time by working on an abridgement of *Seven Pillars* for possible commercial publication and reading German and Spanish for practice—hardly a way to repel suspicion that he was an unusual recruit. When photographers joined the press corps vigil, the commanding officer wrote to the Air Ministry asking—in a triumph of understatement—that Ross be removed from Farnborough because his presence was unsettling.

How aware Lawrence was of the undercurrent of excitement his presence was generating is difficult to ascertain. He had bought a motorbike for possible trips to London, was in chatty correspondence with many of his old friends, and was busy particularly with plans for the *Seven Pillars* abridgement he and Edward Garnett were patching together via the mails. Although these activities complicated his ever-present problems of adjustment from seats of glory to the peonage of the ranks, he was still anxious for Shaw's opinion of his book, and found time to prod the great man with another letter. On December 1, Shaw replied honestly, kindly, and at great length. "My dear Lawrence," he began. "Patience, patience: do not again shoot your willing camel through the head. [*Evidence that G.B.S. had read Chapter LIII.*] The truth is, I havnt read it yet. I have sampled it, but must read it all through. . . ."

There had been many obstacles to Shaw's reading the book: Charlotte's seizing it, other reading and writing tasks, and Shaw's participation on the Labour side of the election campaign. But he had read enough of *Seven Pillars* to be genuinely interested and puzzled about Lawrence's reluctance to publish. He not only considered it a great work, but now worried that the author might withdraw it completely and destroy it. Once he would get to know Lawrence, G.B.S. would realize that such worry was unfounded. Meanwhile he urged deposit of copies in such places as the British Museum and the Library of Congress, threatening that if he thought Lawrence capable of de-

stroying the book he would take the copy he had to his
flat in London and mask his safeguarding of it by setting
the building on fire and reporting that the book had been
among the belongings destroyed in the flames. Anticipating
Lawrence's secret, Shaw shrewdly suggested several variations of the book for publication, including a mass-circulation abridgement. But all this advice, he had to admit, was
on the basis of limited acquaintance with the work. Still
his sampling was so intriguing that he invited Lawrence to
visit him and Charlotte either in London or Ayot, even
offering to drive him the seven miles to Ayot from the
nearest railroad station if given advance notice.

> I am curious as to how you will come out of it—of
> the reading I mean. Take the case of Gordon for
> example. He was a most infernal scoundrel according
> to any workable standard of human morality. . . .
> Have you ever considered the question as affecting
> yourself? . . . You have a conscience which would
> have prevented you acting as Gordon did in China; so
> there will be a deep difference; but I wonder what,
> after reading the book through, I will decide to do
> with you if ever I become one of the lords of the
> east. As I shan't perhaps I shall put you into a play, if
> my playwriting days are not over. [*Letters*, pp.
> 386-87]

Shaw was anxious about a subject for his next play then,
feeling that perhaps his labors over the Wagnerian-sized
"metabiological Pentateuch," *Back to Methuselah*, had
drained his energies and sapped his inspiration. He was
seriously telling friends that he was finished as a playwright, and pointed to his advanced age (sixty-six). Sydney Cockerell pressed a copy of the Joan of Arc trial
records on Shaw, but G.B.S. showed no interest, and
Charlotte took up the battle by leaving books about Joan

everywhere her husband might spot them. Another kind of pressure came from Lawrence's training camp. Answering Shaw's letter in shrewdly meek fashion, Lawrence hastened to assure him that he was not pressing him—that he was only afraid that the hours Shaw might be spending on it might be retarding the muse at the cost of another *Caesar and Cleopatra* or *Heartbreak House*. "Please don't," he wrote, "out of kindness, bore yourself." The book, he confided dramatically,

> won't be so odd as what I've [since] done with myself. I'm now an airman in the Air Force: one of those funny little objects in blue clothes who look forlorn when they walk about the Strand. It keeps me alive (just) and keeps me out of mischief. One of its consequences is that I'm afraid I can't come and see you: they give us very little leave, and rather too much work. At present I'm stationed at Aldershot. As the Press would talk rot about my eccentricity, please don't talk very much of it. It's not a secret, and not common knowledge: you see, people generally took for granted that I had enough money— or the determination to make some: whereas I have none at all, and have never worked for it: and won't. [*Letters*, No. 184]

Further, Lawrence confided, the book was being abridged by Edward Garnett, in the hope that a publisher would find the cut-down version commercial. "If so, I'll become a civilian again. You have no idea how repulsive a barrack is as permanent home. It reconciles me to the meanness of the abridgement."

G.B.S. had not known about the Garnett abridgement. A few days later he visited Constables, his publishers, to discuss prices of some new editions of his books with the two senior partners, William Meredith and Otto Kyllmann. In the course of the conversation, he brought up the subject of Lawrence of Arabia—and to his surprise discovered that Meredith had not only once met Lawrence but knew about the Oxford *Seven Pillars*. He asked why Meredith had not snapped up the masterpiece for his firm. The conservative Meredith replied that it would have been indelicate to press for the book, although Constable hoped it might come their way. Shaw still had not finished *Seven Pillars*. It would take him through the winter and into the spring to do so; yet he expounded upon the book's virtues to his publishers with missionary enthusiasm. To do it justice, he said, it would have to be published, eighteenth-century fashion, in a dozen volumes. Then, after a suitable lapse in time, an abridgement for the general public would have to follow.

Kyllmann and Meredith listened with unfeigned interest, and Kyllmann followed up the meeting with a letter asking G.B.S. to be intermediary for them in forwarding to Lawrence an expression of their interest and desire to know his terms. When Shaw did so, he made it clear to Lawrence that Constable meant responsible publication, not exploitation in the Fleet Street manner. He strongly urged consideration, especially since Lawrence appeared in a mood to return to civilian life if the book's sale were to provide him with sufficient income. Characteristically, Shaw tried to tease Lawrence out of the R.A.F., but found his real feelings uncharacteristically running out of control.

> Nelson, slightly cracked after his whack on the head after the battle of the Nile, coming home and insisting on being placed at the tiller of a canal barge and being treated as nobody in particular, would have embarrassed the Navy far less. A callow and terrified Marbot, placed in command of a sardonic Napoleon at Austerlitz and Jena, would have felt

much as your superior officers must in command of
Lawrence the great, the mysterious, save in whom
there is no majesty and no might. . . .

You talk about leave as if it were a difficulty. Ask
for three months' leave and they will exclaim, with a
sob of relief, "For God's sake, take six, take twelve,
take a lifetime, take anything rather than keep up
this maddening masquerade that makes us all ridiculous." I sympathize with them. . . . [*Letters*, pp.
350-51]

Shaw wrote on December 17. By the time Lawrence
received the letter, although he did not know it, the whole
question of his voluntary departure from the ranks had
become academic. The day before, the commanding officer
at Farnborough reported to the Air Ministry that vigilant
reporters from the *Daily Mail* and *Daily Express* had discovered Ross's identity, and had even tried to discover
through junior officers at the camp whether Ross was in
their mess. Finding out little positive information, the reporters had turned to the airmen. The commanding officer
hopefully appealed for instructions from the Secretary of
State for Air, because the increasing gossip and conjecture
were becoming harmful to discipline and training.

On December 19, the Air Ministry decided to attempt
to let Lawrence's training proceed normally. It was a futile
gesture, for although Lawrence's letters reveal nothing of
the camp situation, it was rapidly getting out of control.
He tried to continue as if the situation were normal, but
the pose barely lasted beyond Christmas Day. On the
twenty-seventh he wrote to Shaw, who wanted information, having become interested in all aspects of Lawrence's
affairs (Why had not Parliament helped with a gratuity of
£20,000? What kind of work had the R.A.F. put him to?).
"One can guess nothing," G.B.S. added acidly, "about a

man capable of anything, like Habbakuk." Lawrence answered that since he had difficulty getting his demobilization payment of £110 from the War Office it was unlikely he could have squeezed twenty thousand out of Parliament. As a result he had told an agent (and ex-comrade), Raymond Savage, to find him £300 in royalties a year to live on from a publisher who would also give him "the last word as to type, paper and format." Since Garnett was an editor for Jonathan Cape's new firm, which was both respectable and interested, Cape was to have first refusal. "It's good of you to have worked Meredith to the point of offering," he added politely, "and I'll tell Savage about it."

The whole letter sounded like business as usual, as Lawrence listed the myriad petty jobs that occupied his time in the ranks—dishwasher, errand boy, garbage and trash collector, clerk, pigsty cleaner, housemaid, camp cinema attendant. Since it was Christmas week, he had the afternoon off, and had taken advantage of it to go to Oxford on his motorbike to visit David Hogarth of the Ashmolean Museum. "Anything does for airmen recruits: but the life isn't so bad, when the first crudeness works off. We have a bed each, and suffer all sorts of penalties unless they are 25 inches apart: twelve of us in a room. Life is very common. . . . Much good humour, very little wit, but a great friendliness. They treat my past as a joke, and forgive it me lightly. The officers fight shy of me: but I behave demurely, and give no trouble." [*Letters*, No. 187]

That day, however, unfortunately for the even tenor of Lawrence's plans for himself, the *Daily Express* front-paged the news that the "Uncrowned King of Arabia" was serving in the R.A.F. as a "private soldier." The famous war hero had become a private, it reported, both to seek peace, and to find material for a book. The newspaper gossip reached proportions which alarmed the government, and while no one was really sure how the news had come out (Lawrence told several friends that an officer gave him away), it was realized that the hide-and-seek Lawrence had played had been an open secret anyway. The notoriety provided a convenient excuse for the Air Force to dispose of its hot potato, whose identity made life awkward for its officers and discipline in the ranks theoretically more difficult to maintain.

Meanwhile, Cape had announced the impending publication of an abridged *Seven Pillars*, resulting in an immediate letter from G.B.S. to Lawrence, ignoring the newspaper sensation completely and insisting that the book first had to be published somehow in its entirety, for if a shorter version appeared first, no publisher would handle a full library edition. Cape should be given back his advance, if any, Shaw wrote, and offered to lend money for the purpose, if necessary. He expressed concern that Lawrence might have committed himself irreparably, and ended with a curt apology for pushing himself into his friend's business—it was the only way he could make himself of the immediate service he felt Lawrence needed, and which, having served ten years on the managing committee of the Society of Authors, he could supply.

Lawrence had another and more urgent reason for wanting to beg out on the arrangement with Cape: to make his position in the R.A.F. more tenable, for he had good cause to worry about his prospects as an airman. All that publication could do would be to make his situation more notorious. On New Year's Day, 1923, a day or two after he received Shaw's letter, he wrote to Cape that he had thought the matter over, and decided that while he remained in the R.A.F.—or at least during 1923—he could not publish anything. [*Letters*, No. 188] By this time the newspaper furor had begun to die down.

Shaw's letter urging the cancellation of the agreement
with Cape also mentioned that Mrs. G.B.S. was a fanati-
cal believer in Lawrence's literary genius. His secretary
Blanche Patch recorded in her memoir that Charlotte had
been ecstatically reading aloud passages from the awk-
wardly type-set *Seven Pillars* as her husband sat ruminating
by the fireside at Ayot. It took her until the last day of
1922 before she could find the courage to write to Lawrence. Very likely her letter was meant, at least in part, to
reinforce G.B.S.'s urging that the book be published first
as a whole, for she made that point clear, after opening
with paragraphs of admiration:

10, Adelphi Terrace W.C.<br>31 Dec. 1922

Dear Mr. Lawrence,

If you've been "mad keen" to hear about your
book I've been mad keen to write to you about it
ever since I began to read it, and I simply haven't
dared. I got from it an impression of you as an Immense Personality soaring in the blue (of the Arabian
skies) far above my lowly sphere, and that anything
I could say in the way of admiration, or comment, or
question, could only be an impertinence. But the latest developments of your career have been so star-
tlingly unexpected, and your later letters so human,
that I take my courage in both hands and send you
a word.

How is it *conceivable*, *imaginable* that a man who
could write the Seven Pillars can have any doubts
about it? If you don't know it is a "great book" what
is the use of anyone telling you so. I believe (though
he has never said anything of the sort) that G. B. S.
thinks you are "pulling his leg" when you ask him.
I devoured the book from cover to cover as soon as I
got hold of it. I could not stop. I drove G. B. S.
almost mad by insisting upon reading him special

bits when he was deep in something else. I am an old woman, old enough at any rate to be your mother; I have met all sorts of men and women of the kind that are called distinguished; I have read their books and discussed them with them; but I have never read anything like this: I don't believe anything really like it has been written before. When I find in your letter such suggestions as "Should it be without the first-person singular?" "Is there any style in my writing?" "Anything recognizably individual?" I think—are you laughing at us! Why, foolish man, it *could* only have been written in the first person singular: it is one of the most amazingly individual documents that has ever been written: there is no "style" because it is above and beyond anything so silly.

You have been the means of bringing into the world a poignant human document, and now—have faith in the Power that worked through you. . . .

Your book must be published as a whole. Don't you see that? Perhaps little bits about the French, and such things as your scarifying account of Meinertshagen (splendid, that is) might be toned down (not left out. . . .) and such like little personal severities, *but don't leave out the things an ordinary man would leave out:* the things people will tell you are "too shocking." Publish the book practically as it is, in good print, in a lot of volumes. I am sure Constables will do it for you that way.

Both G.B.S. and I have lots of experience about books and we would both *like* to put it at your service. By the way, don't call him "Mr." Shaw!

Yours sincerely,
C.F.S.
(Mrs. G.B.S.!)[2]

A few days later G.B.S. threw his heavy artillery at Lawrence, sarcastically reminding him that in the newspaper furor he had just had a demonstration of how impossible it was to hide the Frankenstein monster of a personality he had created under another name and occupation, even if—as he had explained—Lawrence was technically not his legitimate name either. He would be Lawrence to the end of his days, Shaw pointed out; even if the name and fame rankled him, he would have to live with both. Shaw then followed up Charlotte's comments on form and style by construing the idea of publishing *Seven Pillars* as a whole as meaning the entire work minus actionable or scandalous passages. He also made fun of the idea of style by tossing in a free paraphrase of his lines on the subject in the Preface to *Man and Superman*, and adding advice on how to revise without acquiring a self-conscious style. Again G.B.S. apologized for his lengthy advice, but reminded Lawrence that since the only times he seemed to be able to think were those when he was in an Arab tent flattened by dysentery, with the temperature above that of hell, someone had to do his thinking for him.

The Shaws had left for a week's holiday at Bournemouth, but there they could not escape Lawrence. He had kept all his letters from G.B.S. in a neat bundle—a bundle which was found that week on a street in London by a merchant's clerk. Lawrence had stuffed the letters into a slit in his cycling overalls. "The slit is a way to a pocket but not a pocket in itself," he explained to Shaw. When informed that his letters had been found, Shaw wrote to Cope Hand, the finder, that letters were always the property of the recipient, and that he should hold them until they were reclaimed by Lawrence. Charlotte's comment was, "Something extraordinary always happens with that man." On January 9 Shaw wrote to Lawrence, who eventually reacquired his letters (Hand mailed them back). He had, by then, more correspondence from the Shaws to

add, for the exchange—over a dozen years—of hundreds
of letters between him and Charlotte had begun, Charlotte
eventually taking over most of the correspondence as
spokesman for her husband as well as friend in her own
right. Her first letter Lawrence had already shown to his
mother, who, he thought, developed an instant liking for
Mrs. Shaw because of her praise for the book. Soon the
first of many books Charlotte was to send to him arrived
in camp. Why he decided to enlist Charlotte as addressee
(instead of G.B.S.) and assume for her the post of correspondent in his relations with G.B.S., is explained in part
in a letter to her written in 1927, ". . . I won't write to him
again yet. I feel that letters to him must be somewhat
remarkable . . . [to be] fit for him. . . ."[3]

The month of January went by with Lawrence filled
with anxiety, hoping the storm about Aircraftman Ross
had dissipated, but uncomfortably sure it had not. The
Chief of Air Staff, Sir Hugh Trenchard, came to Farnborough and talked privately with the man whose enlistment orders he had given, leaving Ross with little hope
—unless he would accept officer's rank. By the end of the
month he was a civilian named Lawrence again. Almost his
first act in that capacity was an appealing letter to Trenchard through T. B. Marson, his secretary. "I fear it's too
late and the business closed," he wrote on the 28th. [*Letters*, No. 189] But he hopefully suggested (as he also wrote
to G.B.S.) that there might be no further trouble over him
if he were openly posted to "some remote station, where
there are no papers, and no one will have heard of me." On
getting his discharge, Lawrence quietly told Group Captain Findlay, the Adjutant, that he would try again. Flight
Sergeant Chalkley made up the discharge documents, and
later recalled that in all of Ross's papers there was nothing
to connect him with Lawrence. Thus, but for his defiant

remark to Findlay, "Ross's" departure from the R.A.F.*
was as normal as his entrance had been devious.

One week later, on January 30, 1923, he wrote to G.B.S.,
telling him that he had been sacked from the Air Force,
and felt miserable. As a last resort he reported having
written to the Chief of Air Staff for another chance at a
more remote station. Not only was he out of the service,
but nearly out of funds too, and worried that he might
have to "eat" his motorbike. After some details of a new
proposal for publishing *Seven Pillars* (Cape had risen to
his suggestion of a small subscription edition, complete, as
Shaw had advised), Lawrence added that the contract
arrived for his signature the day of his discharge. It was
the most inopportune of moments, for not only was his
mood negative, but he was sending his request for reinstatement and did not want to buy a rejection through the
book's publication. In a different vein he concluded, "Please
give Mrs. Shaw my regards. I tried to call last week end."
[*Letters*, No. 191]

Soon he was calling on the Shaws regularly, filled with
a variety of alternative plans for re-enlistment and plans
as well for production of a private limited edition of the
unabridged *Seven Pillars*, which Shaw was beginning to
intimate that he would revise. At his first meeting with the
Shaws (despite the quickening of their friendship, he had
not actually seen them again since the Cockerell introduction), G.B.S. had nothing but praise for the book, and
Lawrence, wondering whether what the great man said
to him was the same as what he privately told others, asked
the sculptress Lady Scott (later Lady Kennet) to undertake the "pumping" of Shaw, which she did, with the same
result. "To me," he wrote on February 5, thanking her,

---

* See Appendix, page 283 ff., for a discussion of Terence Rattigan's use
of this whole episode in his play *Ross*.

"he would only say cryptic words, all of commendation. Those are nice, like chocolate eclairs or cream puffs, but not a meal. Mrs. Shaw praised even more than he did. I hung on until nearly four o'clock, but not even boredom would show through his courtesy, so that my curiosity came away unfed." Though he knew G.B.S. had read at least half the book, he added, "My private opinion is that she's read it, and he hasn't: and can't: but is much afraid to shock her by letting on." [*Letters*, No. 193]

When Lawrence pointed out to the Shaws in further self-depreciation, that even if his book demonstrated some literary talent, no one would be interested in its subject matter, Charlotte mentioned *The Worst Journey in the World*, the narrative of the adventures of their Ayot St. Lawrence neighbor, Apsley Cherry-Garrard, who had accompanied Scott on his expedition to the Antarctic. The book had benefited from the Shaws' help and had been a popular success. "Why should not sand have the same appeal as snow?" G.B.S. asked.[4]

During February Lawrence tried to find new avenues toward a return to the R.A.F. Trenchard had offered the salve of promising that if he made a good record in another service he might be reacceptable to the Air Force. He immediately sent out feelers toward services as varied as the Army and the Coast Guard (thinking of lighthouse duty as suitable solitude). Holed up in Barton Street, Lawrence put his ingenuity and connections to work (even the armed services of the new Irish Free State were solicited). With his many friends in high places to apply appropriate pressure in Whitehall, ironically for the opposite reason than most such pressure was exerted, it was arranged early in March (via Sir Philip Chetwode, a comrade of Arabian days) for him to enlist as a private in the Royal Tank Corps. It hardly seemed possible that under the circumstances he could get through the red tape and into uniform without being recognized and exploited in the newspapers, but again he chose to enlist under another name than his own.

Toward the end of March, Lawrence wrote to G.B.S. from Bovington Camp in Dorset that he had joined the Army on a seven-year enlistment, and expected to go to India with an armored car unit sometime during his tour of duty. Meanwhile, he reported that his "little team of artists" was still at work on illustrative material for the private unabridged edition he had discussed with Shaw. Intermittently, whenever artists on the "team" needed work or money they would return to his project, on which he had spent almost all of his Colonial Office salary of the year before. Signing his letter as from Barton Street, and as T. E. Lawrence, he carefully omitted a significant fact about his newest incarnation. He had taken the name of Shaw.

*"Even* Saint Joan, *which might seem to be aloof both from the postwar generation and from Shaw, has as its theme the homelessness of genius."* —Eric Bentley

# TWO

## *1923-1924*

The news that Lawrence of Arabia, Prince of Mecca and colonel-turned-private, had enlisted in the Army as T. E. Shaw, leaked slowly into private knowledge and eventually (through G.B.S.'s zest for writing prefaces) into public knowledge. The inevitable speculations about the change of name followed, and—though groundless—these were abetted by false scents helpfully supplied by people representing the entire spectrum of strong feelings about Lawrence and about Bernard Shaw.

Lawrence was Shaw's illegitimate son, one story went, and was finally acknowledging his parentage. This one gained such currency that Colonel Ralph Isham once asked Shavian biographer Archibald Henderson if it were true. Disclaimers of any connection between the adopted service name and that of Lawrence's elderly friends came from the most reliable friends and confidants of both Shaws. It was authoritatively reported to be sheer coincidence—but all stories were different.

The 1934 Liddell Hart biography, which Lawrence both read and contributed to, reported that "contrary to rumour, the choice was not due to his friendship and admiration for Bernard Shaw; he took it at random from the Army List Index while waiting in a room at the War Office. It had the same convenience for pay parade as 'Ross'!" (He would not have to hurry into line because of his remote location in the alphabetical order.) Yet it was reported from the Tank Corps depot at Bovington, Dorset, that the "one fact the men of the depot—quite naturally—did note was that 'Shaw' never appeared on pay parade."[1]

Another suggested motive, hardly less weak, was that, like *Ross*, *Shaw* was a name that appeared far down the duty list. However, Lawrence's record of readiness to do any enlisted man's distasteful job renders this equally inadequate as an explanation. He once told Florence Doubleday (wife of the publisher) that he had chosen a name of four letters but the officer who was to accept his enlistment had that name also, and laughingly said, "I'm not going to let you have my name." "Then give me the telephone book," Lawrence countered, "and I will pick the first name of four letters that I see." The first was *Shaw*, Lawrence confided, adding, "And I have had to apologize to Bernard Shaw many times for having taken his name."

Blanche Patch, Shaw's long-time secretary, is the authority for the story that when a clergyman caller remarked how "very like his uncle" Lawrence was, Lawrence, then about to enlist, exclaimed, "A good idea! That is the name I shall take." Another version of Miss Patch's story is that Charlotte told her that a lady had commented upon Lawrence's striking resemblance to G.B.S., asking whether they were nephew and uncle. In this variation Lawrence's

Portrait of T. E. Lawrence as Private Shaw, by Augustus John.
(*Courtesy of Augustus John*)

exclamation was, "Now I shall take the name of Shaw as I'm looking for a pseudonym." G.B.S.'s own version was that Lawrence was taken for his son one day by a clergyman who was visiting Thomas Hardy (Lawrence was a frequent visitor at Max Gate, Hardy's home). The mistake is understandable, for, although Lawrence was short in stature, there was some resemblance in the bony structure of their faces—a resemblance that G.B.S.'s luxuriant foliage did not conceal.

Bernard Shaw, however, had several tales of his own—public and private—about the reasons for the name change. Lawrence found it difficult to get the armed forces to accept him as a common soldier, he wrote, because he would be "a most embarrassingly uncommon soldier," and because "Private-Colonel Lawrence would make the army ridiculous." For this reason, Shaw concluded, neglecting mention of the earlier, pre-Shavian use of "Ross" for R.A.F. enlistment, "He promptly took another name and wore down the War Office. . . ."[2] An earlier Shavian secretary than Miss Patch, Mrs. Georgina (Judy) Musters, recalled that she heard from both G.B.S. (her cousin) and Charlotte that Lawrence's adoption of *Shaw* was pure accident, and that it had no hidden meaning.

Through the twenties and thirties, once the change of name had become public, there were persistent reports that Lawrence had adopted the name of *Shaw* "because it was his mother's name, according to some versions of the story. . . ." This suggestion continued to appear in print as late as Lawrence's obituary notices in 1935. Richard Aldington's "biographical enquiry" notes that Sir Ronald Storrs gives Lawrence's mother's name as Sarah Maden, and so it appears on his birth certificate, while the birth certificate of one of Lawrence's brothers gives the name as "formerly Sarah Junner." Explaining the name to Captain H. C. Armstrong in 1924, Lawrence wrote: "Any more mysteries left unsettled? No, I don't think so. I call myself Shaw now: it's short as a name. Lawrence wasn't my choice (or my family name) & I find it too long . . . and a bit 'too ripe' for life in the ranks."

Although flattered by the adopted name, G.B.S. realistically pointed out to Lawrence the irony of his attempt to change his identity by a simple change of surname. "You didn't keep quiet," he wrote, in obvious reference to Lawrence's military and public career, self-publicity, and published writings in mass-circulation journals and newspapers prior to his enlistments, "and now Lawrence you will be to the end of your days and thereafter to the end of what we call modern history. Lawrence may be as great a nuisance to you sometime as G.B.S. is to me . . . but you created him and must now put up with him as best you can."[3] Not advertising the change of name as directly related to his own surname, G.B.S. later told his neighbor Stephen Winsten, "He was a strange fellow. He thought that by changing his name to Shaw he wouldn't be recognized, Shaw being a common name." Yet Miss Louise Rumball, another Ayot St. Lawrence neighbor, when interviewed by Allan Chappelow for his *Shaw the Villager* (1961), assumed that it was common knowledge that Lawrence took *Shaw* from Bernard Shaw's surname.

In the great world beyond Ayot, Lord Vansittart, who disliked both Lawrence (to whom he was distantly related) and G.B.S., commented acidly that Lawrence joined the ranks "calling himself Shaw after Bernard, also an exhibitionist." Inevitably, the most imaginative of the rumors spawned by the adopted name had to reach Lawrence in some form, and it did—in a letter from Augustus John: "I hear a report that you are the son of G.B.S. If so he

should have repeated the effort. (I mean this kindly.) . . ."[4]
Whatever the real reason, the Shaws privately accepted the
adoption at face value, G.B.S. once telling Gene Tunney of
his great admiration for Lawrence; and that Lawrence as a
gesture of affection for the Shaws had assumed their name.
The compliment, Tunney was told, was "very, very much
appreciated by both Mrs. Shaw and G.B.S."[5]

The Shaws, in some ways, became Lawrence's substitute
parents (his father had died in 1919, and his mother was
often out of the country at remote missions.) For the
Shaws,  he was a surrogate son—not the first to play this
role in the lives of the childless couple. Although Charlotte Shaw's marriage was (by her command) childless,
her mothering instinct expressed itself in the distaff but
sometimes no less dominant side of several of her husband's
mentor-disciple relationships. Mrs. Musters recalls how,
when Charlotte Shaw met her brother, then about fouteen
years old, she took a "violent fancy" to him and wanted to
shower him with gifts and establish him in a program of
schooling that would lead to any career he wanted. First,
though, the Shaws decided to preface his education with
"a wonderful holiday in Switzerland, where he was killed.
When T.E.L. was killed riding the Shaw gift motor bicycle, I thought of this."[6]

In the first two decades of the century, the Shaws found
themselves responding toward Harley Granville Barker as
surrogate parents, and before, during and after Barker's
marriage to Lillah McCarthy, offered her the same affection. Early in G.B.S.'s relationship with Barker, during
the years of their Court Theatre collaboration, someone
remarked at rehearsal that Shaw was fifty. "You're the
same age as my father," said Barker. On week-ends he
often stayed with the Shaws. Charlotte treated him as a
son, while G.B.S. often engaged in stormy but affectionate

sessions with him, Barker playing the respectful but rebellious offspring. When predatory females attracted
G.B.S., Charlotte often engaged Barker to help drive them
off. Barker once threatened to shoot one of them and leave
the mess for G.B.S.[7]

The Shaws abetted the romance of Barker with Lillah
McCarthy, exulted at their marriage (G.B.S. writing plays
like *Androcles and the Lion* for them), and were heart-
broken when an American heiress left her husband to be-
witch Barker into divorcing Lillah. The break-up came in
1915, but Lillah refused to give Barker a divorce. The
Shaws took it as their tragedy, writing anxious letters to the
estranged pair, G.B.S. in one letter to Lillah assuming that
he was the "proper person to meddle." After the divorce
and remarriage, Helen Huntington, Barker's new wife,
gradually cut him off from his theatrical friends, and
ended his long intimacy with the Shaws. Even the letters
trickled to nothing. When Mrs. Shaw died (at eighty-six)
in 1943, G.B.S. wrote a pathetic postcard to Barker, re-
calling that Charlotte had always been fond of him and had
felt the severance of their relations deeply. "She had not
forgotten you," Shaw wrote, concluding, "You will not, I
know mind my writing this to you." When in 1946, Shaw
heard with sorrow on the radio the news of Barker's death,
he murmured to Miss Patch that he had always hoped they
might come together again. The void in the Shaws' lives
left by Barker in 1918 was to be filled by Lawrence in 1922.

The anonymous *Times Literary Supplement* reviewer of
Margery M. Morgan's study of Granville Barker's plays,
*A Drama of Political Man* (London, 1961), connected
Lawrence with his predecessor, although in reviewing the
book there was no need to mention him. The compulsion
to connect the two is interesting, in the light of the Shaws'
attraction to both:

The now legendary figure of Harley Granville
Barker bears a striking resemblance in many of its
characteristics to the popular image of T. E. Lawrence. As subjects of endless conjecture both men are
assured of immortality. Though both were pre-emi-
nent as men of action, both earnestly desired to be es-
teemed as men of letters. Both, deeply scarred with a
sense of failure and disillusion, withdrew from the
dust and heat engendered by their own enterprise.
Though both were sparing of their affections, both
inspired devotion in their fellow workers. What they
wrote is less likely to survive than the record of
what they did. . . . [November 17, 1961]

It is interesting to speculate upon the relationship between Lawrence and Barker—the estranged "son" and the
younger man now beginning to assume a similar role in the
Shaws' lives. Late in 1923 we find "Shaw" asking Barker
if he would read the early version of *Seven Pillars*. Noting
that he was busy reading a Barker play provided Lawrence
with an opportunity to echo G.B.S. by attacking Barker
for his increasing "retirement" from the stage. By early
1924 an exchange of books had occurred, and Lawrence
remarked that he was amused at the "comic" picture of
"an author and a would-be (would have been?), exchang-
ing books, & tasting each other meditatively." "Shaw (the
real one)," Lawrence then reported, "talked of it [Barker's
*The Secret Life*] with me, deploring your profusion of
material, your introduction of stuff which would have
made eight plays if beaten out thin."[8] Could this have
been Barker's indirect way of channeling his copy to his
old friend and mentor, G.B.S., for comment and criticism,
without risking his wife's wrath? Possibly the last letter
from Barker to Shaw—a kind, although somewhat critical
commentary on *Saint Joan*—was written that year. The

new Mrs. Barker detested Shaw, who reciprocated her feelings. Soon the promising correspondence between Barker and "Shaw" all but petered out, although their friendship never faded completely.

Robert Graves pointed out as early as his 1927 *Lawrence and the Arabs*, that Lawrence "presented a different facet of himself to each of his many friends according to their activities and character. . . ." Inevitably this led to neat oversimplifications of Lawrence's ability to elicit friendship from the most diverse of men. Thus we find Anthony West writing:

> The secret of most successful fascinations or seductions is a simple one; the seducer not only convinces the subject that the relationship under construction is unique but also rapidly fabricates, for the purposes of the operation, a personality entirely composed of answers to the subject's most pressing necessities. Lawrence was more than just a man of unusually delicate sensibilities; he was a chameleon, and his rare capacity for recognizing what was required of him in any situation was equalled only by his capacity for becoming it. In Cairo, among the intellectuals of the Arab Bureau, he was entirely the Oxford don caught up in the war machine, ironically teasing the Regulars at G. H. Q.; in the desert with Colonel Newcombe and the fighting soldiers, he was all plain fighting soldier; with the Arabs, all feckless Arab, warring only when the odds were with him and when the chance of pillage made it seem worth while; with the Robert Graves of *Goodbye to All That*, all disillusioned infantry officer harrowed by the darkness of war; with Liddell Hart, the commander who had in the field arrived at one of Liddell Hart's tactical and strategic theories of the indirect approach; with E. M. Forster, all sensibility

and literary intelligence; with Shaw, the ironic
buffoon indicating with a slapstick the tragic contrast between what man knows he could do and
what he does.[9]

There were many less obscure factors which drew
Shaw to "Shaw." Like G.B.S., Lawrence was remarkably
talented as a self-publicist and as a man of letters. Essentially each was a pacifist who loved soldiery, a born actor
and politician. Like G.B.S., he was ascetic: his major excess
in life was letter-writing, and more than once, as Shaw
actually *did,* he thought of printing correspondence cards.
"Someday," he wrote in 1928, "I dream of putting round
a little printed card to everyone. . . . 'Many thanks for
your letter, which I should have endeavored to answer,
only that I have determined lately to write no more letters
that are not of a strictly business character!' " In 1935, a
few months before his death, he actually did have correspondence cards printed.

Like Shaw, Lawrence was of Irish descent, and, at least
after becoming close to Shaw, was publicly proud of it,
eventually affecting a sort of brogue which his friend
Henry Williamson called "Bernard Shaw's brogue, but
clearer, less Irish." Although he claimed to be "no writer,"
toward the end of his life he accepted membership in the
Irish Academy of Letters. V. S. Pritchett writes: "Other
Anglo-Irish traits [of Lawrence] are suggested by a comparison with Bernard Shaw. There are the continuous
historionic touch and the remorse that follows—an un-
availing remorse because it, also, is theatrical. There is the
merciless mental energy which pours out endlessly in
words or action, and turns upon the character in humiliat-
ing self-criticism. There is the special kind of idealism:
ascetic, bodiless, rational, unromantic, and it keeps a place

for the inevitable cynicism of tactics. Unlike English
idealism it is unsentimental and without hypocrisy."[10]

Though Shaw did not have Lawrence's obsessive, Swiftian preoccupation with the physical, he had (as Lawrence
also did) the often complementary shrinking from it, and
the indications are that both men (in Anthony West's
words) "considered sexuality as a dissipation of vital forces
that could be more profitably engaged in [their] real
business. . . ." A lover of music, Lawrence had no pretensions to musical ability, or to critical authority, but in
Shavian fashion was an advocate of Mozart, Wagner and
Elgar. Much of his record collection came as gifts from
Charlotte Shaw and the record-player he used in India was
a gift from G.B.S. His appreciation of G.B.S.'s own works
long antedated his first meeting with the Shaws, as letters,
memoirs, and inscribed books in his own library indicate.
A catalogue of "confessions" he once prepared for Robert
Graves listed a number which might easily be suspected
as having been prepared by the other Shaw. His favorite
composer was Mozart; favorite dish (ascetically enough),
bread-and-butter; favorite author, William Morris.

Even Lawrence's motorcycling adventures had their har-
rowing parallels in G.B.S.'s narrow escapes on bicycle and
motorcycle. Shaw's indefatigable bicycling is a mine for
anecdotes, but that he was a pioneer motorcyclist is less
well known. In his early years at Ayot (where he settled in
1906) he raced along the narrow country lanes on an All-
days motorcycle, once losing the driving chain, and having
to push the disabled vehicle a mile back to his house. (Miss
Rumball recalled that the chain was later found in a lane
near the Ayot grammar school, where her mother was then
headmistress.)[11]

Whether Lawrence was aware of Shaw's essay, "Killing
for Sport," (1914), or other Shavian writings on the sub-

ject before meeting the author, is unknown; however, it
is clear that they shared a revulsion for the pastime, which
Shaw called "degrading" and "subhuman," the "unbearable stupidity" of "converting an interesting, amusing,
prettily colored live wonder like a pheasant into a slovenly
unhandsome corpse." Lord Winterton in his memoirs recalled a wartime incident in which "Shaw"-to-be spoke
with Shavian authority and Shavian bite:

> Suddenly, we came upon a rare sight, in this arid
> part of the desert, of three gazelles. I told the ar-
> moured car officer to chase them and try to kill one
> with our Lewis gun as we hadn't tasted meat for more
> than a week; as soon as we were in range he opened
> fire but missed. . . . He had only just started firing
> when Lawrence's car came rearing alongside us with
> signals to halt. Lawrence, looking extremely angry,
> got out of the car and said that he would not have the
> gazelles molested in this way; it was cruel and unfair
> in the extreme to try and kill them with a Lewis gun,
> "even," he said, "for a fox-hunter." All my inward
> indignation at Lawrence's attitude this day returned
> after this rebuke and the loss of a chance at a meat
> meal so I saluted with exaggerated decorum and said,
> "Very good, sir," using the term to Lawrence for
> the second and last time in my life.
> . . . Before the day was over . . . my hero worship
> for Lawrence was renewed.
> I reflected as I settled down to sleep on my bed of
> soft sand that this was the first occasion on which I
> had ever received a cross word from Lawrence, and
> how immensely I admired his imperturbable de-
> meanor in the most exasperating circumstances. I
> thought also, chuckling to myself, that it was typical
> of him to show one of his rare bursts of anger at the
> attempted destruction of a gazelle.

Although Shaw's wartime opinions were heretical, even when they were not pacifist, his fascination with military matters was profound, even spilling over from his plays and journalistic writings into his conversation. Shaw had long been attracted to the hero in his role as unconventional military leader. One Sunday evening in the wartime autumn of 1917, at a dinner given for Shaw by his editor-friends Massingham and Nevinson, young Osbert Sitwell listened to the guest of honor expound on this preoccupation of his:

> He spoke much that evening of the great Duke of Wellington, a fellow countryman in whose exploits and conversation he had always been greatly interested: he told us the story of how, on one occasion, when the Duke was asked by an admirer, "How did you really manage to beat Napoleon?" he replied simply, "Well, I'll tell you. Bonaparte's plans were made in wire, mine were made in string"—a very good simile to convey flexibility to a lay mind.[12]

G.B.S., who had already dramatized Napoleon and Caesar, as well as Burgoyne and lesser military heroes, from Captain Bluntschli to Private O'Flaherty, V.C., was in 1923 working on a stage chronicle of another, even more unorthodox, military commander, Joan of Orleans. As far back as 1913 he had expressed interest in the theme, and had even written a letter from the "Joan of Arc country" to Mrs. Stella Campbell in which he anticipated the play's epilogue. But it took further suggestions from Sydney Cockerell and Charlotte before the play was actually begun. By that time Shaw had Lawrence's chronicle at his elbow as he researched and drafted his play. It may have been a coincidence crucial to the play that he was involved simultaneously with two chronicles about unconventional military leaders, mulling over the bulky Oxford recension of *Seven Pillars* (and writing letters of advice about it to Lawrence) while working on his Joan play.

Visitors to Ayot St. Lawrence during 1923 usually were exposed to an admiring display of "the book," as well as a progress report upon the current Shavian work-in-progress. When Sidney Webb week-ended with the Shaws in January, G.B.S. handed him the weighty *Seven Pillars* with the exhortation to read a few pages and form an impression of the contents. After ten minutes, Webb, who scanned a page almost as rapidly as he turned it, looked up and identified the stylistic inspiration as George Borrow. Shaw, who saw Doughty-*cum*-Lawrence, was incredulous, and asked for an explanation. "He described every blade of grass and foot of gravel he walked over," said Webb. When Shaw reported the incident to him, Lawrence worriedly wrote to Edward Garnett, asking for his views about the Borrow parallel.[13] (After Beatrice Webb read *Seven Pillars* she pronounced it "disgusting.")

Meanwhile, Shaw—busy with preliminary reading and planning of *Saint Joan*—had little chance to finish *Seven Pillars* himself. That his enthusiasm for the book survived both sporadic reading and Charlotte's missionary zeal is a key to the playwright's real feelings about the work's literary merits. He took the book in brief nightly stints at Ayot—when he was there—for the Oxford volume was too massive to be regularly carried about to be read on trains, even by stronger, younger men. By mid-April, just as he began the actual writing of *Saint Joan*, he still had forty pages to go, but was convinced, even apart from Charlotte's praises, that Lawrence had written one of the era's great books. Sydney Cockerell, patiently waiting to read the Shaw copy, was put off by a G.B.S. note that the book had to be finished to the last morsel before it could be released.

In May, Lady Augusta Gregory arrived for a stay with
the Shaws, and carefully noted all the details in her diary:

*May 19, 1923.* Came down to Ayot by train. . . .
   G.B.S. drove me home and talked of his Joan of
Arc play. He has not read Mark Twain, is afraid of
being influenced by him. He has read a little of Ana-
tole France and is reading the evidence at the trial, it
was published some years ago. He does not idealise
her as Mark does, and defends the Church, "it didn't
torture her." I think there will be something good
about the English soldiers. He tells me that Lawrence, who fought in Mesopotamia, had been to see
him, is an extraordinary man, very small, living as a
private in the army, having resigned his command,
and has written a wonderful book, has had five
copies linotyped, and lent him one. "It will be one of
the great books of the world. He describes every
blade of grass and flower and noxious insect, and all
the fighting and the terrible crimes of the Turks and
the terrible vengeance he and his men took on them.
He has not a religious mission like Gordon but must
have a touch of his nature. His brother is a missionary in China, or wants to be one, and his mother has
the same desire." He thinks (G.B.S. hears) that all
his family will die out because they are all mad. The
Government did all they could for him, finally gave
him a post in the Colonial Office, but he resigned and
enlisted and for a while it was not known where he
was. His comrades knew but would not give him
away.
*May 20.* He showed me in the evening this book, and
I read a few sentences and said, "It seems as good as
Doughty," and G.B.S. said, "Lawrence is a great ad-
mirer of Doughty." This probably gives him his
style.
   G.B.S. had been working at Joan without talking
[further] about it. . . .

G.B.S. says he chose Joan of Arc because of Bern-hardt and others having played so many parts turn-ing on sexual attraction, he wanted to give Joan as a heroine absolutely without that side. . . .

I am reading the Lawrence book, it is enthralling, each sentence rich and complete.

Charlotte says Lawrence was a Don at Cam-bridge. . . .

He had come to lunch with the Shaws while (as he still is) a private, but dressed extremely well, and although he said that a couple of weeks ago he had been washing plates for the sergeants' mess, she could hardly believe it because his hands were so well cared for. He was charming, but one hears of his thrusting away approaches of friendship with some rudeness. . . .

*May 21.* We have been to Cambridge. Lovely day and a wonderful drive over the smooth roads, not a stone on them, and through hedges and rows of elms and old-fashioned villages. Charlotte is still laid up and could not come. Cockerell met us at the Fitzwilliam Museum and showed us its riches. . . . G.B.S. has given it one of the three John portraits painted at Coole, the Ezekiel one.

Then we had lunch at "The Bull," ordered by G.B.S. Mrs. Cockerell there too, and a daughter of De la Mare. There was a good deal of talk of Law-rence and his book. Cockerell says it (the book) is to be kept secret, but G.B.S. says, "When Lawrence gets into a secret place it is in the limelight. If he hides in a quarry, he puts red flags all around."

Cockerell had met him on Doughty's business. . . .[14]

While, as will be seen, G.B.S. was attempting to pull strings in Whitehall to get Lawrence pensioned out of the Army, he was completing *Joan,* finally writing on August

27 to the young American expatriate Molly Tompkins, "Saint Joan is finished (except for polishing): a magnificent play,—and I thought I should never write another after Methuselah! I am certainly a wonderful man; but then historical plays hardly count: the material is ready-made." By September, 1923, only the arrangement of the stage business remained to be done, and by early October he was staying with Barry Jackson at Birmingham, planning for February (1924) rehearsals.

As he researched and plotted *Saint Joan*, G.B.S. may have sensed the uncanny resemblance which the work in progress (although primarily a religious play) bore to the book at his elbow—the Oxford *Seven Pillars*—and its enigmatic author. Whether the coincidences helped shape the play and its preface can only be surmised, but the parallels are there nevertheless, and perhaps represent Shavian perspectives upon the legendary Maid and the living legend of the ascetic former knight of the desert. As Shaw lived with the records and chronicles of one, and with the chronicle and person of the other, their figures seem in many ways to have merged into a single image, reinforcing for Shaw the timelessness of Joan's experience: the experience of having the spirit within—adventurous, imaginative, contemplative—made use of and then destroyed by a world unready for its idealism except as an instrument to serve the purpose of political realities. In many aspects, it would be difficult to separate the personalities of these two figures, with their immense appetites for glory, their abilities to put people in their pockets, their knacks for unconventional strategy unconventionally set forth. "She lectured, talked down and overruled statesmen and prelates. She pooh-poohed the plans of generals, leading troops to victory on plans of her own. She had an unbounded and quite unconcealed contempt

for official opinion, judgement and authority, and for War
Office tactics and strategy. . . . There were only two
opinions about her. One was that she was miraculous: the
other that she was unbearable." [Preface to *Saint Joan*]
Observers and associates might have also said of the Maid
what John Buchan commented about Lawrence: "His
qualities lacked integration. He had moods of vanity and
moods of abasement; immense self-confidence and immense
diffidence."

In both cases we find the campaign's central figure in the
grip of a nationalistic impulse to create a unified state from
a feudal order, and to set a monarch representative of that
unity upon the throne of the nation-state. Joan's France
under the Dauphin (later Charles VII) may have had as
its modern parallel Lawrence's more naive dream, dashed
at Versailles, of a Pan-Arabian kingdom under Feisal.
Lawrence was embittered by the Paris Conference of
1919, when colonial spoils were cynically divided, and
the assistance the British and French received from the
Emir Feisal and his brothers in defeating the Turks and
ejecting them from Arabia, Syria and Palestine was not
recognized as significant. Finally, in the 1922 Cairo settlement, engineered by Lawrence via Churchill, the loss of
Syria to French domination, and Palestine to Jewish im-
migration (which Lawrence supported), was partially re-
dressed by placing Feisal on the throne of the newly
constituted (from the Palestine mandate) Transjordan.
Possibly it was the resulting easing of bitterness that had
enabled him to think anew of retiring to become a small
cloud of dust on the horizon of public life—a desire first
born in despair.

By the time Shaw had begun *Saint Joan*, Lawrence had
already ascetically retired to his hoped-for obscurity in the
ranks, once saying of himself in a letter to Lionel Curtis

(May, 1923) when he was still attempting to adjust to Army life, that his was a strange form of lay monasticism. "I want to stay here till it no longer hurts me: till the burnt child no longer feels the fire. . . . One used to think that such frames of mind would have perished with the age of religion: and yet here they rise up, purely secular. It's a lurid flash into the Nitrian desert: seems almost to strip the sainthood from Anthony. How about Teresa?" [*Letters*, No. 207]

What might Joan have done, had she lived? In his Preface, dated May, 1924, Shaw pondered, "Had she escaped she would probably have fought on until the English were gone, and then had to shake the dust of the court off her feet, and retire to Domremy. . . ." We may ponder further that Joan, "a young girl, pious and chaste; [whose] . . . excesses have been excesses of religion and charity and not [as the Inquisitor points out in the play's trial scene] of worldliness and wantonness," might have found her postwar world depressing and unsatisfying, and sought fulfillment instead within the walls of a convent.

In 1927, quoting an anecdote about Marshal Foch, Shaw wrote that Lawrence's self-imposed retirement after the First World War saved England a delicate problem—the problem of the young colonel's future. The marshal, the story went, was asked how Napoleon would have fought the war. "Superbly," he said, "but what the devil should we have done with him afterwards?" Flatteringly equating Lawrence's achievement with Napoleon's, Shaw added, "The Prince of Damascus solved the problem for Britannia. He simply walked away and became a nobody again under another name."[15]

It is a striking coincidence that Shaw, several years after connecting the Foch anecdote to Lawrence's situation (in the 1927 G.B.S. preface to the Exhibition Catalogue of paintings from *Seven Pillars*), fastened the story Foch told, not to Lawrence, but to Saint Joan. The occasion then was a B.B.C. radio talk delivered on the five-hundredth anniversary of the burning of Joan at the stake, May 30, 1931. The question of what is to be done with them afterward, Shaw pointed out, arises following the accomplishments of many people of extraordinary ability. He went on to pick a case from the newspapers—that of Leon Trotsky. Stalin's former rival—a civilian whose military exploits from his railway car headquarters, Shaw thought, rivaled those of history's great commanders—was then in precarious exile in Turkey. There were many reasons why, in 1931, it was best for Shaw to leave Lawrence (for the moment) publicly unmentioned—if the omission was a conscious one on Shaw's part. Interestingly enough, we sense a labyrinth of relationships in Shaw's mind in the Saint Joan anniversary talk, for he had just completed the section of his play *Too True to Be Good*, in which Lawrence is caricatured as Private Napoleon Alexander *Trotsky* Meek.

G.B.S. titled one section of his Preface to *Saint Joan* "The Conflict between Genius and Discipline." In it he discussed the charismatic quality of the Maid's personality:

> Outside the farm she had no authority, no prestige, no claim to the smallest deference. Yet she ordered everybody about her from her uncle to the king, the archbishop, and the military General Staff. Her uncle obeyed her like a sheep, and took her to the castle of the local commander, who, on being ordered about, tried to assert himself, but soon collapsed and obeyed. And so on up to the king.

Similar testimonies from Lawrence's military associates and later friends in public life began appearing shortly after the war ended, and persisted until his death. John Buchan (Lord Tweedsmuir), who called him the only authentic genius he ever knew, confided, "I am not a very tractable person or much of a hero-worshipper, but I could have followed Lawrence over the edge of the world."

There was no question about the compelling power of Lawrence's wartime leadership, however unmilitary and informal his Arabian operations were. Still, his irregular status needed administrative sanction, even if *ex post facto.* G.B.S. embellished the facts slightly by raising Lawrence to a rank which, if he held it at all, was a temporary one awarded after he was out of the conflict, but his comment —more theatrical than historical—is nevertheless worth quoting in this context. "As to the British Army," he wrote, "its feelings when, after having to make Lawrence a colonel rather than be ordered about by a nobody, it found him leading his hosts to battle on camel-back in a picturesque Arab costume, can be more easily imagined in messrooms than described by me. Even the camel did not get its regulation meals."[16]

The same charisma manifested itself in Lawrence's final incarnation as "Shaw." An incident of 1929, recorded by Mrs. Clare Sydney Smith, wife of his commanding officer then, indicates as much. Flight-Lieutenant Brecky, who was in charge of Air Force marine craft at Calshot, and Mr. Robertson, of the Air Ministry's Press Section, had gone down to the slipway, discovering there a corporal transmitting some orders about a boat. "Who gave you those orders?" the officer inquired.

> "Mr. Shaw, sir."
> "Who is Mr. Shaw?"
> "Well, sir, Aircraftman Shaw."
> "And why should you, a corporal, take orders from an aircraftman?"
> "Well, sir, it seemed perfectly natural to take orders from Mr. Shaw."

Mrs. Smith drew from the incident what she considered a
key to his "unconscious power of leadership," referring to
Chapter XXV of *Seven Pillars*. There Lawrence had written, ". . . the work suffered by the creation of . . . a bar
between the leaders and men. Among the Arabs there
were no distinctions, traditional or natural, except the
unconscious power given a famous sheikh by virtue of his
accomplishment; and they taught me that no man could be
their leader except he ate the ranks' food, lived level with
them, and yet appeared better in himself." It is unlikely
that these lines escaped G.B.S.

G.B.S.'s Joan, perhaps out of the same instinctive power
of leadership, insists (as play and preface point out) upon
having a soldier's dress and arms, horse and equipment, and
on treating her escort of soldiers as comrades, sleeping
side by side with them on the floor at night as if there were
no difference of sex or rank between them. Yet both
youthful warriors were essentially unmilitary individuals—
novices at war but in love with its trappings and its heady
thrills. To the village girl from the Vosges, Dunois comments, "You have the makings of a soldier in you. You are
in love with war." So, too, in 1916, was the young arche-
ology student from Oxford.

What was quite apparent to those as close to Lawrence
as was Shaw, was that the reports about his disinterest in
such conventionalities of living as love and marriage were
borne out by his choice of friends and his monastic barracks life as much as by his letters. The "conflict of sex,"
as Shaw put it in his description of Joan, was given little
encouragement to manifest itself:

> The evident truth [Shaw wrote of Joan] is that
> like most women of her hardy managing type she
> seemed neutral in the conflict of sex because men
> were much too afraid of her to fall in love with her.

> She herself was not sexless: in spite of the virginity she had vowed up to a point, and preserved to her death, she never excluded the possibility of marriage for herself. But marriage, with its preliminary of the attraction, pursuit, and capture of a husband, was not her business: she had something else to do.

Shaw comprehended Lawrence's design for living only in part—the part represented by such of his heroes as Joan, the type of individual controlled by what Shaw called *moral passion*. This kind of hero does not control his passions by any rational process: his physical passions are overwhelmed by something greater—virtue—which is a passion of the mind. "It must be remembered," a critic writes, "that for Shaw thought is a passion. In *Back to Methuselah* the Ancients agree with Martellus that 'Nothing remains beautiful and interesting except thought, because thought is the life.' Thus Shavian evolution ends in pure thought, a rather boring proposition to the conventional mind which cannot envision excitement without passion. To the conventional mind Shaw would say, as does Raphael at the end of *Farfetched Fables*, 'On the contrary: intellectual passion, mathematical passion, passion for discovery and exploration: the mightiest of all passions.' "[17]

On the other hand, Shaw seemed to see in Lawrence's choice of the ranks a quest for a living martyrdom rather than a quest for an ascetic way of living. To Shaw martyrdom was "a waste of vitality and a triumph of illusion over reality, since it produces a sort of hypnosis upon its witness. Men develop fixations upon the cross, the act of martyrdom itself, while doing their best to ignore the implications of the martyr's ethical conquest. As Joan remarks, 'It is the memory and the salvation that sanctify the cross, not the cross that sanctifies the memory and the salvation. . . . I shall outlast the cross.' Thus while Shaw was hardly a prudent man—among other things, *Commonsense about the War* nearly got him lynched—he nevertheless saw quite clearly the futility of martyrdom, and the value of Joan going far beyond the mere burning of her body."[18] A possible reflection of this attitude is the evidence that as Shaw worked on *Saint Joan* he pressed his efforts to pension Lawrence out of the service and into creative literary work.

Lawrence enjoyed the discipline of sitting for portraits, and the reflected glory of looking at them; yet it is unlikely that he ever saw himself in the Joan G.B.S. shaped. Shaw appears to have modeled Joan's physical appearance after the woman who then managed the Fabian Society Summer Schools. When the play was published he inscribed her copy: "To Mary Hankinson, the only woman I know who does not believe that she is the model for Joan and the only woman who actually was." Lawrence received several copies of the play over the years, the last, "To Shaw from Shaw to replace many stolen copies until this, too, is stolen," was inscribed on February 7, 1934, and was in Lawrence's library at his death. In it was a longer note added by the recipient: "G.B.S. gave me first a copy of the acting version of S. Joan. It was borrowed from me by an R.T.C. reader, who lent it to another, and he to a third. So it disappeared. Then G.B.S. sent me another Joan, like this, inscribed 'To Pte.* Shaw from Public Shaw.' This was one of my chief joys at Clouds Hill: but in 1932 it also vanished. Hence this third copy, with its pessimistic inscription. 2. 34. T.E.S."

A number of parallel occurrences in 1944, shortly after

* The abbreviation for the lowest enlisted rank. The United States Army uses *Pvt.* as its abbreviation for *Private*.

the death of Charlotte Shaw, do not seem to be discon-
nected. When G.B.S., then eighty-eight, gave the letters
from his wife to T. E. Lawrence to the British Museum,
he also presented the shorthand draft of his manuscript of
*Saint Joan*. At the same time his reawakened memories of
Lawrence spurred him to return to a reading of Doughty,
whose *Arabia Deserta* he had consulted when working
with Lawrence on the revision of *Seven Pillars*. To borrow
additional volumes of Doughty, Shaw wrote his old friend
Sydney Cockerell, maintaining in the correspondence that
*Seven Pillars* would either never have been written or
would have been wholly different without Doughty.[19]

Years earlier, at the time of Lawrence's enlistment in
the Tank Corps, G.B.S. had realized that Doughty's literary influence was so marked in the book (which he had
not finished) that any attempt on his part to help prepare
*Seven Pillars* for publication required a preparatory sampling of Doughty. On April 12, 1923, Lawrence, who had
discovered Shaw's enterprise, wrote delightedly to Edward
Garnett: "Good news of Shaw and Doughty. What guts
the man has: to read a great part of my book, and *at once*
to go on to Doughty: magnificent!" [*Letters*, No. 203]
G.B.S. later estimated that it had taken him the equivalent
of ten days to read *Seven Pillars*. The nine months' task
—begun while Lawrence was undergoing Air Force recruit training—had been completed while he was submit-
ting to Tank Corps basic training.

Lawrence—Private Shaw, R.T.C.—despised the Army
but refused to leave it, hoping instead for the "good character" that would gain him re-entry into the R.A.F. His
letters lamented the animal outlook of his companions,
the foul life. At the Bovington Tank Corps depot, Corporal Alec Dixon discovered that "Broughie Shaw" (the
troops admired him for his Brough motorcycle, with

side-car, which represented about two years' pay to his
fellow recruits) was really an ex-colonel named Lawrence,
whose wartime exploits meant little to the other men;
their ranks included a number of ex-officers at a loss for
peacetime occupation. Lawrence confided to Dixon his
desire to return to the Air Force, when it would have him.
He had enlisted, he said, because he equated the modern
army barracks with the medieval monastery, and, "as he
explained with a grin, the medieval monastery provided a
convenient refuge for disillusioned warriors." The work
at Bovington—even basic training—was hardly as exhaust-
ing as his R.A.F. training at Uxbridge, for civilian contract
labor and permanent service personnel performed many
of the menial housekeeping tasks; but army service was far
from exhilarating. During the first months of army recruit
training, Lawrence was desperately unhappy. He was
much older (at thirty-five) than most other recruits, and
felt even older than he was. The monotony of the routine
distressed him. The endless procession of drills and guard
duties were like those of an infantry regiment: he had
not expected to find them in a mechanically oriented corps.
"Nevertheless," Dixon recalled, "he was a good soldier, although sorely tried at times by those whose delight it was
to make life miserable for any recruit who showed more
than animal intelligence."

When on armored car training, Lawrence later wrote
in *The Mint*, he was regularly driven so unskillfully by
others all day, that his nervousness turned by night into
fever and delirium, and he talked "like a river" in his sleep
half the night. The other recruits would not tell him
what he said, but in the morning they would look at him
strangely. He wrote D. G. Hogarth that his barrack mates
were barely tolerable, even to his stomach: "There is an
animal reek here which keeps me awake at night with

horror that mankind should be like it: because I feel that we are the unnatural, & that Hut F-12 is the truth about human-kindness."

To Curtis he reported that recording the acts and conversation of the inhabitants of Hut F-12 would result in a "moral-medical case-book," and that exposure to it had shown him "the truth behind Freud." Though his mind ached with it, and with longing for the slow bugle call for lights out, "like God's providence, a dewfall of peace upon the camp," he could not sleep. The worst of it, he thought, was that although R.A.F. training was severe, he lay at night contented in its exhaustion; even his mind stopped working. Now he was sleepless night after night, "thinking about everything germane." The irony of it all, he emphasized to Curtis, and later to G.B.S., was that "Those fellows are the reality, and you and I, the selves who used to meet in London and talk of fleshless things, are only the outward wrappings of a core like those fellows." His brooding constantly found its way into his correspondence[20] and into the extremity of his after-duty avocations. He discussed his "masochism," which he insisted was of the moral variety only, and ruefully described one letter to Curtis as a "nice, neurotic" one. He found himself unable to eat any meal beyond breakfast. After-duty hours he would pull out his motorcycle and "hurl it top-speed through these unfit roads for hour after hour. My nerves are jaded and gone near dead, so that nothing less than hours of voluntary danger will prick them into life: and the 'life' they reach then is a melancholy joy at risking something worth exactly 2/9 a day."

In his letters Lawrence regularly announced that his decision to remain in the ranks was an economic one. Although his rationalization was certainly not true, he at least partially believed in it, and his friends had little choice but to accept his decision. Why did he enlist? "The security of it first: seven years existence guaranteed," he wrote Hogarth. He claimed to be finished with the "Lawrence episode," and wearied by the life of politics, for which he did not feel "coarse-fibred enough." He was only worth more than three shillings a day when employed in Middle East politics, he thought, and he was finished with that. "Exit Lawrence and there is most of the residue of my earning power gone." The fact that he possessed some considerable literary ability did not escape him, but his attitude toward it was bound up with his desire to remain in the ranks, something not easily compatible with commercial literary success. His own verdict upon the *Seven Pillars* manuscript was (to his friends) a hard one. "The hope that it isn't as good as Shaw says sustains me," he wrote Curtis in a letter filled with the consolations of the private soldier's life:

> The perfect beauty of this place becomes tremendous, by its contrast with the life we lead, and the squalid huts we live in, and the noisy bullying authority of all our daily unloveliness. The nearly intolerable meanness of man is set in a circle of quiet heath, and budding trees, with the firm level bar of the Purbeck hills behind. The two worlds shout their difference in my ears. Then there is the irresponsibility: I have to answer here only for the cleanness of skin, cleanness of clothes, and a certain mechanical neatness of physical evolution upon the barrack-square. There has not been presented to me, since I have been here, a single choice: everything is ordained—except that harrowing choice of going away from here the moment my will to stay breaks down.
> [*Letters*, No. 208]

Though he was busy with plans for *Seven Pillars*, and undecided between publishing an abridgement made for

him by Edward Garnett, or (as G.B.S. urged) a revision
of the complete text, he continued to insist that it was a
"pessimistic unworthy book"—and just as regularly recounted the praises of it sung by Thomas Hardy and
Bernard Shaw. His state of mind is best seen in a letter to
Hogarth, in which, after mention of the unpleasantness of
barracks company, he concluded that his refusal to be
"Lawrence," and to be involved in politics, left him without a trade to follow. Since he refused to do the "two or
three things" for which he was qualified, he reasoned, he
was reduced to soldiering. A literary career was out; he
had already had one, even though it was over somewhat
more abruptly than he might have wished. "When I joined
the R.A.F.," he wrote, "it was in the hope that someday
I'd write a book about the very excellent subject that it
was. At that time I thought my Arab Revolt book very
bad. Since then Shaw has turned my mind slowly to consider it good: and there's another ambition gone, for it
was always in my hope to write a decent book: and if
I've done it there seems little reason to do another. A pity,
for my Uxbridge notes were good & there was the making
of a very good thing out of the life of a squadron. . . ."
[*Letters*, No. 212]

The Shaws brooded with growing, almost parental,
horror over Lawrence's immolation, and G.B.S. again
brought up the matter of a Civil List pension, asking him
how much would suffice to bring about his willingness to
ask for a discharge from the Army. Shaw had chosen his
timing well, for at that time (as Villars describes these
early Army months), "never was a courageous soul less
resigned." Lawrence replied, "with a promptitude which
showed he had fully considered the matter," £300 a year.
Armed with this information, G.B.S. then interceded with
Stanley Baldwin, the new Prime Minister, who had just
been elevated into the premiership. The collapse in health

of Bonar Law, after seven months in office, had forced the King to choose between Baldwin and Curzon. Baldwin had held Cabinet rank less than three years, with only his last ministry, that of Chancellor of the Exchequer, being significant preparation for the highest office. And that was achieved only because the most eminent Conservatives had followed Austen Chamberlain into political exile, forcing Law to form his government from—as Churchill, one of the dissidents, put it—the second eleven. Baldwin—only second choice for the Exchequer—was suddenly the King's First Minister. As an irreverent contemporary history commented:

> Only clairvoyant intuition could have recognized Mr. Baldwin as a man of destiny. Indeed, he had so little to distinguish him, in physical or mental features, from the rank and file of Conservative members that the public was hard put to identify him when his leadership made some sort of identification necessary. If it had not been for his habit of smoking a pipe hardly anyone would have been able to keep in mind who he was. The pipe was invaluable. Its projection provided the only abruptness of contour in the square, smooth figure, and the cartoonists were duly thankful for this small mercy. It typified Mr. Baldwin's kinship with the millions of steady, slow-but-sure, house-holding, tax-paying, bread-winning, pipe-smoking, proudly ordinary English voters. [John Collier and Ian Lang, *An Informal History of Great Britain Since the War*, London, 1932]

It may have surprised Baldwin to receive a private memorandum from a political foe, G. B. S.—a letter which had been carefully read and corrected in some details by Lawrence's friend Hogarth. Dubiously, Hogarth had written about the gesture to Shaw: "The fact is that money weighs much less with him than his mode of life. I cannot conceive any Government post, such as the P.M. could offer, which L. would accept, or if accepted, retain. He begins at once to talk of 'moral prostitution' and quits! . . . Lawrence is not normal in many ways and it is extraordinarily difficult to do anything for him! In some measure the life of letters is best suited to him. He will not work in any sort of harness unless this is padlocked on to him. He enlisted in order to have the padlocks rivetted on to him." [*Letters,* pp. 351-52]

Undeterred, G.B.S sent his letter, dated May 31, 1923, the last day of Baldwin's first precarious month in office. No meek supplication, it expressed indignant concern at Lawrence's situation:

> Clearly this is a bad case of Belisarius begging obols in an ungrateful country . . . the fact remains that he is serving as a private for his daily bread; and however much his extraordinary character may be accountable for this, it strikes all who know about it as a scandal that should be put an end to by some means. They feel that the private soldier business is a shocking tomfoolery and are amazed to find that Lawrence is not in a position of a pensioned commanding officer in dignified private circumstances. [*Letters,* p. 446]

A few days later Sydney Cockerell commented on the Shaw-Hogarth memorandum in his diary:

> Called on Bernard Shaw and had a good talk about T. E. Lawrence, on whose behalf he has written a long letter to the new Prime Minister (Stanley Baldwin). He showed me a copy of this letter, in which, after giving a fairly accurate outline of Lawrence's exploits and antecedents, and a great eulogy of his (unpublished) book, he states that L's only desire is

to have an assured income of £300 a year from the Government in return for his astonishing war services in the East. (This all comes from my introducing Lawrence to Shaw on 25 April 1922.) He is now Private Shaw of the Tank Corps, Bovington Camp, Dorset, and has refused £7000 from Jonathan Cape for the publication of his memoirs. He is an absolute puzzle and enigma—an undoubted genius of incredible bravery—perhaps a little mad.[21]

Lawrence's enforced and well-publicized discharge from the R.A.F. was of very recent memory. Obviously in a difficult political position, even with a majority of eighty-eight in Commons, Baldwin was not likely to rush into the creation of adverse newspaper headlines. But Bernard Shaw, a lion of the burgeoning Left, was a man to be listened to politely; and so Baldwin did, while G.B.S. asked for a pension of £500 for Lawrence, perhaps hoping to compromise down to the sum he mentioned in his letter. "Baldwin," the petitioner recalled, "pipe in mouth and always agreeable, approved of all I said, but feared that Parliament might object. I, instructed in parliamentary procedure by Lord Olivier, explained how it could be done without raising any question. He very kindly left me under the impression that the petition would be granted.

"It never was. That was Baldwin's way, and the secret of his promotion. He could always be depended on to smoke amiably and do nothing."[22]

Not only Baldwin's gracious manner of receiving him, but the speed with which his quiet diplomacy had effected the meeting, had encouraged G.B.S. His letter had resulted in an interview within the week, and by the seventh of June he was writing to Cockerell that the Prime Minister had seemed "cordial and, I think, really interested." Baldwin, Shaw reported, was going to Oxford shortly, and would talk about the matter with Hogarth.

The "Belisarius" image in the letter to Baldwin was a carefully calculated one. G.B.S. late in 1922 had been solicited, along with every other public figure in England, to contribute to a fund-raising enterprise, *The British Legion Album in Aid of Field-Marshal Earl Haig's Appeal for Ex-Service Men of All Ranks*. Whether G.B.S. had Lawrence's new condition in mind at that time is unkown, but what he penned for the *Haig Album* parallels his romanticized despair over what was to Lawrence a reasonably comfortable situation. A secret poet (and really no poet at all), Shaw produced a set of verses on Belisarius, the Byzantine general known for his Lawrence-like hit-and-run tactics; his ability to achieve conquests at little cost and with small units; his temperate, brave and chaste character; and his lamentable end (as tradition in Constantinople preserves it). Belisarius's eyes were put out, and, unrewarded by his own people, he passed the rest of his days begging in the streets, his words "preserved" in a metrical romance by Tzetzes. Shaw's poem was reproduced in facsimile in the *Haig Album*:

> Justinian in History's view
> Your fame is not worth half a snowball
> Because, ungrateful monarch, you
> Grudged Belisarius his obol.
> Again the veteran begs his bread
> From you, who swore he ne'er should rue it.
> For shame! It was for you he bled:
> It is for you to see him through it.

Baldwin, who knew the *Haig Album*, then on sale, could not help but sense the bold, and perhaps disturbing, refer-

ence to Belisarius in Shaw's letter. Neither could it have
escaped Lawrence, who was soon to see a copy of the letter.
He had read and translated parts of the histories of Pro-
copius (Belisarius's military secretary) as a schoolboy, and
later claimed he had learned tactics from them. And it is
interesting that in 1928 he wrote to Robert Graves from
India, "Send me another poem whenever you remember
Belisarius. To desire such obols is not to deny my satisfaction." Five years later, in a letter to Liddell Hart, we see
perhaps an unconscious tie to the poem in the *Haig Album*:
"A general can learn as much from Belisarius as from Haig
—but not a soldier."

Pleased with himself, G.B.S. had sent a copy of the
"Belisarius" letter to Lawrence, who, the reference notwithstanding, was unhappy with the intervention. He disapproved the portrait of him Shaw daubed for Baldwin, and,
now that his recruit training was over, apparently felt relieved that he was still in uniform. "I'm not intractable and
rebellious:" he wrote to G.B.S., "ask any of my officers for
witness! There is not a humbler little beast. . . ." Turning
on Shaw—but gently—for a favor that was now unwanted,
Lawrence suggested that it was Irish stubbornness that made
him what he was, and Irishmen could persuade the rest
of the world, but not other Irishmen. He was genuine in
his desire to serve in the ranks, he insisted, and wanted no
part of the civil or military responsibilities offered him as
alternative callings. Changing the subject, he commented
on *Back to Methuselah* (Shaw sent him an inscribed copy
a month later): "We aren't going that way, if the fellows
here are an indication, and I suppose they are extracts of
the widest English class." [*Letters*, No. 235] Whether
Lawrence recognized it or not, the last play in the *Methuselah* series, *As Far As Thought Can Reach*, suggested
traits in the long-lived race with which Shaw peopled the

world of 31,920 A.D. that could already be seen in Lawrence. It was in no way intentional, for the play had been written before the two men had met, and the anti-romantic asceticism Shaw saw in the humans of the future was possibly as much wish-fulfillment as the free-lovers with whom Shaw's friend H. G. Wells (no ascetic he) peopled his future worlds. Lawrence disliked physical contact, recoiling even from the shaking of hands, and had no interest in romantic love. It would have been interesting to have had recorded his impressions of the world of *As Far As Thought Can Reach*, whose people (like him) did not concern themselves with physical comfort as an end in life, and whose reactions to romantic love, once they left infancy, were much like Strephon discovered in the Maiden:

> STREPHON. Listen to me [*he puts his arm around her*].
> THE MAIDEN [*extricating herself*] Dont. We can talk quite as well without touching one another.
> STREPHON [*horrified*] Chloe! Oh, this is the worst symptom of all! The ancients never touch each other.

Later in the play the artist Martellus (at four years of age) enters adulthood in Shaw's precocious world, and announces, "The body always ends by being a bore. Nothing remains beautiful and interesting except thought, because thought is the life." Lawrence might have added that he was "going that way," but answered Shaw only by indirection: the others in his barracks were not.

Probably G.B.S. had not misunderstood Lawrence's past lack of enthusiasm for Army life. What he had not realized was that Lawrence's attitude had changed drastically after the sixteen weeks of recruit training were followed by an appointment as quartermaster's clerk: soft, dull employment with leisure for working over the revision of *Seven*

*Pillars.* Even the after-hours were more pleasant. Lawrence, on one of his motorcycle jaunts through Dorsetshire, had come upon a tumbledown cottage, hidden by huge rhododendrons, in the Hardy country just over a mile from camp. Determined to acquire it, he sold to Lionel Curtis a gold dagger he had brought back from Mecca, thereby raising funds for the cottage's purchase and renovation. Nearby was the home of Sergeant Knowles, one of his new friends, who helped him patch the tiled roof, whitewash the bricks and build bookshelves in the one room downstairs, narrowing the tiny cell. "Clouds Hill" fast became the repository for a bed, two chairs, his phonograph (and record collection), his pictures and his many books. Built-in was a wide mantelshelf for his use as a table (to eat at standing).

G.B.S. had asked him what he did in his spare time, and T. E. answered that he belonged to the Army until six each evening, but spent Sundays and afternoons-off (actually every day from 4:30 to 9:00, also) either riding or in the cottage reading or writing. He could also now receive friends, and ended his letter on that note. Would the Shaws come to Clouds Hill? Mrs. Shaw had been writing him regularly, and he added a thank-you for her latest letter and check. He could not visit them, for one of his mates had borrowed his cycle and wrecked it.

Shaw, apparently still convinced that only pride kept Lawrence from begging out of the service, kept both at the critical reading of *Seven Pillars* for the projected limited edition, and at wire-pulling to acquire a pension for the quartermaster's storeman-clerk who protested that he really liked his job after all. By this time, Shaw, deeply immersed —with Charlotte—in the problems of refurbishing *Seven Pillars,* was more concerned, because of the ensuing gain to letters he envisaged, with returning its author to full-time literary activity than with his obvious loss of interest in leaving the service. Lawrence wrote Edward Garnett, who had worked on what he thought was a commercially viable abridgement, that the text "will be revised, but only in petto. No good cuts or noble changes, no re-writing: just punctuation, and insect-blemishes removed." It was diplomatically less than the truth, which might have hurt the kind, conscientious Garnett. It failed to mention that the changes were being initiated by Bernard Shaw, who had just unknowingly struck another, more cruel blow. Garnett, who had never been a success at fiction or (his real love) drama, making his considerable reputation as editor and critic, had just had his interest revived in his 1911 play, *The Trial of Jeanne d'Arc*. He was sending it to theatre managers when Shaw announced to the press that he had completed *Saint Joan*. This made it impossible for any management to risk putting on Garnett's Joan play.

In early January, 1924, a month before the *Saint Joan* rehearsals were to begin, Shaw called on the Prime Minister, Stanley Baldwin, again, and pressed the matter of Lawrence's pension. Baldwin, in the last, rocky fortnight of his first tenure of office, could hardly have been receptive, even after Shaw presented him with a copy of Robert Graves's short-lived magazine *The Winter Owl*, which contained a sample of the magnum opus. Again Shaw insisted on the incongruity of Lawrence's lowly situation, and on his willingness to accept a pension, which understanding he claimed to have had from Lawrence personally, although he feared Hogarth might have been intimating otherwise. Lawrence, he told the Prime Minister, felt that he could only make a writing career by exploiting his Arabian adventures, and, although he wanted a literary vocation, he would rather have his country recognize his past military services in the traditional manner.

Baldwin politely set aside the idea of a Civil List pension,

as not only inadequate, but intended less for services rendered than as near charity. Commons, which could vote a
special pension, he pointed out, obviously was too busy
trying to bring him down to consider another controversy.
Shaw countered with the suggestion of a military pension,
and Baldwin offered to look into it, jotting down a note
on the subject, and promising pleasantly to take his *Owl*
with him to read at Chequers.

The Prime Minister vacated Chequers two weeks later,
a no-confidence vote in the House ushering in the brief first
Labour government of Shaw's Fabian friend, Ramsay Mac-
Donald. With Baldwin went the *Owl* and the note.

Whether Lawrence would have fared better under Baldwin's ministry, had it not fallen spectacularly (although out
of office only briefly), is open to speculation. His changing
attitudes toward his service and literary careers prevented
pressures on his behalf for a pension (but not toward other
ends) for the rest of the decade. It was clearly unsound for
Shaw to press for a military or civil pension for a relatively
young man in his mid-thirties who was still hardy enough
to withstand recruit training in both the Air Force and the
Army within a year, and who had literary talents which
were as commercially useful as they were undeniable.
Further, though G.B.S.'s efforts were sincere, he had been
dealing with an unusual Prime Minister. During the war,
while in Parliament and in a sub-cabinet post, Baldwin lived
through the prevailing cynicism to experience "something
like a spiritual conversion. He felt that it was the duty of
men of his age to supply the loss of that 'missing generation,' which could in ordinary circumstances have guided
Britain's future. . . ." After brooding for some months after
the war, he had quietly, during the summer of 1919, written
a pseudonymous letter to *The Times*, announcing that he
was making a voluntary levy upon his estate—a "thank-

offering"—of twenty per cent of its value, to be given to
the nation's treasury to help pay the war debt. He appealed
to others to do the same, but had few imitators.[23] Shaw
could not have known this, but the request to place a young
man of great potential—and who had survived the war
gloriously—on the Civil List, must have rung hollow to the
idealistic new Prime Minister.

G.B.S.'s efforts did not go over well with Lawrence
either. He had already insisted that he was content to remain in the Army until the Air Force would have him.
Now he sent Shaw a plea for no further intercession. "If
I won't do that sort of thing for myself, other people should
not do it for me. It's awfully good of you . . . but awfully
bad for me. Please let up on it all. The army is more or less
what I ought to have, and in time I'll get to feel at home in
it." The copy of *The Winter Owl* which G.B.S. had prof-
fered to Baldwin had been purchased by Charlotte, who
had been indignant on discovering that her twelve-and-
sixpence was not buying anything new, but only an abridgement of three chapters of *Seven Pillars*. Still, it had served
its use, and Lawrence asked Shaw to "please tell Mrs. Shaw
that if ever I write anything new (I try hard not to) I'll
send her a copy direct. This will save her wasting money on
owls or Doughty's [to read Lawrence's new introduction
to *Arabia Deserta*] in the future." A week before the hope
was to be realized, "Shaw" ended his letter to Shaw: "May
Ramsay MacDonald soon succeed Baldwin. . . ." [*Letters*,
No. 239]

One of the ironies of politics is that when MacDonald
did succeed Baldwin, Shaw felt that since he had worked
hard to establish the Labour Party in power, any intervention into politics by him at that juncture would have been
interference. As he wrote Beatrice Webb, whose husband
became Minister of Labour in the new cabinet, "The arrival

of a Labour Government puts me definitely out of politics just as it puts Labour members and candidates definitely into politics. But my own peculiar position remains stronger than ever. . . ."

Shaw's political position turned out to be weaker than ever with regard to MacDonald, whose two tenures of office as Prime Minister alienated him first slowly, then completely, from the Fabian-Labour supporters who had nurtured his political career, only to see him as he reached the top to be utterly unlike their image of him. David Garnett writes [*Letters*, p. 446] that Shaw continued—without success—to press MacDonald for a pension for Lawrence, but it seems unlikely that Shaw could have made as serious an attempt with MacDonald, whom he soon regarded as an apostate, as with Baldwin, whose Opposition views he respected as such. G.B.S. even suggested that the fall of Baldwin was regrettable—with respect to Lawrence's interests. [*Letters*, No. 235] For Ramsay MacDonald as Prime Minister, as A. J. P. Taylor writes, "was to prove the left-wing counterpart of Baldwin, equally devoted to tranquility and freedom from adventures and commitments. In 1922 he still seemed securely on the Left; still lunching every day at the 1917 Club; still frowned on by the respectable for his supposed pacifism during the Great War. In presence he was, in Shinwell's phrase, a prince among men. He had a ravishingly musical voice, every syllable ringing of Utopia."[24] Little happened in MacDonald's first brief ministry in 1924. As a saying went, Labour was "in office, but not in power." Finally the affair of the apparently forged "Zinoviev letter" forced Labour into a general election which, fraudulently discredited, it lost. Soon Baldwin was back in office again, not to play musical chairs with MacDonald again until 1929.

Quietly, on March 1, 1924, Lawrence petitioned the Air

Ministry for reinstatement in the R.A.F. The application was considered with care, and one high official, Air Vice-Marshal Sir Philip Game, reported that he had no objection, even suggesting that Lawrence be sent to a squadron stationed abroad, and that its commander be informed in advance of Lawrence's identity. But Game apparently was a minority of one, leaving for Shaw later opportunities to intervene politically for "Shaw." More important to both Shaws now, however, was the revision of *Seven Pillars*, which would be completed, Lawrence hoped, by the end of the year. Subscribers to a limited edition had already been solicited. By the beginning of February, twenty had already been acquired and block-making for the illustrations begun. Both Shaws advanced upon Damascus.

# THREE

---

## *1924-1926*

The Shavian advance upon Damascus began in earnest with the ending of G.B.S.'s entreaties to Baldwin. In December, 1923, Lawrence had written to Shaw that he had definitely decided to print a thirty-guinea edition for subscribers, and not to accept Shaw's subscription: he would mulct only the extremely wealthy. The volume would have about fifty portrait illustrations, and be corrected only in style: nothing would be added, nothing censored. Further, Lawrence added, he would not need to worry about libelous passages, for a private soldier was not liable for damages, and prison could hardly be more unpleasant than the Tank Corps. Ebulliently, "Shaw" had signed the letter "TE?".[1]

G.B.S. was annoyed both with Lawrence's intractability with regard to the pension (temporarily a lost cause with Baldwin's ouster) and with some of Lawrence's plans for *Seven Pillars;* but he realized that for the time being his efforts had to be literary rather than political, and he counted on his having more influence upon Lawrence in person than by letter.

London was 126 miles away from Bovington Heath, more famous as Egdon Heath in Hardy's novels. Army training (and service companions) had made Lawrence so miserable that often, even when he had only a half-day free, he would race eastward on his motorcycle to London in under three hours, and race back in time for evening roll call. He had "really struck bed-rock" in the Army, for it was unspeakably animal, more so than he imagined possible in a body of Englishmen. But he concluded that the new life he hated was "good medicine" for him. To forget it, however, he would visit Thomas Hardy (to whom Robert Graves had introduced him); or race to his more distant friends Augustus John or Bernard Shaw, with whom he would discuss illustrations for *Seven Pillars* or changes in its text. Fresh from Doughty and Lawrence, G.B.S. would interrupt work on *Saint Joan* to playfully tease Lawrence that Doughty was a beachcomber, and that Lawrence's own description of the prima donna qualities of the Arab tribal chieftains made their origins obvious: an Italian opera company had once been lost in the desert, "and bred a posterity of Beduwy. Auda, for instance, was clearly a Verdi baritone."[2]

Once recruit training was over Lawrence had more freedom, visiting the Hardys for tea every third Saturday or Sunday, and staying overnight and week-ends at Ayot St. Lawrence so often that the servants began calling one of the second-floor guest rooms "Lawrence's Room." At camp his leisure-time activity paradoxically involved reinforcing the memories of Army life (which he would usually leave camp in order to forget) by writing long letters to his friends about the horror in which he lived. He had a permanent midnight pass, and usually used it to the limit. The only proof of his presence during off-duty hours was the roar of his motorcycle, as he raced from camp or to camp along the Wool Road, which led to his cottage. There remained little of the physical horror Lawrence had felt during his first months as Private Shaw, for his clerk's duties were easy, his week-ends were spent away from camp, and his meals were taken anywhere but in the ranks' messroom. Even this latter practice failed to excite suspicion, a private recalled.[3] He had achieved the maximum of privacy his introverted self could find in a situation where there were no private bedrooms, and latrines—even when they had partitions—had no doors.

Although his routine was little altered, by 1924 his letters had radically changed into plans and announcements for the limited edition of *Seven Pillars* (Robin Buxton, of Martin's Bank, who had been a colonel with the Imperial Camel Corps, had agreed to handle its fiscal affairs). Early in the year, while he was awaiting a new motorcycle and was temporarily without transportation, he was able to mail to Hogarth from Clouds Hill the new total of subscribers along with the news that "Shaw (the genuine one) was here lately: full of quaintness upon the supposed oddity of my position in camp (now absolutely normal, though I haven't been able to make myself like the rest in mind or manner). Also very bracing, though such sureness of success has closed his pores." Lawrence's friend Corporal Alec Dixon, who was then on leave, heard on returning to camp that "the Great Spadebeard" had been to Clouds Hill, and had approved of the place. "He came in," said Lawrence, "sniffing the air and taking stock of everything like a sergeant-major. I really think he liked it, you know." After the visit Lawrence received a package of delicacies from Gunter's in London. The donor was anonymous, but he wrote his thanks to Mrs. Shaw.

Dixon recalled later (in *T. E. Lawrence by His Friends*) that Private Shaw's conversations and opinions at Bovington Camp and Clouds Hill seemed already to reflect the impact of acquaintance with G.B.S.'s works and words. "Shaw" often "spoke of literature in terms of music" and once told Dixon that every novelist-to-be should study the movements of a Beethoven sonata before committing himself to paper. A similar suggestion, Dixon thought, had been made in one of G.B.S.'s prefaces, and Lawrence may have borrowed it unconsciously. His advice to Dixon again recalled G.B.S.—this time the drama criticism—when he advised reading "some Shakespeare every day—he's sheer music, you know!" Shaw's symbolic farce, *Heartbreak House*, was one of Lawrence's favorite works—even before he met G.B.S. It gained stature in his eyes through the years. He was a generation ahead of critics and theatre-going public, who cited the play as a talky failure. In 1928 he wrote William Rothenstein that he had been "studying *Heartbreak House:* whose first act strikes me as metallic, inhuman, supernatural: the most blazing bit of genius in English literature. I'd have written that first, if I had choice." [*Letters*, No. 347] His Labourite political sympathies then recalled G.B.S.', but he became disillusioned with communism long before Shaw would admit to any flaws in the reality of the communist dream. By the time of Shaw's trip to Russia in the early thirties, Lawrence was faintly praising Bolshevism as noble in aspiration but lacking in common sense. In Bovington Camp days, however, he would shock Dixon and other Clouds Hill companions by remarking casually, "When history comes to be written, Lenin will probably take his place as the greatest man of our time."

Ten years later, curiously enough, the young W. H. Auden (reviewing in proletarian fashion the 1934 Liddell Hart biography of Lawrence in Cape's *Now and Then*), paired Lawrence and Lenin—no mean intellectual feat. Auden compared the asceticism of the two as modern approaches to more natural human relationships. "The self

must first learn to be indifferent," Auden wrote, and quoted
Lenin's dictum that one had "to go hungry, work illegally
and be anonymous." This was absolute modernity. "I mentioned Lenin," Auden went on. "He and Lawrence seem to
me the two whose lives exemplify most completely what is
best and significant in our time, our nearest approach to a
synthesis of feeling and reason, act and thought, the most
potent agents of freedom and to us, egotistical underlings,
the most relevant accusation and hope."

On one G.B.S. visit to Dorsetshire, the Shaws—all three
of them—went on from Clouds Hill to a more famous local
address—Max Gate. A journal entry by Florence Hardy for
December 30, 1923, notes that the Shaws and "Col. T. E.
Lawrence" lunched at Max Gate and spent several hours
there. Lawrence had earlier refused the opportunity to
spend Christmas at Max Gate. Though his reason was
largely that he wanted to release a family man for the holiday, he added another in a letter to Sydney Cockerell. "It
is not good to be too happy often," he wrote from camp on
Christmas Day. "May see Shaw tomorrow," he added, "if I
can wangle a pass to Bournemouth, and transport thither."[4]
The friendship with the Hardys almost resulted in another literary adventure for Lawrence. Hardy was in his
middle eighties, and his prudent wife, knowing of his fond-
ness for Lawrence, once asked the latter if he were interested in editing her husband's diary, "written quite
intimately before he became famous, but showing, very
wonderfully, the growth of his mind and the slow accumu-
lation of its knowledge." [*Letters*, No. 264] Lawrence
confided the information later to Jonathan Cape, because of
his contractual relationship with Cape, but intimated that
his answer would be a *no*, "since I haven't much desire to
undertake so difficult a scissors and paste job . . . but its anonymity appeals to me: and if I felt at a loose end, say two

years hence, then I might try my hand as an editor." It was not his forte, and nothing ever came of the suggestion, for he loved lingering over the discriminating choice of an adjective, and found joy in stylistic changes that would have tortured the patience of most other writers.

A letter to Eric Kennington, his art director for the book, reflected his discussions with G.B.S. about the possibly libelous passages in *Seven Pillars*. Shaw had suggested toning down or removing anything that might provoke a libel suit. Later in the summer, after Manning Pike, the printer, had delivered the first page proofs of the revised text, G.B.S. blue-penciled the entire first chapter, concluding that the second chapter made a better beginning than the first. Shaw grounded his decision on the comparative effectiveness of the "furious rush of words" opening the second chapter, compared to the personal and political introspection of the first. This becomes clear in the notes G.B.S., years later, added to the flyleaf of Charlotte's subscription copy. The opening chapter

> was a record of the stirrings of his [Lawrence's] very sickly conscience (Ibsen's phrase) instead of estab-lishing, as in a play, the who and when and where and how and what which readers must know if they are to understand what they are reading. He ac-cepted this. . . .
>
> As to the sickly conscience I have his own author-ity for it. I asked him whether he felt any remorse for blowing up trains with innocent civilians in them as well as uniformed Turkish troops. He answered emphatically that he did.
>
> With this clue to his mind I was able to under-stand his determination to make no money by the Seven Pillars, much as it could place within his grasp. This was not a refusal to coin his blood into drachmas: for he had shed none that he could not

spare. But the gesture led to a belief that he would
not accept payment for his services on any terms.
I knew better. . . .[5]

The first seven chapters were immediately renumbered to
reflect the excision, which, in spite of G.B.S.'s regular
denials, seems to have had a political as well as a literary
basis. Shaw may have felt that it was neither tasteful nor
politic for Lawrence to open his epic with a statement of
his disillusionment with British Machiavellian diplomacy,
especially since he ought to be on good terms with a government which he wanted to restore him to the R.A.F. Jean
Beraud Villars, writing from the perspective of the historian, pointed to the contradictory nature of statements in
the introductory chapter, in which Lawrence insisted on
the subjective qualities of his history. Bernard Shaw, Villars
thought, realized "that these preliminary statements would
remove all credence from the work." The Frenchman regretted the chapter's posthumous publication. To him it was
a naive gesture, and was "to the great concern of future his-
torians." The suppressed chapter, bitter and sad, was published in a posthumous miscellany of Lawrence's writings,
*Oriental Assembly:*

CHAPTER I

The story which follows was first written out in
Paris during the Peace Conference, from notes jotted
daily on the march, strengthened by some reports
sent to my chiefs in Cairo. Afterwards, in the autumn
of 1919, this first draft and some of the notes were
lost. It seemed to me historically needful to repro-
duce the tale, as perhaps no one but myself in Feisal's
army had thought of writing down at the time what
we felt, what we hoped, what we tried. So it was
built again with heavy repugnance in London in the

winter of 1919-20 from memory and my surviving
notes. The record of events was not dulled in me and
perhaps few actual mistakes crept in—except in details of dates or numbers—but the outlines and significance of things had lost edge in the haze of new
interests.

Dates and places are correct, so far as my notes
preserved them: but the personal names are not.
Since the adventure some of those who worked with
me have buried themselves in the shallow grave of
public duty. Free use has been made of their names.
Others still possess themselves, and here keep their
secrecy. Sometimes one man carries various names.
This may hide individuality and make the book a
scatter of featureless puppets, rather than a group of
living people: but once good is told of a man, and
again evil, and some would not thank me for either
blame or praise.

This isolated picture throwing the main light upon
myself is unfair to my British colleagues. Especially
I am most sorry that I have not told what the non-
commissioned of us did. They were inarticulate, but
wonderful, especially when it is taken into account
that they had not the motive, the imaginative vision
of the end, which sustained the officers. Unfortunately my concern was limited to this end, and the
book is just a designed procession of Arab freedom
from Mecca to Damascus. It is intended to rationalise
the campaign, that everyone may see how natural the
success was and how inevitable, how little dependent
on direction or brain, how much less on the outside
assistance of the few British. It was an Arab war
waged and led by Arabs for an Arab aim in Arabia.

My proper share was a minor one, but because of
a fluent pen, a free speech, and a certain adroitness of
brain, I took upon myself, as I describe it, a mock
primacy. In reality I never had any office among the

Arabs: was never in charge of the British mission
with them. Wilson, Joyce, Newcombe, Dawnay, and
Davenport were all over my head. I flattered myself
that I was too young, not that they had more heart
or mind in the work. I did my best. Wilson, Newcombe, Joyce, Dawnay, Davenport, Buxton, Marshall,
Stirling, Young, Maynard, Ross, Scott, Winterton,
Lloyd, Wordie, Siddons, Goslett, Stent, Henderson,
Spence, Gilman, Garland, Brodie, Makins, Nunan,
Leeson, Hornby, Peake, Scott-Higgins, Ramsay,
Wood, Hinde, Bright, Macindoe, Greenhill, Gris-
enthwaite, Dowsett, Bennett, Wade, Gray, Pascoe
and the others also did their best.

It would be impertinent in me to praise them. When
I wish to say ill of one outside our number, I do it:
though there is less of this than was in my diary,
since the passage of time seems to have bleached out
men's stains. When I wish to praise outsiders, I do it:
but our family affairs are our own. We did what we
set out to do, and have the satisfaction of that knowledge. The others have liberty some day to put on
record their story, one parallel to mine but not mentioning more of me than I of them, for each of us
did his job by himself and as he pleased, hardly seeing his friends.

In these pages the history is not of the Arab movement, but of me in it. It is a narrative of daily life,
mean happenings, little people. Here are no lessons
for the world, no disclosures to shock peoples. It is
filled with trivial things, partly that no one mistake
for history the bones from which some day a man
may make history, and partly for the pleasure it gave
me to recall the fellowship of the revolt. We were
fond together, because of the sweep of the open
places, the taste of wide winds, the sunlight, and the
hopes in which we worked. The morning freshness
of the world-to-be intoxicated us. We were wrought

up with ideas inexpressible and vaporous, but to be fought for. We lived many lives in those whirling campaigns, never sparing ourselves; yet when we achieved and the new world dawned, the old men came out again and took our victory to re-make in the likeness of the former world they knew. Youth could win, but had not learned to keep: and was pitiably weak against age. We stammered that we had worked for a new heaven and a new earth, and they thanked us kindly and made their peace.

All men dream: but not equally. Those who dream by night in the dusty recesses of their minds wake in the day to find that it was vanity: but the dreamers of the day are dangerous men, for they may act their dream with open eyes, to make it possible. This I did. I meant to make a new nation, to restore a lost influence, to give twenty millions of Semites the foundation on which to build an inspired dream-palace of their national thoughts. So high an aim called out the inherent nobility of their minds, and made them play a generous part in events: but when we won, it was charged against me that the British petrol royalties in Mesopotamia were becoming dubious, and French Colonial policy was ruined in the Levant.

I am afraid that I hope so. We pay for these things too much in honour and in innocent lives. I went up the Tigris with one hundred Devon Territorials, young clean delightful fellows, full of the power of happiness and of making women and children glad. By them one saw vividly how great it was to be their kin, and English. And we were casting them by thousands into the fire to the worst of deaths, not to win the war but that the corn and rice and oil of Mesopotamia might be ours. The only need was to defeat our enemies (Turkey among them), and this was at last done in the wisdom of

Allenby with less than four hundred killed, by turning to our uses the hands of the oppressed in Turkey.
I am proudest of my thirty fights in that I did not
have any of our own blood shed. All our subject
provinces to me were not worth one dead Englishman.

We were three years over this effort and I have
had to hold back many things which may not yet be
said. Even so, parts of this book will be new to
nearly all who see it, and many will look for familiar
things and not find them. Once I reported fully to
my chiefs, but learnt that they were rewarding me
on my own evidence. This was not as it should be.
Honours may be necessary in a professional army, as
so many emphatic mentions in despatches, and by enlisting we had put ourselves, willingly or not, in the
position of regular soldiers.

For my work on the Arab front I had determined to accept nothing. The Cabinet raised the
Arabs to fight for us by definite promises of self-
government afterwards. Arabs believe in persons, not
in institutions. They saw in me a free agent of the
British Government, and demanded from me an en-
dorsement of its written promises. So I had to join
the conspiracy, and, for what my word was worth,
assured the men of their reward. In our two years'
partnership under fire they grew accustomed to believing me and to think my Government, like myself,
sincere. In this hope they performed some fine things,
but, of course, instead of being proud of what we
did together, I was continually and bitterly ashamed.

It was evident from the beginning that if we won
the war these promises would be dead paper, and had
I been an honest adviser of the Arabs I would have
advised them to go home and not risk their lives
fighting for such stuff: but I salved myself with the
hope that, by leading these Arabs madly in the final
victory I would establish them, with arms in their

hands, in a position so assured (if not dominant) that expediency would counsel to the Great Powers a fair settlement of their claims. In other words, I presumed (seeing no other leader with the will and power) that I would survive the campaigns, and be able to defeat not merely the Turks on the battlefield, but my own country and its allies in the council-chamber. It was an immodest presumption: it is not yet clear if I succeeded: but it is clear that I had no shadow of leave to engage the Arabs, unknowing, in such hazard. I risked the fraud, on my conviction that Arab help was necessary to our cheap and speedy victory in the East, and that better we win and break our word than lose.

The dismissal of Sir Henry McMahon confirmed my belief in our essential insincerity: but I could not explain myself to General Wingate while the war lasted, since I was nominally under his orders, and he did not seem sensible of how false his own standing was. The only thing remaining was to refuse rewards for being a successful trickster, and, to prevent this unpleasantness arising I began in my reports to conceal the true stories of things, and to persuade the few Arabs who knew to an equal reticence. In this book, also, for the last time, I mean to be my own judge of what to say.

On publication day of *Oriental Assembly* in 1939, the press sought out G.B.S. for an explanation of the excision. Again he insisted that his advice was made because the omitted chapter "was a bad opening"—that it had nothing to do with "political reasons." Pressed for other details about his help, he added, "I advised various cuts in the same way one cuts the first draft of a play. There were many libelous passages, and Lawrence was delighted when I suggested I should rewrite them and allow him to say all he wanted to say in perfectly legal phraseology."[6] Apropos of nothing,

G.B.S. confided to reporters the ill-kept secret that he often thought that Lawrence was a boy who never grew up— "like G. K. Chesterton," he added. He probably never knew how much Lawrence would have disliked the comparison, for Shaw's friend and debating rival for three decades, the rotund knight of English Catholicism, was anathema to him. Before he had met Shaw, at the time when he was first becoming enveloped in the Lawrence of Arabia legend, a woman had written to him to request his autograph, boasting that among the signatures of the great she had already acquired was that of Chesterton. Lawrence complied, but requested that she not place his signature next to Chesterton's.

Throughout the second half of 1924, pages of copy and proof of *Seven Pillars* passed back and forth between "Shaw" and the Shaws. Most came by mail, some via the new motorcycle on which Lawrence had raced to London in early March to see *Back to Methuselah* acted at the Royal Court Theatre in Sloane Square. It took five successive evenings to present the gargantuan work, and he managed to race in from Bovington Camp to see two of the parts before financial disaster overtook the experiment in playgoing hardiness. In March, too, the exchange between "Shaw" and G.B.S. had gone briefly in the other direction: Lawrence received a rehearsal copy of *Saint Joan*, which he praised—all but Joan's dialect, which he thought beneath the nobility of her conception.

Twice, while in London to see parts of *Back to Methuselah*, he called at Adelphi Terrace, only to be shunted away by doormen who looked suspiciously at the figure in the grimy cycling rig and announced that neither of the Shaws ever saw anyone without an appointment. When Lawrence finally did get to see the Shaws, he politely evaded G.B.S.'s offer to read to him from *Saint Joan*, which the playwright had begun rehearsing for a March 26 opening. Shaw loved to read from his plays to friends, and Lawrence, sensing that he had wounded G.B.S. in a sensitive spot, felt compelled to write to Mrs. Shaw in explanation. It was partly because he felt literarily worthless in relation to G.B.S., he apologized, but more because he felt that he had to shun pleasures, in expiation of his personal defilement at Deraa, when he had been captured by the Turks and homosexually abused. Although it had been the torture which forced him to give way, he confided, he felt forever unclean. The revelation must have shocked Mrs. Shaw. This was something he could not force himself to make so explicit in his book despite her earlier protestations that he should forego the conventional writer's reticences in *Seven Pillars*. G.B.S.'s comments to the press on publication of *Oriental Assembly* seem to indicate that he had not seen this letter to Charlotte, or that he intentionally attributed Lawrence's "sickly conscience" to other causes. He was certainly surprised (he confided later to Hesketh Pearson) by Charlotte's lack of reticence in the letters to Lawrence he first read after her death; he may have been equally astonished by those letters from Lawrence he recalled only from her having read them to him. He did once confide (on a blank leaf of Charlotte's copy of *Seven Pillars*) that Lawrence had told him that the account of the "revolting sequel to his capture by the Turks" (G.B.S.'s words) as set down in Chapter LXXXI was not true—something Shaw attributed to his being an "actor," rather than "a monster of veracity." But, added Shaw, "I forebore to ask him what actually happened." Where Shaw forebore, others have since conjectured.

Terence Rattigan in *Ross* indulges in some speculation, based on his interpretation of Lawrence's writings on the episode, and the personality of Lawrence revealed elsewhere, that when he was whipped and abused at Deraa, his will was broken by the traumatic awakening he experienced: he recognized himself as a latent homosexual. Further, Rattigan deduces, the Turkish commander ordered the torture of Lawrence not primarily because he fancied him himself and was refused by his prisoner, but rather to break down the will of the self-styled Circassian whom Rattigan deduces the Turk knew all the time was really his enemy, Lawrence. In the Rattigan version, the General tells Lawrence, who is half-conscious, face down on the floor:

> You can hear me, I think. . . . You must understand that I know. . . . I do pity you, you know. You won't ever believe it, but it's true. I know what was revealed to you tonight, and I know what its revelation will have done to you. You can think I mean just a broken will, if you like. That might have destroyed you by itself. But I mean more than that. Far more. (*Angrily.*) But why did you leave yourself so vulnerable? What's the use of learning if it doesn't teach you to know yourself as you really are? . . . For you, killing wasn't enough. (*He lifts Lawrence's head again.*) You had to be—destroyed. . . . The door at the bottom of the stairs through there is unlocked. It leads into the street.

The Rattigan theory is that all of Lawrence's life thereafter constituted a series of attempts to achieve personal triumphs of the will—the will that the Turks had assumed they had destroyed. It assumes, however, that the Turkish general knew who Lawrence was, feared him as an enemy, but believed that the best way to destroy the Arab revolt would be not to kill its inciting force, but to return him to the Arabs broken in body and spirit, depriving them not of Lawrence's physical presence, but of his value as a rallying and unifying factor, thus inverting his usefulness. Would a general indulge in the hazard of returning the enemy's field commander, when he could do away with him? We have to accept this premise to accept the theory at the core of *Ross*.

In May, Lawrence had an unexpected opportunity to come to London. The Air Ministry had suggested that he was the right person to write its official history of the R.A.F. role in the World War, and hinted that perhaps this work would gain him readmittance into the R.A.F. Lawrence went to discuss the proposal, and discovered that he would only be guaranteed a three-year stay as an Air Force *officer*. With an evening to think it over, he went to the New Theatre to see *Saint Joan*. Back in Bovington Camp he wrote Charlotte that he had received, and declined, the R.A.F. offer, and had seen the play which he felt was "final, inevitable, like the other plays, but this time with a ripeness which only The Tempest (please don't tell G.B.S.) in other work has for me. The Elizabethan age was Shakespeare and his fellows: & I feel that this age will be Shaw & his fellows, when the detractions of the next 150 years are passed. His stuff has to be taken without question, like air or light. How they will hate it, in thirty years!"[7]

By then subscribers had reached thirty-four of a hoped-for hundred. Lawrence continued to busy himself with paring his text by ten to fifteen per cent, while collecting more subscribers, including a subscription from a rich American lady sent to G.B.S. From Shaw in July came the first edition copy of *Joan*, with the "Public Shaw to Pte. Shaw" inscription. Lawrence was beside himself with delight, and could not resist displaying it about the barracks, gathering laughs wherever he took it. At the end of the month he cycled to London to see *Joan* again, and was even more impressed than before, especially with the audience response. He noticed that people in the audience, each having his own point of maximum impact, cried at different moments in the play.

The work on the revision went on, Lawrence insisting on the importance of the appearance of the printed page. Like G.B.S. he disapproved of too much white space, particularly "rivers" in the type, like broad cracks running down the page. Both men gave way to William Morris-inspired enthusiasm for the book beautiful, but Lawrence went even further than G.B.S. by desiring to alter what he had to say, if necessary, in order to achieve the appearance he desired the page to have. Once he wrote the Shaws that it was necessary to keep his rules in mind when changes were made in order to make Manning Pike's work easier, as Pike had to follow the same injunctions. They included a page of a uniform thirty-seven lines, each beginning with a new paragraph. Most pages had to begin with an ornamental capital, so that when the book lay open its two pages would balance in appearance. The last line of each page had to be solid, with the last lines of other paragraphs running beyond the middle of the line, again to avoid blocks of white space. Words were not to be split at the ends of lines, and every chapter had to end with a page format like the others—at the bottom right-hand corner. "Incredible meticulousness," Vyvyan Richards later wrote, "—reducing all writing to an absurdity—it really seems. But there is almost no trace of these Procrustean games in the actual text—he had an amazing command of word and phrase. The most careful reader of the later popular edition, where, of course, all this typographical precision is dropped, would never suspect that the text had been so forced."

A sampling of the two texts shows the changes made by the combined efforts of the three Shaws. What specific stylistic changes were effected by each one is impossible to tell, except through the comments of Lawrence and G.B.S.

## Oxford Text

But when at last we anchored in the outer harbour off the white town, hung between the blazing sky and its reflection in the mirage which swept and rolled over the wide lagoon, the heat of Africa came out like a drawn sword and smote us speechless. It was mid-day, and the noon sun in the east, like moonlight, put to sleep all the colours. There were only lights and shadows, the white houses and the black gaps of streets dividing them: in front the shimmering whiteness of the haze on the inner harbour; behind, the dazzle of league upon league of featureless sand, running up to a hedge of low hills, dimly suggested in the distant mist of heat. Just north of Jiddah was a second group of black-white buildings, moving up and down like pistons in the mirage as the ship rolled to her anchor and the intermittent puffs of wind shifted the heat waves in the air. It looked horrible and felt horrible.

The Muadhins began to send their call through the

## Subscribers' Edition
### [from VIII]

But when at last we anchored in the outer harbour, off the white town hung between the blazing sky and its reflection in the mirage which swept and rolled over the wide lagoon, then the heat of Arabia came out like a drawn sword and struck us speechless. It was midday; and the noon sun in the East, like moonlight, put to sleep the colours. There were only lights and shadows, the white houses and black gaps of streets: in front, the pallid lustre of the haze shimmering upon the inner harbour: behind, the dazzle of league after league of featureless sand, running up to an edge of low hills, faintly suggested in the far away mist of heat.

Just north of Jiddah was a second group of black-white buildings, moving up and down like pistons in the mirage, as the ship rolled at anchor and the intermittent wind shifted the heat waves in the air. It looked and felt horrible.

### [from CXX]
Later I was sitting alone in my room, working and think-

warm moist night over the feasting and illuminations of the city. From a little mosque quite near there was one who cried into my open window, a man with a ringing voice of special sweetness, and I found myself involuntarily distinguishing his words: "God alone is great. I testify that there is no god but God, and Mohammed the Prophet of God. Come to prayer. Come to security. God alone is great. There is no god but God."

At the close he dropped his voice two tones, almost to speaking level, and very softly added, "And he is very good to us this day, O people of Damascus." The clamour beneath him hushed suddenly, as everyone seemed to obey the call to prayer for the first night in their lives of perfect freedom; while my fancy showed me in the overwhelming pause my loneliness and lack of reason in their movement, since only for me of the tens of thousands in the city was that phrase meaningless.

ing out as firm a way as the turbulent memories of the day allowed, when the Muedhdhins began to send their call of last prayer through the moist night over the illuminations of the feasting city. One, with a ringing voice of special sweetness, cried into my window from a near mosque. I found myself involuntarily distinguishing his words: "God alone is great: I testify there are no gods, but God: and Mohammed his Prophet. Come to prayer: come to security. God alone is great: there is no god—but God."

At the close he dropped his voice two tones, almost to speaking level, and softly added: "And He is very good to us this day, O people of Damascus." The clamour hushed, as everyone seemed to obey the call to prayer on this their first night of perfect freedom. While my fancy, in the overwhelming pause, showed me my loneliness and lack of reason in their movement: since only for me, of all the hearers, was the event sorrowful and the phrase meaningless.

As the Shaws edited (Charlotte proofreading, G.B.S. making textual changes), each alteration meant more rearrangement by Lawrence to satisfy his esthetic principles. For the most part he had plenty of time. As the summer of 1924 drifted on he found his storeman-clerk's job ideal for reading proof. Now and then surprises occurred, such as the day of his thirty-sixth birthday, when Air Marshal Salmond and his wife and his brother (also an air marshal) came calling at Bovington Camp and took the khaki-clad Private Shaw out to dinner.

Meanwhile, Pike and an assistant worked in a reconverted shop near Paddington station, setting type by machine, and adjusting and readjusting each page. September was the month for Pike's vacation in Cornwall, and when pages of proof ceased coming in to Lawrence, he forwarded all he had on hand (forty pages) to the Shaws, with the injunction to "Please alter, mark, erase, add, abuse anything which hits you: either technical, or literary, or moral, or intellectual. . . ." The extent of the changes was beyond his expectations; and when the proof was returned to him, he admitted to being staggered with more than gratitude. In the middle of October he confessed to Sydney Cockerell that G.B.S. had read the proof and "left not a paragraph without improvement . . . but some nearly died in the operation. Not a trace of anaesthetic! Bracing of him to treat me by his standard. . . ."[9]

G.B.S. said little in public about the extent of his help, but must have intimated something to Siegfried Trebitsch, his friend and German translator, after Trebitsch met Lawrence at a Malvern Festival in the early thirties. Later Trebitsch, in his autobiography, wrote about Lawrence and his *Seven Pillars* that it "was written with a masterly skill that did honour to his eminent friend Bernard Shaw."

One surprise to greet Lawrence in the pages Shaw returned to him was a cavalcade of semicolons. Like G.B.S., he loved the colon, and could not remember ever having used the lesser form, unfairly blaming Pike for its rare appearances in the pre-Shavian proof. Accepting Shaw's semicolons with good-humored sarcasm, he vowed to acknowledge this phase of editorial assistance in a preface. Eventually he did. The 1926 Preface to the Subscribers' Edition offered his particular thanks "to Mr. and Mrs. Bernard Shaw for countless suggestions of great value and diversity: and for all the present semicolons."

Lawrence mourned the loss of his first chapter, especially since the second page contained his Homeric catalogue of names—those figuring in the event to whom he wished to pay homage. Rather than protest the excision, he planned to include the names elsewhere. Eventually they, too, found their way into the brief preface along with the Shaws and their predilection for semicolons. The punctuation changes rankled Lawrence more than the others. Stops, he insisted to the adamant G.B.S., were not actually necessary—just a matter of literary taste. But the semicolons remained, and though Pike groaned at the renewal of his labors, "everything was so clearly better that his repining was short."[10]

Lawrence forwarded more proof from Clouds Hill to Ayot St. Lawrence. With it was a letter (written the same day as the unhappy one to Cockerell) brightly encouraging more excision, as the text, he pointed out, was still not only longer than *Back to Methuselah*, but longer than *Methuselah* added to *Saint Joan*, *Heartbreak House* and (inexplicably) *Cashel Byron's Profession*. The Shaws took the page proofs with them on their vacation in Madeira.

Costs, meanwhile, were mounting. Even at thirty guineas a copy, the project would not pay for itself, and Lawrence began thinking again of a popular edition of an abridged text in order to raise more money (he also intended to replace his Brough motorcycle with the £200 newest model). Learning of the prospect of the abridgement, G.B.S. telegraphed his unhappiness, and offered to guarantee payment of any overdraft resulting from the limited edition. Lawrence shied away from the idea, writing to G.B.S. (via Charlotte) that borrowing money he could not repay was worse than selling indecent merchandise—his cut-down text. Since Jonathan Cape was offering him a £3000 advance for a book made from the Subscribers' Edition, but only half as long, he considered that he was morally fair to the subscribers. Still, he wanted G.B.S. to see the contract. The elder Shaw was delighted: contractual wrangling with publishers was a sport he loved.

The timing of the discussions about the abridgement seems to have been carefully planned by Lawrence, for he was trying to wangle his way back into the Air Force. He calculated that to be successful he would have to accomplish the transfer before any abridgement, with its inevitable publicity and reviews, was published. On February 6, 1925, he had written to Air Marshal Trenchard to inquire about his chances for transfer or re-enlistment. "February is supplication month. . . ," it began, and detailed at considerable length his clean record in the Army, and the fact that he was not the only misfit in the armed forces. Significantly he mentioned that although he could get influential individuals to plead his case with the Air Ministry, he did not want to. [*Letters*, p. 471] Favorable action, he then wrote Charlotte Shaw, would elevate him to the "seventh level of happiness." It would be settled in May, he wrote to her and to Robin Buxton.

In spite of his forswearing political influence to Trenchard, he had no intention of completely ignoring its possibilities. Late in March he wrote to Edward Marsh, confidential secretary of his former employer, Winston

Churchill, indicating that the long letter was really for Churchill, when Marsh found the time opportune. Also at that time the second draft of the contract with Cape arrived at Clouds Hill, and was forwarded to the Shaws. Since G.B.S. was hostile to any abridgement, Lawrence explained that the important section was Clause 10, for it gave him the right to halt further publication and sale of the book in England once he had made enough money to clear his obligations resulting from *Seven Pillars*. It had not occurred to him before, but he now queried his namesakes— as earlier possessors of the name—"By the way, what name should I call myself in it?"

G.B.S., rising to the challenge with gusto, both edited and altered the language of the three-page contract, removing the incongruous "Esq." following Lawrence's name, boldly lining out large passages and inserting new ones.[12] In the happy process he undoubtedly became more reconciled to the abridgement, which he had up to this point advised against. The agreement for "War in the Desert" ("War" became "Revolt" later) had originally been drawn up— not by Cape but—by Raymond Savage, acting as agent for Lawrence. The contract called for delivery of a 120,000-word manuscript by March 31, 1926. This gave Lawrence about a year to effect his re-entry into the R.A.F. When he arrived in London to sign, as first fruit of the agreement he borrowed enough money from Jonathan Cape to buy a ticket for the revival of *Caesar and Cleopatra* at the Kingsway. Cedric Hardwicke was the Caesar, and Gwen Ffrangcon-Davies the Cleopatra. Happy at the contract-signing which insured the viability of *Seven Pillars*, he thought the play the best entertainment he had ever had.

May came, and Lawrence was filled with anxiety, awaiting a decision from the Air Ministry. Hearing from the Shaws that both were ill with influenza, he decided to com-

bine a free day with the desire to forget his premonitions
about the R.A.F., and dashed off to London, only to find
the Shaws both out. Dejected, he returned to camp, and
learned that he had been turned down. His gloom turned
morbid. The following Sunday he was in London again,
and accidentally met another service friend, John Buchan,
in the street. Impulsively he appealed to Buchan about his
longing to return to the R.A.F., hoping Buchan's connections with Downing Street would help. Returning to
Clouds Hill, he followed up his personal appeal with a letter.
"The difference between Army & Air," he insisted, "is that
between earth & air: no less." Precisely, he set down the
alternatives. He had come into the Army to earn his way
back to the Air Force. It would be the ranks or nothing, as
he would rather be dead than hire himself out for his wits,
as the Air Force wished him to do by accepting their offer
of a commission to write their wartime history. And he had,
he thought, proven himself fit for the ranks by his toughness
and his conduct. [*Letters*, No. 265]

Though Buchan had forwarded the appeal to Stanley
Baldwin (again Prime Minister), it was at first not taken
seriously, not even the "rather be dead" phrase. Perhaps not
even Lawrence took that part of it seriously until, in the
bitterness of the defeat of his aspirations, he began to brood
about it during the early days of June. Earlier, he had written brightly to Edward Garnett, telling him, tongue-in-
cheek, of his method of paring down the Oxford Text for
the Subscribers' Edition. "My abridgement," he intimated,
"consists in cutting out every fifth word of the old text:
when possible. If the fifth won't go out, the sixth probably
will." [*Letters*, No. 262] Now—it was the thirteenth of
June—he wrote a different kind of letter to Garnett, full of
contempt for his own "furry" editorial judgment, and the
"irredeemable, irremediable" trash he had written. Any

Fleet Street scribbler could have improved on it, and put more "fire and colour into every paragraph." Then came the real reason why the taste of the new page proof had turned to ashes. Trenchard had withdrawn his objection to Lawrence's rejoining the R.A.F., but Samuel Hoare, the Minister for Air, had returned from Iraq to unmake the decision on the reasonable grounds that it was not in the best interests of the Air Force. That, and his new look at *Seven Pillars* convinced him, Lawrence told Garnett, "that I'm no bloody good on earth. So I'm going to quit: but in my usual comic fashion I'm going to finish the reprint and square up with Cape before I hop it! There is nothing like deliberation, order and regularity in these things.

"I shall bequeath you my notes on life in the recruits camp of the R.A.F. They will disappoint you." [*Letters*, No. 266]

Garnett took the suicide threat literally, and immediately wrote to Bernard Shaw. On June 18, G.B.S. reported to Garnett on the action he had taken:

> I saw the Prime Minister about it during his former term of office. . . . But I heard nothing more.
> I have now sent on your letter to Downing St with a card to say that some decision should be made, as there is the possibility of an appalling scandal, especially after Lowell Thomas's book.
> I don't see what more I can do. Can you suggest anything.
>
> G.B.S.[13]

When Lawrence heard that the Chief of Air Staff wanted to see him in London on Wednesday, July 1, he began to live in new suspense—a suspense, however, which did not prevent him from working five hours a day on various stages of the *Seven Pillars* proofs. At the Air Ministry

Trenchard informed him that permission would be granted to transfer his current seven-year enlistment in the Royal Tank Corps to the R.A.F., the seven-year term considered as having begun in March, 1923, with his entry into the Army. It left him nearly five years of his current enlistment to complete in the R.A.F., with the further opportunity of extending his active duty an additional five years by serving his obligatory reserve time on active duty. Almost ten years of future responsibility foregone, he thought. For him it was paradoxically a kind of freedom. Leaving the Air Ministry he leaped astride *Boanerges*, his motorcycle, and pushed it, in his exultation, up to one hundred and eight miles an hour on the way back to the no-longer-forbidding Bovington Camp.

Later he wrote in his R.A.F. journal, *The Mint*, "The trouble I had to get into the Air Force at all! Surely for less work I could have had my seat in the Cabinet!"

On the Saturday after his return to camp, he wrote Charlotte that the R.A.F. had agreed to let him back into the ranks, and not knowing (nor, apparently, did he ever know) that G.B.S. had intervened again, praised the effect of Buchan in accomplishing the Air Force's change of attitude. About the second step in the intervention he was more correct. He suspected that Stanley Baldwin had put pressure on Air Minister Hoare. He had.

The relief from tension ended his impulse to finish the *Seven Pillars* task by the end of the year. As he volunteered to Charlotte (and, through her, to G.B.S. as well), he planned now on living for some additional years. Strangely, he admitted to the Shaws that he had consciously begun, before the suicide threat about which he never told them, to wind up and tidy up his affairs. It seemed to be something he assumed they understood; and they understood more than he knew. Now he was eager to see them again:

> About coming to you. Ayot is it? I'll try to get
> away next Saturday . . . early enough to reach your
> house about 6 p.m.: and must start back at noon on
> Sunday. Will that do? I'd like to see you and G.B.S.
> very much. There are so many things one can't put
> on paper. . . . [14]

It had been a fine week-end, he reported to them later
from camp. His only regret was having talked too much and
listened too little.

The day after he had written the Shaws about his reinstatement he began sending out his notes to friends in appreciation for services rendered. John Buchan received the
first, and Edward Marsh the second. After the formal approval of his transfer was signed by the Chief of the Air
Staff on July 16, 1925, and Lawrence was ordered to apply
for the transfer through his commanding officer, he wrote
to Edward Garnett, comparing himself and his new sense
of peace with Jason's old ship *Argo* contentedly drawn up
on the beach after her wanderings had ended.

Happily visiting friends, Lawrence popped in and out of
country houses within motorcycling range. The sculptress
Lady Kennet (Kathleen, Lady Scott) noted in her diary
for Sunday, July 11, that she had been in her bath when
her maid tapped on the door and reported that Mr. Shaw
was there. Automatically she said, "Mr. Bernard Shaw, all
right." No, it was not Bernard Shaw, the maid corrected;
and Lady Kennet called to her to find out what the man's
business was. Shortly the maid returned, reporting that the
man would not tell what his business was, and was gone.

"Probably a beggar," said Lady Kennet.

"I don't think so. He was in Air Force [*sic*] uniform."

"Colonel Lawrence! Dash after him."

Off flew the maid to retrieve Lawrence. Brought back to

the house, he explained that he could not imagine what to say his business was, for obviously he had none. "He has signed on as an unskilled mechanic for seven years," Lady Kennet told her diary. "He is to go to India in the autumn. He sweeps the floors. I asked if there were other educated men there. He said, 'Yes, mostly in for repairs—money, war or health.' He is happy, living ten in a hut."

A few days later she had lunch with G.B.S. and mentioned the surprise visit from Lawrence, whom she had not known had become *Shaw*. The talk turned to *Seven Pillars*, and G.B.S.'s part in it. Other than suggesting that a part be cut out, Shaw said, he had little share in it. But Lady Kennet confided to her diary for July 15 that Lawrence had told her (in a familiar phrase) otherwise—that "there was scarce a paragraph that G.B.S. had not amended." Apparently not arguing the point, she noted only that she and G.B.S. "went on to see the Epstein dollies."

Private Shaw had little to do while his transfer application was being processed. With few service duties to get in the way, revision went more smoothly than he had expected. By the time Pike left for vacation, he had delivered sheets of the post-Shavian revisions through Book VII, and Lawrence had mailed proofs of VIII to the Shaws. Only two books remained untouched, one of them the difficult Book X, which described the entry into Damascus, and his total disillusionment with both Allies and Arabs— something G.B.S. had been unwilling to see explicitly set down in the first chapter.

By the end of August, Private Shaw had become Aircraftman Shaw—a transformation which required a trip to an R.A.F. depot in London; a week-end at familiar Uxbridge, where he was reoutfitted in Air Force blue; and a journey to his new station, the R.A.F. Cadet College at Cranwell in Lincolnshire. He was beside himself with joy and triumph: "How can any man describe his happiness?" he wrote in the preface to the R.A.F. journal he renewed making. He wrote his friend Private Palmer of the Tank Corps that Cranwell was not a literal heaven, but there were no bugles and no reveille, no guard duty, no kitchen duty, no P.T.; while kit inspection, hut inspection and marching order parade came up only once a month. The food was better, too; and while at Bovington he had eaten almost every meal in a canteen, or at Clouds Hill, out of cans, he could now stomach the regular mess. His identity was well-known in camp, and he made no effort to hide it. The result was a total lack of internal or external difficulty about his unpublicized assimilation into the ranks. Curiosity about him faded rapidly as he fitted into his excitingly drab new job.

But Cranwell was far from both Clouds Hill and Max Gate, and he had more regrets than his craving for release from Bovington Camp led him to expect. There would now be little chance to visit his cottage on the heath, and little time left to visit with the aging Thomas Hardy. He had not even had time to say good-by to the Hardys, and instead wrote to them from his new station: "You see, it has happened! Quite suddenly at the end: so that I was spared a visit of farewell. It is best to go off abruptly, if at all." [*Letters*, No. 272]

There was little in the nature of his new duties to account for his pathological desire to return to the R.A.F. His "B" flight was one of many that serviced and maintained the school for Air Force cadets. Though living conditions were an improvement, his own work was of the same clerical variety as at Bovington Camp. In his flight there were a sergeant, a corporal and fourteen aircraftmen to service a hangar and six training planes used by fifteen cadets. As junior man he was runner and bookkeeper for his flight. The fact that it was the R.A.F. was satisfaction enough. "Odd that a man should be so ungrateful," he wrote about the Tank Corps to Palmer, "for the R.T.C. was very good to me. . . ." In his new peace he wrote little, except in his R.A.F. journal, in which life at Cranwell appeared much more bleak than in his joyous letters.

In September King Feisal of Iraq visited England, and Aircraftman Shaw, who had known Feisal well when both were in highly different circumstances, received a pass to see him. They had lunch at Lord Winterton's home, Lawrence, in R.A.F. uniform, feeling uncomfortable among the reminiscences. The situation caused him to picture Colonel Lawrence as a stranger he once knew, and whose posthumous papers he was now editing.[15] Work on the "posthumous papers" was still going on, with G.B.S.'s part of the task in process first in Scotland, where the Shaws took an early fall holiday, and then back at Ayot. By November the revision was nearly completed, and he was able to tell Edward Garnett that he would have the revision to examine as soon as the Shaws sent it back. He was nearly finished with Books IX and X, and Pike had returned revised page proof of Books VI and VIII. Still to be done was the index, a map, collation of illustrations and binding. Early in December he wrote to the Shaws that he wanted to see them about Book X, and wanted to come down (he was now north of Ayot) on *Boanerges* some afternoon to discuss it. The Shaws had spent little time in England, going from Scotland almost immediately to Lake Maggiore in Italy, and they planned to spend Christmas away as well.

Lawrence never got to Ayot in December, and work on *Seven Pillars* slowed down. The day after he paid a Sunday visit to E. M. Forster at Cambridge he was thrown from his motorcycle. On a dark wet night, at 55 miles an hour, he skidded on a patch of ice, damaging *Boanerges* and him-

self. The repairs to his arm, knee and leg took longer than
the repairs to *Boanerges,* and until he could bend his
bruised leg again, he was confined to camp, where he hob-
bled about his duties. At Christmas leave-time he had the
hut to himself, and divided his time between reading T. S.
Eliot, correcting proofs, and sampling a holiday assortment
of delicacies delivered by Gunter's from an anonymous
donor whom he felt sure was Charlotte. The day after
Christmas he wrote to ask her if the word "GUNTER"
awakened any feelings of guilt in her.

Writing again on New Year's Day, 1926, he wondered
when the Shaws would return from Falmouth, where
they had been spending the holiday, as there were things
about the last two chapters he could discuss better in person. It would take too much correspondence, he thought,
to do otherwise, although he knew G.B.S. might possibly
begrudge the time. Shaw had been working, since the completion of *Joan,* on an extravagantly long prose work, which
was to become *The Intelligent Woman's Guide to Socialism
and Capitalism.* Because it was not a play, Lawrence felt
that however happily G.B.S. indulged his time in its writing, it would leave him unsatisfied, for Shavian polemics
belonged in his plays and prefaces. Shaw intended the *Guide*
to be an elongated preface, the *summa* of his social philosophy, and the time and vigor which were put into it (had
not the well of his dramatic inspiration been low) might
have resulted in several major plays, even though he was
now nearing seventy.

January weather was bad, with temperatures dropping
at night to zero, and many roads still snowbound; but Lawrence had promised to spend a week-end at Ayot. Before
the end of the month he had done so, winding up the
*Seven Pillars* revision and planning the abridgement for
Cape, which by March he had put together from *Seven*

*Pillars'* proof in scissors-and-paste fashion with the help of cooperative airmen. It was sent for criticism first to the Shaws and then to Edward Garnett, who had done the previous abridgement. Many months later Garnett suspiciously queried him on the deletion of the grim passages about the cleanup of the Damascus hospital and removal of the unburied dead, assuming that Mrs. Shaw had had a hand in cutting them out, even though they remained in *Seven Pillars*. But Lawrence (by then in India) answered that she had not been consulted on the point. He had removed the hospital passages himself to avoid ending *Revolt in the Desert* with an emotional climax. Again Pike set the result in type.

Fortunately the business had been accomplished in January, for other distractions occupied Lawrence in February of 1926. Early in the month Doughty died, and T.E. had gone, in the cold rain, to the funeral. Charlotte and then G.B.S. took to bed with flu, and Lawrence became a victim of an epidemic of measles at camp. There were ninety cases, and he rationalized that, since the measles forced the cancellation of Sunday church parade (one of his few objections to Cranwell), it had some real value. Possibly his report to the Shaws that he was in bed with the measles remained in the back of G.B.S.'s mind when he wrote the opening "measles scene" of *Too True to Be Good* several years later, in which an adult is bedridden with the affliction.

Other afflictions dogged him now that his major writing tasks were behind him. In mid-March he fractured his writing (right) arm, an event which drastically curtailed his correspondence and further curtailed his usefulness to the Air Force. While out on *Boanerges* he had stopped to help an old man restart his stalled car, and was caught on the wrist by the flying crankhandle. Gritting his teeth, he cranked with his left hand, and got the car going. Then, arm dangling, he left-handedly cycled back to camp, after someone helped him get *Boanerges* started. By the end of the month he was writing letters—though his wrist ached —with his right hand, after a week of frustrating left-handed correspondence.

While his arm was still mending, he chanced the long journey from Lincolnshire to Max Gate. A few months later Virginia Woolf heard about the visit when she was there, and noted in her diary how

> Colonel Lawrence, bicycling with a broken arm "held like that" from Lincoln to Hardy, listened at the door to hear if there was anyone there. "I hope he won't commit suicide," said Mrs. Hardy pensively, still leaning over the tea cups, gazing despondently. "He often says things like it, though he has never said quite that perhaps. But he has blue lines around his eyes. He calls himself Shaw in the army. No one is to know where he is. But it got into the papers." "He promised me not to go into the air," said Hardy. "My husband doesn't like anything to do with the air," said Mrs. Hardy. [July 25, 1926]

G.B.S. was still not well, and ailed through April. Lawrence was reluctant to visit Ayot and disturb the patient. Work on the text had slowed anyway, he informed the Shaws. Only the index, maps and illustrations were left to be done. The color plates to be made from his and Kennington's final selection of illustrations were not scheduled to be ready until August. Even that date was optimistic, for Whittingham and Griggs, the printers, like almost every other business in England, was suddenly crippled by the General Strike. It was paralyzing but futile. The Trades Union Congress, supporting a miners' strike, had ordered strikes in other vital industries, including printing and transport services. Baldwin's government met the challenge by organizing volunteers and readying the Army for stopgap employment, and the strike began petering out after ten days. Even Cranwell had been alerted, and all leaves canceled. Lawrence and the others at Cranwell passively awaited the government's order for their use, but it never came.

Additional subscribers were still being added, and during the spring he entered King George V on the list, although he intended to return the check forwarded by His Majesty's Librarian. The King remained on his mind, as he resented His Majesty's interference with a planned trip to the Shaws on the first week-end in June: he had to help the R.A.F. cheer the King on his official birthday (Saturday, June 5). After the ceremony T.E. raced southward to Ayot. The Shaws had passed up the opportunity to visit H. G. Wells on the chance that Lawrence might turn up.

Few knew at the time, but T.E. had already been told that he was to be transferred to India in November. It meant that both *Seven Pillars* and *Revolt in the Desert* had to be ready for publication by the time of his departure, as conducting business from India would be impossible. He did not even tell the Shaws. Toward the end of June, with everything going well, he sent them a facetious foreword he had written, supposedly for the Cape abridgement. "Will this do?" he inquired. It began: " 'Why did I never think of that way to advertise a play?' said G.B.S. when told that I meant to hold up my book ten years. . . ."[16]

In July the news belatedly broke that Lawrence was back in the Air Force, but the information was romantically garbled, and created no stir at Cranwell. Across the ocean the *New York Times* published a copyrighted story headlined "Col. Lawrence Again Becomes Army Private."

" 'Uncrowned King of Arabia' is British Air Mechanic," it reported; "His Book to Cost $150 a copy."

> London, July 21.—Colonel Thomas Edward Lawrence, known as the "uncrowned king of Arabia" and the "mystery man of the World War," is now serving again as an ordinary mechanic in the Royal Air Force.
>
> Under the name of Ross he entered as a mechanic in 1922, but obtained a discharge after six months.
>
> The reason for this famous soldier's return to the service is that it keeps him fit.
>
> The incident is but another in the adventurous life of the man long regarded as an enigma. Lawrence's superiors are aware of his identity, but he has asked for no privileges, doing all the routine of an enlisted man.

Nowhere did the article indicate Lawrence's replacement of *Ross* with *Shaw*, nor his current duty station. Lawrence's book, it noted, "reported to be one of the most remarkable yet produced" on the World War, was now in the hands of the printer.

A *Times* reader reproved the newspaper for its inaccuracies and its air of sensationalism in reporting the story. In a letter to the editor on July 24, 1926, F. J. H. O'Rorke contributed his emendation of the facts, which again suffered a sea-change:

> With reference to the article in today's issue regarding Colonel Lawrence, it has been a matter of public knowledge for some considerable time that Lawrence was a mechanic in the Royal Air Force, which he joined under the name of Shaw not Ross. His identity was discovered by some busybody and the story given to the cheap press with such head-

lines as "Prince of Mecca on Rifle Parade," &c. This
unwished-for publicity caused his resignation and
subsequent re-enlistment in the Tank Corps, where
he still is, now as Private Marks.

Further, added the *Times*'s correspondent, the *Seven Pillars*
had already been published, "And it has been said that
George Bernard Shaw was one of the first to get a copy of
the 30 guinea edition in return for the gift to Lawrence of
a copy of 'St. Joan,' inscribed 'From Public Shaw to Private
Shaw.' "

The summer had rushed by for Lawrence. Every free
week-end meant cycling to visit someone on business or for
a farewell. In August he made a seven-and-one-half hour
journey on *Boanerges* from Cranwell to Edinburgh, to see
the map-making firm of Bartholomew, which was adapting
a War Office map for *Seven Pillars*. Meanwhile, only three
color plates remained to be produced. One had twenty-three
color variations. Otto Kyllmann, G.B.S.'s publisher-friend,
admired some of the prints when he visited the press at Chis-
wick doing the work, and wondered aloud why his firm
(Constable) never got any work of that quality. He could
have it, too, he was told, at a cost of ten shillings per print!
Kyllmann was shocked into silence.[17]

The Shaws continued spending much of their time away.
Although G.B.S. was trying to give as much time as he
could to his *Intelligent Woman's Guide*, he was actually able
to do little work, not having regained his strength after his
winter illness. For a while he wondered if he were going to
survive long enough to reach his seventieth birthday, on
July 26. Shortly after his birthday, he and Charlotte left for
two months at Stresa, on Lake Maggiore, where he found
himself moderately renewed in the triviality and leisure of

resort life; and stood (rather than sat) for sculptor Prince Paul Troubetskoy, who had a studio there.

While in Scotland, Lawrence wrote to the Shaws about India, but gave few details. Not until early October did he know them himself. He was already getting pre-embarkation inoculations, in preparation for an early December departure, and expected to be on leave for most of the month before that. He had more time for reading (rather than proofreading) now, and reported that he had just finished a "great book"—D. H. Lawrence's *The Plumed Serpent*. Later in October he suddenly found himself free late on a Wednesday afternoon, and sped to Ayot without advance warning. It was evening when he arrived. G.B.S. was home alone, just having returned from viewing a prize-fighting film, and he happily related all the details, after which the two spent the rest of the evening discussing boxing. Whether G.B.S. also brought up the matter of another political intervention by him, this time to cancel Lawrence's sailing orders and permit him to remain in England, cannot be traced, although there is a hint in one of Lawrence's letters of the period, in which he insisted that the Cabinet could now do nothing for him or against him; it could only let him alone.

November was his month for the private distribution of *Seven Pillars*, complete and sumptuously bound. Copies were of two varieties: the subscription copies, complete in number (though variant in order) of plates; and the incomplete copies (missing some or most plates), given to comparatively impecunious friends who had served with him in Arabia, or to others in acknowledgment of services rendered (Baldwin received a copy). The 280,000-word production had cost him £13,000. Reproducing the plates alone had cost him more than all the subscription income—at thirty guineas each—had brought in, which made clear why success of the popular abridgement was so necessary. "The *Seven Pillars*," he reported in a note to subscribers, a pamphlet dated April, 1927, "was so printed and so assembled that nobody but myself knew how many copies were produced. I propose to keep this knowledge to myself. Newspaper statements of 107 copies can be easily disproved, for there were more than 107 subscribers: and in addition I gave away, not perhaps as many copies as I owed, but as many as my bankers could afford, to those who had shared with me in the Arab effort, or in the actual production of the volume." David Garnett reported a distribution of one-hundred-and-twenty-eight subscription copies and thirty-six gift copies of the complete book, with an additional twenty-six incomplete copies given away by the author. [*Letters*, p. 295]

A curiosity of the Subscribers' text was that it had no Chapter XI: the renumbering of the chapters after Shaw's excision of the first went only as far as the first ten chapters. The error had gone unnoticed.

The distribution of copies was an undertaking so vast, coming at the same time as Lawrence had to straighten out other business affairs prior to departure, that he had barely enough time to race to Dorsetshire to spend half an hour at Clouds Hill and half an hour at Max Gate. Hardy, eighty-six and frail, must have sensed that the good-by very likely was his last. He was, Florence Hardy chronicled,

> much affected by this parting, as T. E. Lawrence was one of his most valued friends. He went into the little porch and stood at the front door to see the departure of Lawrence on his motor-bicycle. This machine was difficult to start, and, thinking he might have to wait some time Hardy turned into the house to fetch a shawl to wrap round him[self]. In the meantime, fearing that Hardy might take a chill,

Lawrence started the motor-bicycle and hurried
away. Returning a few moments after, Hardy was
grieved that he had not seen the actual departure,
and said that he had particularly wished to see Lawrence go.[18]

The Shaws, too, wanted to see him before he left, and he
visited them in London late in November. Off on another
visit from there, he "got into a trough in the paving" on a
street in the north of London, and cracked up, reinjuring
his knee slightly. He sold the wrecked motorcycle for
£100, and was without transportation a few days earlier
than he had anticipated. Limited now to the mails, he recalled in a farewell note early in December that Charlotte
—on his last visit to London—had impulsively betrayed the
anonymity of her Christmas packages. Nevertheless, he concluded that he had managed his good-bys with the Shaws
very well.[19]

His leave ended on December 4, and three days later he
was on the troopship *Derbyshire,* en route to Karachi, as
anonymous as he could want among twelve hundred airmen, another name and number on the manifest.

*"The limelight of history follows the authentic hero as the theatre limelight follows the* prima ballerina assoluta." —Bernard Shaw

# FOUR

---

## *1927*

With Lawrence en route to India, and the *Seven Pillars* distributed, plans were made early in 1927 to release the popular abridgement amid publicity that would have embarrassed yet delighted the author had he been in England. The *New York Times*, under the heading, "Shereef Lawrence's Book," editorialized on January 2: "Well, let earnest souls pine for Oxford copies; and purple plutocrats like Shaw hug their luxurious specimens, the abridgement will be good enough for us."

The fanfare in advance of the March 10 English publication date of *Revolt in the Desert* featured an exhibition of paintings, pastels, drawings and woodcuts illustrating the *Seven Pillars*. Assembled by Eric Kennington, it held forth at the Leicester Galleries in Leicester Square from February 5 to February 21. The newspapers treated the exhibition as, in large measure, Bernard Shaw's show, and quoted paragraphs from G.B.S.'s long preface to the exhibition catalogue, in which he indulged happily in tongue-in-cheek

111

hyperbole. Since Lawrence had politely rejected Charlotte
Shaw's unsolicited suggestion that James Barrie do the preface to *Seven Pillars*, and had hinted strongly that he wanted
no one's preface, not even Bernard Shaw's, G.B.S.'s only
opportunity was the catalogue, where he was in his merriest
prefatory manner:

> The circumstances of the present exhibition are so
> extraordinary that if most of them were not un-
> questioned parts of recent history I should certainly
> be accused of inventing them for the entertainment
> of the visitors.
> In the war of 1914-18, all those of the belligerent
> Powers which were holding alien peoples in subjec-
> tion, for their own good or otherwise, had to face
> the risk of such peoples seeing in the war their op-
> portunity to rise and strike for independence. The
> Germans banked on a rising in Ireland. What is more
> to the present point, they considered the possibility
> of a nationalist rising in Algeria against the French.
> If they could have brought that about, the conse-
> quences might have been serious. But the steps they
> took to provoke it were futile, ending in a merely
> literary propaganda which was easily and effectively
> countered, not from France but from England: I
> myself being concerned in the affair in a comic
> opera manner as a reputed Prophet. Nevertheless the
> thing could have been done had there been a man of
> genius on the German side to do it.
> The proof of this is that England, having a man of
> genius at her disposal, succeeded in effecting the
> parallel operation of stirring up a nationalist rebel-
> lion against the Turkish Empire in Arabia. The
> genius in question was a young archeologist with a
> careless fancy for calling himself by any name that
> came into his head at the moment. His mission caught
> him when he was T. E. Lawrence, and immortalized

him under that name in spite of all his subsequent
efforts to discard it, which included, by the way, an
avatar as Shaw. As this caused him to be taken for my
son one day by a clergyman at the house of Thomas
Hardy, I had better, perhaps, explain that we are two
different people, not related in the way of vulgar
consanguinity.

Lawrence, like the Prophet of the Latter Day Saints,
had a passion for digging up old civilizations, to
gratify which he had to go to the East, where such
excavations are not obstructed by precarious and extremely uninteresting new civilizations. He picked up
some Arabic, and found out the sort of people the
Arabs are. Knowing already only too well the sort
of people we are, he saw that if he came to our rescue
by making the Arabs revolt during the war he would
have more trouble with us than with them: for British public opinion and official routine disapproves intensely of geniuses, even when they have been hall-
marked at Oxford. . . .

The limelight of history follows the authentic hero
as the theatre limelight follows the *prima ballerina
assoluta*. It soon concentrated in its whitest radiance
on Colonel Lawrence, *alias* Lurens Bey, *alias* Prince
of Damascus, the mystery man, the wonder man, the
man who . . . did, when all the lies and all the legends are subtracted, authentically and unquestionably in his own way and largely with his own hands
explode and smash the Turkish dominion in Arabia
and join up with Allenby in Damascus. . . .

. . . Any country with a Valhalla or a spark of
gratitude would have rewarded him with a munifi-
cent pension and built him another Blenheim. The
British Government left him to pension himself like
any ex-minister by writing a book about it all and
living on the proceeds.

Now it happened that Lawrence's genius included
literary genius; and that his maddeningly intense con-

scientiousness obliged him to write the book. . . . It
was a prodigious task; and the result was a masterpiece of literature. Commercially it was worth to the
author a very large sum. . . .

Lawrence made up his mind to lose money by it.
He set able painters to work to make portraits of his
Arab comrades in arms, and imaginative draughts-
men to let their fancy play on illustrations in black
and white. He had the portraits reproduced in colour.
He had paper specially made, and directed the printing himself in the manner of Morris or Caxton.
Finally he produced a private subscription edition of
one hundred copies after bringing the cost per copy
up to ninety pounds or so, the subscription price being
thirty. It was scarcely out when advertisements appeared in *The Times* offering £5 a week for the loan
of a copy.

The pictures in this exhibition are those he had
procured for the book. Except a few which belong to
the artists, they are the property of a Trust set up by
Lawrence to liquidate the bankruptcy which he had
so ruthlessly contrived. Perhaps you would like to
buy them and pay extravagant sums for them over
and above their value to you as works of art with
the intention of benefiting Lurens Bey in his own
despite. You will not succeed: the Trust is to devote
all its residual assets . . . to a fund for the relief
of the Belisariuses of the Air Force. . . .

If you ask me, as you well may, how all these
extravagances were financed, I can point only to the
subscription, and to a mortgage on the popular
abridgment of the book which is to be issued by the
firm of Jonathan Cape, and which will presently
take its place among our treasures of military chronicle, travel, confession, and ethnology. An Oxford
grant which Lawrence refused to exploit for his private ends, and some remnants of his own property,
were sunk in the enterprise. . . .

How, then, did he live whilst all this expenditure was going on? Well, how does a nobody live when he had made himself totally unintelligible to commercial civilization? The Government was not wholly ungrateful; but it did not understand. It offered him all sorts of jobs he did not want. . . . In the Middle Ages Lawrence would have gone into a monastery as a retired *condottiero*. Living as he was, and is, in the Dark Ages, he deliberately chose the lot of a common soldier. It was objected that this was not fair, as he would be a most embarrassingly uncommon soldier, and that Private Lawrence would make the Army ridiculous. He promptly took another name, and wore down the War Office as he had worn down Headquarters in Egypt. As a private soldier living humbly with his comrades (though I must confess that when he invited me to tea he looked very like Colonel Lawrence with several *aides-de-camp*) he finished the great book, and directed its manufacture even to ordering a different binding for every copy, so that there might be no "first edition" in the collector's sense. He then transferred his patronage from the regular army, changing into the Air Force, and becoming Aircraftman XXXX, still refusing any position in which he would have to give an order, and still making me wonder whether he ever did anything else. At all events, having made up his mind to run away to India from the book and its inevitable rekindling of the Lawrence limelight, he ordered his regiment (or whatever they call a regiment in the Air Force) thither, and is now out of reach of this exhibition and this preface, which is perhaps lucky for me, as I am able to say all these things behind his back.

What will happen in India next, Heaven only knows.

G.B.S.

The period just before and during the Leicester Galleries Exhibition was a high-water mark for Public Shaw and Private Shaw publicity, for the preface to the exhibition catalogue had been written by the newly announced winner of the Nobel Prize for Literature. G.B.S. had fanned the publicity in November, 1926, by rejecting the most coveted of literary awards, remarking that he did not need the money and that the prize probably had been given to him for not writing anything during the previous year. Then, competing with each other for newspaper space from December, 1926, through March, 1927, were stories about the long-waited release of the mysterious *Seven Pillars* and Shaw's decision to accept the Nobel Prize after all, if his prize money could be diverted to a useful purpose. Soon the Anglo-Swedish Literary Foundation to secure English translation and publication of significant Scandanavian works was founded with the unacceptable prize money. At about the same time the American publisher George Doran announced the publication of a limited American edition (twenty copies) of *Seven Pillars of Wisdom* at $20,000 a copy. Not surprisingly, there were no takers. The intention had been to secure copyright (and publicity) for the unabridged version of the book. The scandalously impossible price tag for the American edition was highly newsworthy. It was not a coincidence that the publication date in New York for the abridgement, *Revolt in the Desert*, was only a few weeks away, at the end of March. Public Shaw and Private Shaw had few peers in luring the limelight.

Though Lawrence complained from India about the Blenheim Palace remark "and other sad things" in Shaw's catalogue remarks in a letter to Eric Kennington, he wrote his mother that it was "a very excellent preface." Like Shaw's best prefaces, it was not all meant to be taken literally, though much of it was more than a mere frolic with the facts. In one sense, it may have been very damaging to Lawrence: it trumpeted to the general public that Lawrence, "the mystery man, the wonder man," was *in India*, in the ranks, and cloaked in intriguing anonymity. Under the title, "This Man Lawrence," Shaw's exhibition catalogue preface was featured in the April, 1927 issue of the popular magazine *The World's Work*. An editor's note announced that G.B.S. had "gladly consented" to the reprinting. In the same issue was an excerpt from *Revolt in the Desert*—"With Lawrence's Guerrillas"—and a contribution by Lowell Thomas in the tradition of his illustrated lecture: a piece about the attack on Deraa titled modestly "How Lawrence Helped to Frame the Greatest Hoax since the Trojan Horse."

Speculation as to what Lawrence was doing in India began as soon as his whereabouts became public knowledge. G.B.S. alone could have placed him again so prominently before the public, but in addition, parts of *Revolt in the Desert* were serialized in the *Daily Telegraph* in December, 1926, and the exhibition, followed by publication of *Revolt* in March and preceded by a winter frenzy of newspaper comment about the mysterious Subscription Edition, insured that people would wonder what Lawrence was doing in India.

Sales of the abridgement of *Seven Pillars* were brisk (over forty thousand copies in the first three weeks). The reviews were generally laudatory, though (in the nature of all reviews) they often contradicted each other. The author compiled the contradictions from cuttings forwarded by Charlotte, and sent selections to his friends:

"Obscure, to the point of affectation." *Tatler*.
"Effortless, artless-seeming, adequate prose." Gerald Bullett.
"Has none of Doughty's biblical or Elizabethan anach-

ronisms." John Buchan, *Saturday Review.*
"So imitative of Doughty as to be near parody."
Leonard Woolf, the *Nation.*
"Writing as easy, confident and unselfconscious as a
duck's swimming." *Literary Digest.*
"Gnarled texture twisted with queer adjectives and
adverbs." Leonard Woolf.
"A scholar's style, simple, direct, free from orna-
ment." H. W. Nevinson, *Manchester Guardian.*
"Positively breezy." Bernard Shaw, *Spectator.*
"A cool, distinguished prose." Eric Sutton, *Outlook.*
"Style here and there affectedly abrupt and strenu-
ous, but mostly without affectation." Edward Shanks.
"The style is like music." C. F. G. Masterman.
"Style has a straightforward fierceness, an intrepid
directness." Ellis Roberts.

Even praise of his style often irritated Lawrence, when it
came from the wrong persons. In a book written while T.E.
was in India, *Three Persons,* by Andrew MacPhail (London
and New York, 1929), there was praise for the book as
literature, and condemnation of it as history. "What does he
know about prose that he dare praise mine?" Lawrence
complained. MacPhail's comments, as representative of the
favorable contemporary consensus, are worth repeating in
part:

> Nor is it what Lawrence saw in the desert that
> gives value to this book; it is what he thought of the
> things he saw. They passed through his mind. The
> desert and all that it contains have been described a
> hundred times, but never so delicately or with so
> sure a touch. He describes not things themselves, but
> the inner meaning and beauty that lie in them. The
> mid-day heat; the blaze of sun on basalt, rock or
> sand; the abomination of desolation; the pain of body;
> the glare from shining mud; the blackness of night

and the brilliancy of stars; the cold of snow; the small
grass that comes in a green shimmer after rain; the
rich herbage along the rivulets—anyone may see
these, but Lawrence saw them through different
eyes, through the eyes of a patriarch or prophetic
Arab, and in detail, as one might say, through the
eyes of a camel. Any man may walk in the woods;
it is given to few to see what Orlando saw in the
Forest of Arden.

Robert Graves, working then on a popular biography of
Lawrence (with his help, although Graves declared otherwise until after his subject's death), told Lawrence that
G.B.S.'s editorial work on *Seven Pillars* had spoiled the
book; and it was inevitable that others should make the
same judgment. For many, the conclusion implied the special
knowledge (and special favor) of having read the rare, semi-
secret Oxford text, and was as much an announcement of
having been "let in" as it was literary criticism. The earlier
version still retains advocates, because of its more complete,
ur-text quality, and the comfortable feeling that no Procrustean games were played with its vocabulary and sentence structure.

During his overseas stay, Lawrence, with time on his
hands and distance from home increasing his appetite for
news, hungered after critical comment on his book—all
three circulating versions of it. Later in the year, writing to
Edward Garnett, he confessed his annoyance at a review of
his book by Herbert Read, who accused him of "ruthlessly
cutting his text to suit his page." The cutting, he insisted,
was always based on how to better the prose, and most
persons had told him that they thought the later version was
superior to the earlier. Also, he pointed out, in reference to
carping about the text as subservient to the format, there

were many cases where the initial letter was not in the top
left-hand corner of the page. He claimed he was "careful,
exact, ambitious; and a hopeless failure because his aim was
so high," "overthinking and overtrying" rather than indulg-
ing in "Max Beerbohmish little perfections." [*Letters*, No.
327] Max had much the same opinion of Lawrence, telling
S. N. Behrman that the "mixture of genius and insanity was
too heady for him to do more than sample it."[1] About Lawrence's later translation of *The Odyssey* Max once wrote a
friend, "I would rather not have been that translator than
have driven the Turks from Arabia."[2]

Bernard Shaw's own review of *Revolt in the Desert*, a
book which happened to be an abridgement of one which he
had helped rewrite, appeared in *Spectator* on March 12,
1927. Because of his role in seeing to it that few paragraphs
escaped improvement, the declaration that the book "has not
a dull or empty sentence from end to end" sounds suspiciously like self-praise. It was the lead review in *Spectator*'s
literary supplement (and was reprinted in the *New York
Evening Post*'s *Literary Review* on April 16, 1927):

### The Latest from Colonel Lawrence

*Revolt in the Desert.* By T. E. Lawrence. (Jonathan Cape. 30s)

This abridgement of the famous Seven Pillars (itself
an abridgement) contains as much of the immense
original as anyone but an Imam has time to read. It is
very handsomely and readably printed, and has not a
dull or empty sentence from end to end. It contains
sixteen reproductions of the illustrations to the Seven
Pillars, including a portrait of Feisal, the superb
drawing of Mr. D. G. Hogarth, and a magical one of
the author by Mr. Augustus John; a remarkable
Chino-Johnion group by Mr. Cosmo Clark; three
portraits by Mr. W. Roberts, which are triumphs of
the draughtsmanship that sprang from Cubism; and

seven of the portraits of Arab chiefs which Mr. Eric Kennington went into the desert to make so consummately and humorously skilful in their combination of the popular style of the pavement artist (to disarm the chiefs) with his own very original and independent modernity: the Perfect Futurist turned Perfect Screever. The book does not, like the original, leave you with a sense of having spent many toilsome and fateful years in the desert struggling with Nature in her most unearthly moods, tormented by insomnia of the conscience: indeed it is positively breezy; but that will not be a drawback to people who, having no turn for "salutary self-torture," prefer a book that can be read in a week to one that makes a considerable inroad on a lifetime.

Among the uncommon objects of the worldside, the most uncommon include persons who have reached the human limit of literary genius, and young men who have packed into the forepart of their lives an adventure of epic bulk and intensity. The odds against the occurrence of either must be much more than a million to one. But what figure can estimate the rarity of the person who combines the two? Yet the combination occurs in this amazing age of ours in which we sit holding our breaths as we await wholesale destruction at one another's hands. In Mr. Apsley Cherry-Garrard's *Worst Journey in the World* we have a classic on Antarctic exploration written by a young man who endured it at its blackest. And within ten years of that we have "Colonel Lawrence" (the inverted commas are his own) appearing first in the war news from Arabia as a personage rather more incredible than Prester John, and presently emerging into clear definition as the author of one of the great histories of the world, recording his own conquests at an age at which young company officers are hardly allowed to speak at the mess table.

The fate of the man who has shot his bolt before he is thirty, and has no more worlds to conquer, may be compared curiously with that of the genius who dies unwept, unhonored, and unsung, and is dug up and immortalized a century later. Nobody will ever be able to decide which is the more enviable. But it is mitigated if the hero has literary faculty as a second string to his bow; and Colonel Lawrence has this with a vengeance. He can re-create any scene, any person, any action by simple description, with a vividness that leaves us in more complete possession of it than could 'the sensible and true avouch of our own eyes.' He packs his narrative with detail that would escape nine hundred and ninety-nine out of a thousand observers; so that when he has made you see the start of Feisal's motley legions as plainly as he saw it himself, he has also left you with an exact knowledge of how an Arab mounts a camel and arranges his outlandish clothes for riding, and how he manages to carry a slave with him (when he has one) as a westerner might carry a portmanteau. As to the landscape painting, no padding novelist gravelled for lack of matter ever approached Col. Lawrence's feats in this art. And the descriptions are not interpolated: they are so woven into the texture of the narrative, that the sense of the track underfoot, the mountains ahead and around, the vicissitudes of the weather, the night, the dawn, the sunset and the meridian, never leaves you for a moment.

You feel, too, the characters of the men about you: you hear the inflections of their voices, the changes in their expression, all without an instant of reader's drudgery. There is a magical brilliance about it; so that you see it at once with the conviction of reality and with the enchantment of an opera. Auda after his roaring camel charge, with his horse killed, his field glass shattered, and six bullet holes through his clothes, unhurt and ascribing his escape (under

Allah) to an eighteen-penny Glasgow Koran which
he had bought as a talisman for a hundred and twenty
pounds, is at once a squalidly realistic Arab chieftain
and a splendid leading baritone. The description has
the quality of orchestration. Lawrence's own famous
camel charge, which was checked by his having the
camel shot under him, and ended, after a whole
Arab tribe had thundered over him, in the irresistible
anti-climax of the discovery that he had shot the
camel himself, makes a page that reduces Tenny-
son's Charge of the Light Brigade to minor poetry.

These blazing climaxes of adventure stand out
from an inferno of tormented bodies and uneasy
souls in which one is glad to meet a rascal for the
sake of laughing at him. The subjective side which
gives Miltonic gloom and grandeur to certain chapters of The Seven Pillars, and of the seventy and
seven pillars out of which they were hewn, plays no
great part in this abridgement: Lawrence's troublesome conscience and agonizing soul give place to his
impish humor and his scandalous audacities; but it
will interest the latest French school of drama to
know that their effect remains, and imparts an otherwise unattainable quality to the work, even though
they are not expressed.

The political side of the revolt, important and
extraordinary as it is, need not be dwelt on here: it is
now public property; and the value of the national
service rendered by its author is patent to everybody,
except, apparently, those whose function it is to give
official recognition to such services. It is characteristic of the author and hero of this book that he has
provided most effectively against the possibility of
his ever making a farthing by it; and it is equally
characteristic of the powers that be, to assume that he
is amply provided for by it. He is left in his usual
ultra-scrupulous attitude; but the nation can hardly
claim to have left itself in a generous one. For it is

England's way to learn young men not to know
better than their elders. Nothing could have been
more irregular than the methods by which Lawrence disabled Turkey in the Great War by hurling
an Arab revolt on her rear; and to encourage and reward irregularity would be to set a bad example to
the young.

> G. Bernard Shaw.

Because of its size and bulk in the only editions until recently available, the full text of *Seven Pillars of Wisdom* has
been more discussed than read. It is an erratic book (Jeddah,
for example, is not always spelled the same way), overpopu-
lated by adjectives, often straining for effects and for "art."
A reviewer of G.B.S.'s *The Apple Cart* once complained
(summing up a school of criticism of Shaw's dramaturgy)
that the hero of the play was really the brain of Bernard
Shaw, endlessly ratiocinating, its many cerebral facets sparkling like a diamond in the center of the stage. V. S. Pritchett, writing about *Seven Pillars* a quarter-century after its
publication, thought he saw in it "the will at work, hour by
hour. Throughout a masterly narrative, packed with action,
character and personal emotion, we have the extraordinary
spectacle of a brain working the whole time. It is as if we
could see the whole campaign thought by thought. The
close texture of genius in action has rarely been so livingly
done by an active man; it has been left, as a rule, to the self-
watching invalids."[3] In a way, the work was also that of a
"self-watching invalid," for, as Richard Aldington observes,
"the book imposes on its readers the . . . strain of watching
the author's painful mental and spiritual contortions as he
suffered the onslaught of a severe nervous breakdown," a
collapse "brought to consciousness" by the "hardships, responsibilities and dangers" of the Arab rebellion.

The mannered prose, Aldington also points out, is not the

pseudo-Elizabethan of Doughty, though the diffuse structure of *Seven Pillars* may be Doughty-ish. Lawrence "was aware of the drawbacks to Doughty's style" and Doughty's use "of hundreds of Arab words which have perfectly good English equivalents. Lawrence's dictum: 'Camel is a better word than thelul,' should be obeyed by all writers tempted into verbal local colour."[4]

Most of the criticism of *Seven Pillars* has concerned itself with its synthesis of man of action and man of letters, creating a psychology which will usually preclude a narrowly literary approach to the work. This seems at first to force literary opinion into an uncritical channel, but the facts of the work's conception and development challenge a purely literary judgment. R. A. Scott-James would go further. *The Seven Pillars* to him is not merely the rare product of a man of action who was also by chance a man of letters: "The distinctive qualities which fitted him for literature were qualities without which he could not have succeeded in Arabia; and his literary ability needed, or appeared to need, important events shaped by himself for subject matter. He had an epic theme to handle; there would not have been this epic theme if he had not forced events to take that shape; and he produced the epic. His book is as full of heroes as the *Iliad*, and its Achilles is the author himself. What amazing egotism, one may be tempted to say, what colossal arrogance. . . ." After some discussion of Lawrence's Doughty-inspired prose, Scott-James writes of the work's "muscular" language and "drama and splendour in the portraits of the chiefs," concluding that "The story has the distances of heroic legend, yet the closeness of autobiography. . . ."[5]

It is the marrying of the "distances of heroic legend" with the "closeness of autobiography" that makes *Seven Pillars* (despite the technical flaws close analysis of its text and texture may uncover) unique in literature. Whether or not facts were falsified or magnified, invented or suppressed, belongs to history rather than to literature. Sir Winston Churchill called the book "this treasure of English literature. As a narrative of war and adventure . . . it is unsurpassed. It ranks with the greatest books ever written in the English language. If Lawrence had never done anything except write this book as a mere work of the imagination his fame would last. . . ." It gleamed, thought Churchill, "with immortal fire."[6]

The combination of profound introspection and naked confession in *Seven Pillars*, Jean Beraud Villars wrote, reminds one of Proust or Gide. Villars found—six years before Anthony Nutting's *Lawrence of Arabia* (New York and London, 1961) focused attention upon the author's masochistic streak—

> curious analogies between Lawrence and Gide. Faced with a sentence like "I punished my flesh cheerfully, finding greater sensuality in the punishment than in the sin, so much was I intoxicated with pride at not sinning simply," it is not easy to tell which of the authors wrote it.[7]

Villars thought Lawrence's "balance between romanticism and naturalism was the essence of a new form of literature" to be seized upon by a generation of writers who were reacting from an upbringing on naturalism yet found themselves unable to withstand its attractions. Lawrence gave dignity to horror. It was a strangely mixed blessing, Villars implies, that Lawrence

> plucked at fibres that were not accustomed to vibrating. Into the *Seven Pillars* he dragged in the musty smells of homosexuality, of cruelty, and of death. A certain sadism which had been carefully expurgated from the accounts of the other war writers, who by

tacit consent presented themselves as martyrs and paladins that were not supposed to have such troubled sensations.

Lawrence proved to be the forerunner. Before Malraux, the Koestler of *Darkness at Noon*, Kafka and Jean-Paul Sartre, before the writers of the Resistance and those who described the Nazi and Soviet atrocities (without speaking of recent commercial novels, hybrid offsprings of brutality and pornography), he invented a style which was to be largely exploited by a whole generation of writers.[8]

Richard Aldington's iconoclastic *Enquiry* marvels that "a style so high-flown and exacting" could have been maintained "through so long a book," but accuses the author of "verbal dodging," factual inexactitude and an "unscrupulous" use of words (such as his "appeal to puritan prejudice of the word 'clean' "). The Aldington conclusion: "He might have written much better if he had not striven so painfully to write too well."

A 1961 reappraisal of *Seven Pillars* by Malcolm Muggeridge makes previous hostile criticisms of Lawrence and his book seem timid, for Muggeridge complains of the "hollowness" and "total solemnity" of the prose, and the feeling he had that the events described were "happenings too remote from reality for one to care whether they are true or false." Yet an insight not totally hostile, whatever its intention, rewards the reader. Though the campaign Lawrence engineered in Arabia, Muggeridge points out, "proved historically and militarily insignificant, . . . it provided a flickering afterglow of antique warfare which was going to be flattened out, and perhaps obliterated, by the totalitarian sort."[9] But this insight considers *Seven Pillars* as history.

Muggeridge's observation was not unique. More than a quarter-century earlier, E. M. Forster reviewed the post-

humous public edition of *Seven Pillars*, mentioning, among
other things, that it was a pity the author removed the opening chapter, "for it was a helpful piece of writing and pro-
pelled the reader easily into the action." Although Lawrence
had told Forster in a letter from India that G.B.S. had caused
the cancellation,[10] no mention of G.B.S. appeared in the
review. After considering *Seven Pillars* a *Moby Dick* of a
book, for Melville's masterpiece was ostensibly about catch-
ing a whale and "round this tent-pole of a military chronicle
T.E. has hung an unexampled fabric of portraits, descriptions, philosophies, emotions, adventures, dreams. . . ," Forster (this was in 1935) found a unique non-literary element
in the book:

> He has also contributed to sociology, in recording
> what is probably the last of the picturesque wars.
> Camels, pennants, the blowing up of little railway
> trains by little charges of dynamitte in the desert—it
> is unlikely to recur. Next time the aeroplane will
> blot out everything in an indifferent death, but the
> aeroplane in this yarn is only a visitor, which arrives
> in the last chapters to give special thrills. A personal
> note can still be struck. It is possible to pot at the fat
> station master as he sits drinking coffee with his
> friends . . . good . . . got him . . . he rolls off his deck
> chair! Steal up behind the shepherds and score their
> feet, so that they do not carry the news! Hide under
> the bridge in the rain all night! This is not only
> agreeable to the reader, it is important to the historian.
> Because it was waged under archaistic conditions, the
> Arab revolt is likely to be remembered. It is the last
> effort of the war-god before he laid down his god-
> head and turned chemist.[11]

Again, although it is a man of letters speaking, it is with an
historian's insight into the work.

One of the problems created by the addition of *Seven Pillars* to the monuments of literature is that, with its inexactitude, it is, nevertheless, a work of history: it has the poetry of history. The German historian Mommsen, who lived and worked through the revolutions of 1848, once admonished academicians who complained of partisanship and inaccuracies in his monumental *History of Rome*, "Those who have lived through historical events, as I have, begin to see that history is neither written nor made without love and hate." G.B.S. seems to have hoped of *Seven Pillars* that the result would have been history on the Thucydidean model, where the events were brought to vivid life, however great the cost was in the loss of particularities; but Lawrence's book of the Arabian revolt is only history as is the *Iliad* history.

*Seven Pillars of Wisdom*—as literature—does not approach so great a work as the *Iliad*, but rather has the inaccuracies, extravagances, diffuseness, artificiality—and sustained genius for language—of a Miltonic epic,[12] misplaced in time: misplaced because in its frank subjectivity and its naturalism we see its peculiarly twentieth-century aspect. Lawrence's letters to friends asking, in effect, "To publish or not to publish?" inspired Jean Beraud Villars to compare the question with Rabelais' Panurge, asking each of the winds in turn whether or not he should marry. "Bernard Shaw, with his vigorous moral health," Villars went on, "played the role of Brother John in the debate: 'By God! Marry!'" A not inconsiderable debt is owed G.B.S. for helping to shape *Seven Pillars* and bring it to birth. But a new edition should restore the major cut G.B.S. insisted on and in which the author acquiesced—the eloquently wrongheaded introductory chapter. Even without it, English literature is the richer by *Seven Pillars of Wisdom*'s remaining 280,000 words.

*"It is not G.B.S.' programme for me. . . . It is hard for him, with all that inherent force and courage, to credit a man's being worn out at thirty-five. . . ."*
—T. E. Lawrence to Charlotte Shaw, March 29, 1927

# FIVE

## *1927-1929*

The voyage to India on the *Derbyshire* turned out to be even more unpleasant than Lawrence had envisioned. The nine hundred passengers (including dependents of servicemen) had become twelve hundred, with the addition of a group scheduled for disembarkation at Port Said; and he was revolted by the "smell of stabled humanity" and the heaving of the sluggish ship on the month-long journey. He filled out his time not occupied with the routine housekeeping tasks assigned enlisted men on a troopship by reading the small library he had brought with him: *War and Peace*, Pepys' *Diary*, the Bible, and Synge's book on the Aran Islands. And he found some solace in penciling a few sardonic descriptive notes about the voyage, apparently for a never-completed final section for *The Mint*, to be called "Leaves in the Wind."

In India, he found himself in a familiar occupation: again he was a messenger clerk at an R.A.F. depot, this one the dusty airfield at the aptly named Drigh Road, seven miles from Karachi. The heat made a short working day (7:30–1:00) necessary. While the others could blankly stare and yawn the hours away, Lawrence found the surfeit of leisure intolerable, and sent home for books in Greek to brush up his language proficiency. Nostalgically, he recalled "Ayoting"—his former "monthly debauch," when "G.B.S. could edge in a word," while he "maundered."[1] It was "nominal winter," and, though both hot and cold winds blew dust clouds about, he was told genially that summer weather was "dust-soup." [*Letters*, No. 296]

In the evenings he wandered out alone along the four-mile-wide valley of the aerodrome to hang his topee on a cactus branch and listen to the sounds of the camel bells from Drigh Road until night, and quiet, came. Karachi had no off-hour attraction for him. Instead, he resolved never to leave the camp—probably not "for some incomprehensible reason, probably out of a taste for self-mortification," as biographer Villars concludes. It was an easy decision for one who lived within himself, as Lawrence did, especially since the drabness of Karachi and its colorless environs, which he had seen on arrival, held no fascination for him. Leading Aircraftman B. V. Jones recalled only one time in two years that Lawrence voluntarily went beyond the confines of his camp.

Working in the engine repair shops, he became more clerk than messenger, following the course of each motor overhaul by noting on a lengthy form all the work accomplished. Each man's labor and all replacement parts had to be accounted for, as well as the results of the work shown on shop test. A nontechnical man (his motorcycles notwithstanding), he found following the bench work and learning the nomenclature as fascinating, in their ways, as text-over-hauling.

In the first mail deliveries to follow the *Derbyshire*'s arrival in India were press cuttings about the *Seven Pillars* exhibition catalogue, with G.B.S.'s preface. By early spring Lawrence professed to be astonished by the exhibition's financial success, which he diplomatically attributed to G.B.S.'s sponsorship. He was less diplomatic in a letter to Charlotte about lines in the preface which he read as the beginning of a new attempt by Shaw to pull wires and pension him out of the service. Like many of the letters to Charlotte, it was meant for G.B.S., who knew it and replied that the villain was newspaperdom, which paraphrased a new meaning out of his preface. He was not aiming at Lawrence's involuntary return to civilian life, Shaw wrote; but with the wisdom of old age he knew that Lawrence would soon be ejected from his monastery, and at forty would be too old to make a new battle for readmission practical. If the nation had not by then made provision to support him, the Shaws (or someone else) would have to support him—"and though we should like that, you wouldnt."[2]

Shaw had recently returned from a bachelor dinner fellow-playwright James Barrie had given for Baldwin, Sir Donald MacLean and Sir Edward Grey. There Baldwin told Shaw how pleased he was at receiving a copy of the *Seven Pillars*, and felt that he had to write to thank the author, forgetting in the warmth of after-dinner conversation the horrendous solecism of Prime Minister writing to Private. Shaw, still intent on getting the pension for Lawrence, warmed to the idea and gave Baldwin the address and a copy of the exhibition catalogue.

By early March G.B.S.'s *Intelligent Woman's Guide* had stretched to 180,000 words, but was still a chapter from its end. Being a defendant in a lawsuit and having Charlotte ill at Ayot had slowed him down. Confined to bed, Charlotte occupied herself by reading Lawrence's letters from India, and then having G.B.S. sit by her bed to read the letters aloud to her. Scanning the journals and newspapers, she clipped the latest reviews of *Revolt in the Desert* (including G.B.S.'s in the *Spectator*) and mailed them to Lawrence. On the sixteenth, she was out of bed, and G.B.S. had written the last words of the *Guide*, proofs of which would occupy him through midsummer.

Lawrence passed much of his time in reading (especially reviews sent him) and in keeping up with a prodigious correspondence, the postage sapping most of his service pay. Mrs. Kennington sent him *Ulysses*, and Charlotte (at his request) sent him Wyndham Lewis's *The Lion and the Fox: the role of the hero in the plays of Shakespeare*. He liked the "long dreary slow-marching books" (he wrote Eric Kennington), because time marched similarly for him in India. In the middle of May, though, life brightened briefly; he was able to indulge his love for mystery about himself when Air Vice-Marshal Salmond, whom he had known since 1916, arrived for an inspection of the Karachi depot. Salmond, then in charge of R.A.F. operations in India, knew T. E. was stationed at Drigh Road, but Lawrence, learning of the inspection, kept out of sight.

> "By the way, how is Shaw getting on?" the Air Vice-Marshal asked the depot commandant.
> "Shaw? Shaw? I do not think we have here any officer of that name."

So Lawrence recorded the incident.[3] The commanding officer was probably alone in the camp in his detachment from Lawrence's notorious—but obviously quiet—presence, if the tale is not merely an addition to the Lawrence apocrypha. Though the R.A.F. was supposed to clear his presence with his commanding officers, it is possible that, like many service transactions, this clearance went only as far as the depot adjutant. Certainly the adjutant knew Lawrence, and, in addition, demonstrated no hostility toward him. Soon after Salmond's inspection, the adjutant called him in and asked him if he were interested in becoming clerk to the British air attaché in Kabul, Afghanistan—a two-year plain-clothes engagement. Begging off, Lawrence said that he was not proficient enough as a clerk. Actually he wanted to stay where he was, where there were no private English homes or persons, and he was surrounded by miles of unoccupied government land.

Distant as he was from England, he was nevertheless affecting relationships between his friends. Earlier he had in-troduced two sages of English letters, Thomas Hardy and Bernard Shaw, and closened relationships between G.B.S. and many others among his friends in the literary world. Now, during his early months in India, G.B.S.'s collabora-tion with Eric Kennington in the Leicester Galleries exhibi-tion led to Kennington's doing art work for Shaw's new book. While the "Socialism book" was at the printer, Shaw worried that its closely packed pages needed the kind of life art could provide. He came away from his first talk with Kennington with a tentative assent, but on the second found Kennington protesting that he had been hypnotized by Shaw. Finally, the artist agreed to read the book to see if it might revive his interest in the project. To a limited extent it did, for, although he contributed no illustrations to the text, the first edition of the *Guide*, handsome in binding and typography, was dressed in a colorful dust jacket created by Kennington.

The Kennington-designed four-color dust jacket of the *Guide*, although satisfactory to Shaw, provoked protests from some readers because it displayed a nude woman peer-

ing into a well, apparently searching for truth. The classic
letter of outrage, reported by Blanche Patch in *Thirty Years
with G.B.S.*, came—as might be expected—from Dublin:
"You may not know that the paper cover of your book
presents the picture of a female making a copious display of
bare breasts and indolently scratching a swelling on her right
forearm. She does not look Intelligent." Shaw wrote T.E.
that "nobody could live with Kennington's jacket, though
nobody could pass it on a shop counter or in the window
without stopping to find out all about it." The model for the
jacket was Mrs. Kennington, and Shaw thought her appearance was "an admirable piece of design; but the lady (Celan-
dine) frights the isle from its propriety. Some suppose her
to be my sister-in-law: others identify her with whatever
lady they suspect of being my mistress. But all the people
with a sense of design are delighted, and never dream of her
being anybody in particular. My only part in the matter,
apart from the selection of Kennington, was to tell him I
wanted a woman looking into a well, with all the Powers
and Principalities trying in vain to distract her attention
from the Truth: otherwise my book. He did just the right
thing. I shall make a lot of money by that jacket. And he
has had twenty guineas: all he asked!"[4]

The binding, designed by Douglas Cockerell, was more
decorative than any of G.B.S.'s many preceding volumes.
Obviously G.B.S. wanted to call attention to the book as his
major nondramatic work. Beyond doubt the book's elabo-
rate production was influenced by his work with *Seven
Pillars*. In later works, both prose and drama, Shaw—now
interested in illustrating those of his books he thought could
benefit by it—turned to other artists, John Farleigh and
Feliks Topolski the best of them.

It seems also a reflection of G.B.S.'s work with Lawrence
on *Seven Pillars* that he worked over the appearance of the

printed page as carefully as he did. He had always been interested in enhancing the impact of his words by having them appear on the page to their best advantage, but in an interview published in the *Daily Mail* on May 23, 1928, he revealed a typographical exactitude in which Lawrence would have taken pride. "About my new book," he announced, "there is one thing about which I am very proud. It is the care I have taken to eliminate as many blank spaces as possible, caused by short lines in the letterpress. You know that a true craftsman is proud of his work and wants it to be as perfect as possible. You would not credit the time I have put into reading and altering the proofs of this book to get the spacing just right."

Charlotte's correspondence with Lawrence intensified during the early months he was in India, although much of the evidence on her side of the exchange fails to survive. Lawrence kept little more than a dozen letters from her. His service existence did not make it easy to retain large files of letters from each of the many who wrote to him. He kept some of the more significant of her letters, while she preserved almost all of his—more than three hundred over a dozen years. Their reticences were almost as interesting as their words. Charlotte, lonely in the midst of a busy life, needed someone to share her confidences and her impulsive generosity; Lawrence, deliberately lonely yet hungry for vicarious immersion in the society of interesting people, played surrogate son and looked eagerly in each mail delivery for her gossipy letters. After the first few, neither one ever deliberately used a salutation, going instead directly (and self-consciously) from the date to the body of the letter. Charlotte signed her letters "C.F.S."; Lawrence his as "T.E.S." Unquestionably his letters to her were intended as a record for posterity, as well as for Charlotte and (often) G.B.S., for by August of his first year in India he had written her, "Any letters I send you are yours, to destroy, to keep, to make public, according to your sense of fitness. . . ."[5] It seems safe to conclude that what he wrote to her was what he wanted to survive him. So, too, she assumed, and bequeathed them to the British Museum.

One of her letters to him, in May, 1927,[6] must have been as much a shock to him as his earlier letter to her about the episode at Deraa. She had long wanted to confide in someone about her wretched childhood and youth. Her affection and pity for her gentle, dominated father, who died when still a comparatively young man; and her long-suppressed hatred for her managing, selfish mother (whose treatment of her husband determined Charlotte never to marry), welled up as never before. Marriage of unequals—Nature's means of stabilizing the race, she impulsively wrote Lawrence—was unnatural and disastrous, and her own home life had convinced her that marriage for the purpose of begetting children was, regardless of its necessity for the human race, the most physically repulsive of all concepts to her. She had married G.B.S. after obtaining his agreement that the marriage would never be physically consummated. He knew her strong feelings on the subject, but as a man of forty-two (with many affairs behind him) marrying a woman nearly forty, he had neither illusions nor objections. Nevertheless he could not have shared her feelings, as could the celibate Lawrence, whose sense of revulsion extended to almost every kind of physical contact with another human being. In this respect he was as much a kindred spirit to Charlotte as, in his asceticism, romanticism and love of the histrionic, he was a kindred spirit to G.B.S. To both elderly Shaws, he may have appeared more and more as substitute son; and to T. E., who must have sensed these feelings, Charlotte appeared as well to be the ideal confidant—well-placed in circles that interested him, wife to a sage he regarded (along with David

Hogarth) as one of his masters, motherly in an unpossessive, outgoing manner. As Felix Grendon, who knew her, writes, "She had great charm of spirit and great delicacy, although she was as decided in expressing her opinions as Lesbia in Shaw's *Getting Married*" (1910). Such was her delicacy that G.B.S. discovered, after her death (after forty-five years of marriage), from her diary and her letters to Lawrence that there were parts of her character—and, he added, "her soul"—that he did not know. Apparently Charlotte Shaw had had no intention of making them known publicly or privately during her lifetime. In 1938, when David Garnett was collecting Lawrence's correspondence for publication of a selection from them, she was one of two important Lawrence correspondents who refused to make letters available (although she cooperated in other ways). The other recipient who withheld Lawrence's letters was Winston Churchill.

During the summer of 1927, while Charlotte and Bernard Shaw vacationed again at Stresa, Lawrence was occupying part of his time in India in making his adoption of the "Shaw" surname legal. He wrote to his solicitor, Edward Eliot, in London, who replied that one did not have to register his deed poll at Court, or advertise it in the *London Gazette*. Unsure of what procedure to follow, but certain that he wanted to make his name change permanent and legal, he wrote again to Eliot, who assured him that the formality of registration and advertisement was unnecessary, and that it would be cheaper and quieter to ignore both. David Garnett, who in his *Letters of T. E. Lawrence* records the queries to Eliot, reports that on August 30, 1927, Lawrence officially changed his name by deed poll to Shaw. Lawrence gives a slightly earlier date to the action in a letter to Charlotte, writing on August 12 that he had executed the deed poll "the other day" and felt relieved that he was now

"Shaw only." On the same day he wrote to his mother, but mentioned nothing about the deed poll. Ninety per cent of his letters, he told her, were about business affairs, while the other ten per cent were either to her or to Mrs. Shaw "who is very good about sending me books and things (you should meet Mrs. Shaw some day: she is oldish, & plain-thinking, and interesting, and Anglo-Irish from somewhere near Cork. She would like to meet you, because she found me queer, & would like to study my surviving parent! And you would like her, and admire G.B.S. her husband)."[7]

By the end of the summer *Revolt in the Desert* had earned a surplus of thousands of pounds, after repaying the *Seven Pillars* loans and wiping out the mortgage on a parcel of property Lawrence owned in the London suburb of Ching-ford. Robin Buxton, writing to him for the trustees of the *Revolt in the Desert* fund, reported sales of over thirty thou-sand copies in the English edition within ninety days of publication, and suggested that the enabling clause allowing the author to halt further printing of the English edition be put into effect. Lawrence was delighted. His new book, *The Mint*, was being reshaped, and his attention was turning from the Arabian books, although the letters he received were still full of references to them which impelled his further comment.

His Uxbridge notes, he wrote Edward Garnett, were being condensed, recopied and regrouped in a notebook intended as a Christmas gift to him—for whatever Christmas followed his completion of the project. Meanwhile, he had plans for another Shaw book—one by Bernard Shaw. Hav-ing heard from Charlotte that G.B.S. had completed the *Guide*, he wrote to her that she ought next—before the playwright decided on his next task—convince him to write a play about Irish patriot Sir Roger Casement. The story had the potential for an even greater work than *Saint*

*Joan*, he insisted. Casement, who was hanged by the British, was an Irishman who had gone to Germany in 1914, before war began, to seek aid for the cause of Ireland's independence. He wanted German intervention, including a landing to coincide with a rebellion within. The Germans went only as far as putting Casement and two companions ashore by submarine in 1916, and Casement was almost immediately captured and tried, not as a prisoner of war, but as a traitor. Petitions and letters to the editor flooded England in his behalf. Shaw was among Casement's most vehement defenders, even preparing a legal defense and a dramatic speech to be made from the dock ("I am not trying to shirk the British scaffold: it is the altar on which the Irish saints have been canonized for centuries. . . ."). Casement had his own futile approach to his defense, and carefully annotated Shaw's draft before deciding instead upon his own path to the noose, a path made easier by the revelations of Casement's secret "black diaries" (with their descriptions of sexual perversions) leaked by individuals in the government who wanted to see the Irishman hanged. The Webbs were disgusted by what seemed to them Shaw's lack of seriousness concerning the martyrdom of Casement. When Beatrice and Sidney were helping to raise funds for Casement's defense, Shaw had declined to contribute, commenting that the fight was futile, and that he and the Webbs could order their mourning clothes. But, G.B.S. concluded, the prisoner had the opportunity to speak in his defense after the guilty verdict was rendered, and he offered magnanimously, "I will write him a speech which will thunder down the ages."[8]

Had Lawrence known the full story, he might not have made the suggestion to Shaw that he thought that the tragedy of the Irish patriot was susceptible of the *Joan* treatment. Charlotte wrote T.E. a long letter, detailing the facts about Casement. She had first shown her letter from Lawrence to G.B.S., and his response was that Lawrence overrated Casement, who had not, even before the "black diaries" wrecked his reputation, the qualities T.E. saw. Shaw felt "a slightly amused contempt, and a semi-conscious dislike" for all the Irish nationalist leaders, confided Charlotte, and dared Lawrence to write his own book on Casement.[9] Later E. M. Forster independently suggested to T.E. that he "do" Casement, but still the suggestion failed to take.

Lawrence (who also unsuccessfully suggested a Venus and Adonis play to Shaw) had his own projects in mind. Still, he never gave up the idea of a book about Casement, as letters late in his life indicate. From India he vainly pressed the matter further, although G.B.S. was obviously out of sympathy with it. He gave Shaw—unconsciously—better material for a play when he reported—a few months later—that he had been promoted to aircraftman first class—the highest rank (he noted with glee) one could reach without passing an educational test. When G.B.S. created his Private Meek character out of Lawrence several years later, the educational test was to come up again in their deliberations on the play.

Late summer and early fall had brought the monsoon season to the Karachi area. Chill, interminable drizzles were punctuated by brief cloudbursts. Temporarily the ground turned green and spongy, and clouds of gnats were spawned. Now and then a wan, yellowish sun, once framed by dust clouds, was hidden by thunderheads. Along with the rainy season came dysentery, which Lawrence—to his misery—acquired.

For the Shaws early fall brought two events of interest to him. The first was a grim visit to the Golder's Green crematorium, which he had visited for the funeral of Doughty.

The Shaws had attended the cremation of Jane Wells, which Charlotte described as an agonizing experience because of the endless self-torturing ceremony, during which bereaved husband H. G. Wells had broken down.

The second event was the Shaws' move from Adelphi Terrace to massive, fashionable Whitehall Court, overlooking the Thames Embankment. In brighter rooms, Charlotte complained, her furniture looked shabby.

Working on revising and adding to *The Mint,* Lawrence asked Charlotte to return the Cranwell notes he had left her, yellow slips of paper describing a hoisting of the colors ceremony, guard inspection and his comments on a wing commander's sermon on the death of Queen Alexandra (widow of Edward VII). A more remunerative editing job had come his way, but he rejected it as he had the proposal of Florence Hardy earlier. Colonel Ralph Isham, who had bought the Malahide Castle Boswell papers, offered him part of the editorial work toward getting the papers into publishable form. It was not for him, answered Lawrence, admitting surprisingly that he had never read anything by Boswell. Isham reported on Lowell Thomas's book about him, and he answered that there was some competition for it, as he had just finished looking over "several parts" of a biography of him by Robert Graves. It was fairly accurate, but "On the whole I prefer lies to truth, so far as concerns myself." [*Letters,* No. 326] Actually he had annotated the entire manuscript of Graves's book. Graves had also asked for the help of the other Shaw, and for his pains received a curt postcard telling him that he might as well write a funny book about Mark Twain, for "T.E. had got all out of himself that is to be got." Write a book, G.B.S. helpfully suggested instead, about "the dullest person you know; clerical if possible." Frugally, Graves published Shaw's note in his youthful autobiography, *Good-Bye to All That,* a few years later, then sold the postcard. By Christmas week of 1927 Graves's Lawrence book was out and selling ten thousand copies a week. Later, G.B.S. admitted that he had confused Graves with his brother who worked for the *Daily Mail*.

Isham had several queries about Lowell Thomas's book, one of them about which branch of the service Lawrence had hidden away in; he replied with modest understatement that he had been in the Tank Corps and then returned to the Air Force. "Exchanges from Service to Service are not difficult to arrange." To another query he helpfully replied that he had chosen the name of Shaw "at random." [*Letters*, No. 326]

Christmastime was a horror to Lawrence, who suffered several days of drunken companions. Reminding himself of the holiday seasons he survived in the Tank Corps, he counted his blessings. Life had not been bad that December. Air Vice-Marshal Salmond had stopped by on a visit; T.E. had perfected touch-typing on his office typewriter by typing in predawn darkness; he had received the Cranwell notes from Charlotte, and was setting them into his Uxbridge notebook for Edward Garnett; he had accumulated by Christmas a personal free lending library in India (mainly through gifts from the Shaws and Edward Garnett) of nearly two hundred books, of which less than twenty had been stolen by book-loving "irks." Only the failure of Bernard Shaw to see the possibilities of a work on Roger Casement still rankled him, and he again tried to set Charlotte on influencing G.B.S. Casement could be made, he pointed out in vain, "the epitome of all the patriotisms and greeds and lusts and passions of man. . . ."[10] G.B.S., who saw in Casement only a pitifully weak man, refused to bite.

Late for Christmas, but in time for the New Year, came the inevitable anonymous parcels from Fortnum and Mason. Lawrence swore to his hut-mates that he did not know who sent the candy and sweets. Technically, he did not. The cake was cut into fourteen pieces, one for each occupant of the hut, and his bed was spread with chocolates and *marrons glacés.*

On January 4 (1928), he mailed Charlotte the first twenty thousand words of his condensed Uxbridge chronicle. Obviously the manuscript was intended less for Charlotte than for G.B.S.'s critical eye: "If G.B.S. sees any of the chapters & says anything related to them, will you tell it me, uncensored? There will be no reviews of this book, to fail to tell me anything about myself as a writer. I fancy it better, in shape and strength, to the war-book: but I confess I do not see in either of them more than the psychological interest of souls in travail."[11]

It was more than three months before the rest of *The Mint* could be mailed to the Shaws, in a version Lawrence transcribed on his office typewriter. It was seventy thousand words—shorter than the hand-written version Charlotte was to keep, along with a copy of the typescript. The original was to be delivered to Edward Garnett, as he had promised; but with his love of mystery and melodrama, he asked Charlotte and G.B.S. to ship it, after reading it, in a plain wrapper, with no evidence of sender. Meanwhile, he had written to Garnett to let him know that the typescript was en route "by an official by-pass for safety." Why the circuitous route was safer is unknown, but Charlotte (who had been in North Wales) had Blanche Patch mail the package of manuscript from London.[12]

In its near-final form Lawrence's book followed the pattern of recruit training, but amalgamated similar incidents as taken from notes and from letters to the Shaws into a single more emphatic experience. He reduced the fifty names in his notes to fifteen, both to avoid confusion and to protect himself in some places from too obvious identification. He tried to balance his scenes of contentment with Air Force life and his scenes of splenetic rage at the desecration of a recruit's essential inviolate humanity. He described dehumanization as a good, but probed the service's means toward that end—the metaphor of minting conveying the idea (as he wrote Trenchard early in 1928) of men being stamped into the R.A.F.'s image of what the man in the ranks should be, "violently stamping an indelible mark on coarse material"—the molding "of a soldier's body and soul into a uniform pattern," as Villars describes it.

Lawrence also aimed at what he called the "feel" of a camp for recruit training, balanced by the "feel" of service at an R.A.F. station. The complex of balances was worked out in short, journal-entry chapters, the lyrical ("landscape passages," he called them) opposed to the oppressive and the humdrum, the sentimental opposed to the stark and the obscene. As G.B.S. later told him, *The Mint*, in seeking that balance, wobbled between a document for the files and an artistic work. What Shaw suggested was a rewriting to add the humor in life T.E. deliberately ignored but which was needed to make the work readable, and to scrap the gratuitous bad taste which precluded the book's publication for a mass audience.

In Zolaesque naturalism (with some lapses into fine writing), which he probably thought to be much closer to Swiftian satire than to Zola, Lawrence evoked the barracks and its inhabitants while—through the act of setting it down on paper—exorcising some of his morbid urge to brutalize and humiliate himself. He never abandoned planning new touches for *The Mint*, toward its eventual publication. He was convinced it was his authentic claim to literary survival on his own merits, and not on the accident of war.

He had not expected the revision to take as long as it did,

but several factors—emotional and physical—intervened. In the middle of January he learned of Thomas Hardy's death. It was something he had been expecting for a month, having heard that the eighty-eight-year-old sage was ill, but the news affected him deeply. After the funeral in Westminster Abbey, Charlotte sent him a long letter describing it and G.B.S.'s place in it as pallbearer, along with Galsworthy, Kipling, A. E. Housman, Barrie, Edmund Gosse. Baldwin, the Prime Minister, was there too, and Charlotte thought he was the only one in the Abbey who looked unimpressed by the pomp and dignity. One by one, Charlotte called the roll of the mighty who were present, and described their reactions to the ceremony, ending with a description of her awe at the concluding organ music—Handel's "Dead March" from *Saul,* when music had the last word by paying the ultimate tribute beyond words.[13]

Two other factors intervened also—Lawrence's suffering from fever in late February and early March, and his growing restlessness with his duty station. He still had not left the camp, after more than a year in India. And he was having increasing difficulty with his officers, because of his pyramiding publicity, first about his books, and then about the press's belated discovery of his whereabouts—something that he feared would cause him trouble again in Whitehall. *The Daily Express,* his old nemesis, had printed a story about how "perfectly happy" he seemed to be at the Karachi air depot. The lure of the desert had again captured this "dreamer," it went on, as when other men would leave the base for local jaunts, he would go off to the "edge of the desert" to meditate, with only the company of "a pocket full of cigarettes purchased out of his daily pay of a few shillings." Now and then he chatted with the villagers, and joined in "their profound Eastern meditations."

On receipt of the newspaper clipping he returned it to the editor, Ralph D. Blumenfeld, with succinct, wry annotations. It was all romantic nonsense, he pointed out. Besides, he did not smoke, and did not meditate in the Eastern way, for villagers "in all countries" centered their meditations on food and sex. [*Letters*, No. 339] Apparently the Karachi area was not remote enough, he began to think, and began centering his personal meditations on reassignment.

While at the Drigh Road depot, he was once officially but quietly lifted out of his obscurity long enough to act as a consultant to the British government. It was the kind of incongruous scene he loved. Transcontinental commercial air travel was then in its infancy, and aircraft used had short ranges, requiring many refueling and maintenance stops. British Imperial Airways had been temporarily stymied in seeking a route to India that would include a stop in Persia, and sought a temporary landing site across the Persian Gulf on the Arabian peninsula. Finding a suitable location required the services of an Air Force survey team. This group, commanded by an R.A.F. squadron leader, arrived at Karachi after completing its mission. It knew the geography, and had a good idea of the sites it thought suitable but needed background information on how practical each one was from other than geographical considerations. Armed with its reports and photographs, including some of the affected Arab tribal chiefs, it arranged a conference with the British resident for the Persian Gulf area —and Aircraftman Shaw. His task was to help assess the influence and trustworthiness of the local shiekhs, to enable the government to decide with whom to negotiate. Why he was called in is difficult to understand, since he had never been in that area of Arabia, and having him involved in a conference with political and military officers was bound to prove awkward and exasperating.

The commanding officer at Karachi furnished the setting for the conference—his house. But Lawrence worried about the privacy of the talks—particularly, he was worried that there might be curious women around, before whom he would feel on exhibit. Squadron Leader Hurley, the adjutant at the depot, checked, and put T.E.'s mind at ease, whereupon he allowed himself to be introduced to the conferees—as Aircraftman Shaw, and in his normal working garb of aircraft-hand's overalls.[14]

Flora Armitage, in *The Desert and the Stars* (New York, 1955), finds a "piquancy in this summoning . . . of an airman-clerk in overalls for a political conference with diplomats; it is not unlike the situation which George Bernard Shaw was later frivolously to exploit in the play, *Too True to Be Good*. . . ." Later in 1928 G.B.S. responded to a Lawrence description of his modest duties at an Indian frontier station with a skepticism that again seemed a premonition of the play to come: "I note that you have again moulded the world impossibly to your desire, and live like a Mahatma. Also that you are a clerk, which means, I suppose, that Colonel Lawrence is Acting Adjutant. There is no end to your Protean tricks. . . ."[15]

In February the press notices of the German reception of the Arabian book began to get to Lawrence (through the Shaws). It was through his relation to G.B.S. and G.B.S.'s laudation, that Germans understood him, he concluded, for they understood Shaw before the English did, and revered his words and his works. Acknowledging the cuttings to Charlotte he wrote, "I feel that I should get up and acknowledge that he mainly taught me writing, & that the master's opinion of the pupil is sometimes partial."[16] G.B.S.'s full opinion of *The Mint* was yet to come, for it was not until the Easter holidays of 1928 (while in Wales) that he finished the book.

From the Oakwood Park Hotel in Conway, Shaw wrote a letter of business and literary advice. *The Mint*, he began, was a work of literary power, as well as of value for the experience it recorded. Any kind of reticence was wrong. It should be preserved as a document, even if only a bowdlerized version could be published. As for his literary opinions, Shaw contented himself with suggesting two excisions, both from later parts of the manuscript. "Police Duty" (Part III, Chapter 12) was a retelling of a military policeman's story of a London adventure in which a tart concealed her dead infant in her bed while entertaining the corporal on a couch. Not condemning the tale as gratuitous bad taste, G.B.S. attacked it instead for its purple patchy descriptive passages, which read like a student effort. "Funeral" (Part III, Chapter 9), which G.B.S. also suggested scrapping, described a parade service Lawrence and his comrades were subjected to (including a long sermon on the Queen's reputation for beauty and virtue) on the day Queen Alexandra was buried. Hating what he considered to be folly and imposition even in good weather, let alone on a morning of chilly autumn fog (earlier, when the news had reached camp, they had to stand at attention while drums rolled and rolled, and the flag crept down agonizingly to half-mast), he recalled his last memory of the aged Queen, mummified-looking in her last, pitiful years. It was in bad taste, Shaw warned, and was unnecessarily cruel, savage and ignoble to so write of the infirmities of senility—which required instead man's most humane understanding.[11]

Since *The Mint* was not published in Lawrence's lifetime, there is no way of knowing whether Shaw's most sweeping suggestions would ever have been carried out. That this is doubtful is indicated by the revisions T.E. began making in his last years, and the favorable earlier reception of some of the passages objected to by G.B.S. by such friends as Siegfried Sassoon, who thought the Queen Alexandra section was "wonderful," and E. M. Forster, who called the Queen Alexandra piece "brilliant." T.E. retained the passages,

making only minor alterations. Other comments by both
Charlotte and G.B.S. pleased T.E. more, for both thought
the book generally spare and severe—a parallel to the service uniform and the barrack room, T.E. thought. The
patches of over-writing annoyed Shaw, who labeled them
"Literary Lawrence" and suggested as title for one chapter
that he thought reeked of the lamp, "Literary to the Last."
He worried over the high adjective count, and the surviving manuscript shows stylistic changes in G.B.S.'s hand—
mainly his concretizing T.E.'s diction. For example, "stay
put for ages" became "stay put indefinitely."[18]

His long letter to Lawrence about *The Mint* arrived in
India early in May, and was answered in an equally long
letter which seems to show the frank terms on which each
man dealt with the other. Lawrence saw through the public
Shaw to the private one, and referred to King Charles II
and later himself as Shavian characters in ways that may
have stuck in G.B.S.'s mind until he had written them out
into two plays of the thirties.

*Karachi*

7.5.28
Dear G.B.S.,
    Your letter was a great delight to me, but you have
read too much of yourself into me. So parts of what
you say do not seem to me to fit *The Mint's* circumstances, or my situation.
    *You say 'record of fact' or 'work of art' . . .*
Neither, I fancy. When I had writing ambitions, they
were to combine these two things. *The Seven Pillars*
was an effort to make history an imaginative thing.
It was my second try at dramatizing reality. *The Mint*
is my notebook of preparation for another try. After
1923, when I re-read *The Seven Pillars* in cold print,
and saw that it did not begin to be what I'd intended

and hoped:—then I gave up the notion of writing a book about the R.A.F.: or of writing any sort of book about anything. Don't imagine that because *The S.P.* may be better (in another direction) than my private judgment of it, I thereby become a writer.

'*What to do with it?*' Why, nothing. Garnett asked me for the notes, as a personal souvenir: but for that they would have been burned years ago. Now they are copied out clean and given to him. Surely the job is finished? I can't conceive of their being of any value to humanity. The experience they recount is open to anyone who likes to enlist. If Garnett loses them by lending them to someone prudish, not one of my hairs will turn. Writing books seems inevitable, somehow: but publishing them is an indulgence.

So, neither your '*place on record*' or '*save from destruction*' seems to me worth the expenditure of anyone's time or money. You suggest printing 20 copies for record. Cui bono? Harm to the R.A.F., for fools would not see the solid kindness behind the troubles they inflicted on us: and the R.A.F. is my home, of which I am very fond. I am like Charles II, too old to go wandering again. *The Mint* is not an episode in history, like *The Seven Pillars*, which had to be put on record. My enlistment was a personal experience, only. Libraries like the W.O. (to which you suggest a copy might go) are open only to the officer-class, whose supremacy is based on their not knowing or caring what the men think and feel.

'*Revise*', you suggest, for general publication? I do not think it interesting enough for anyone's revision. Nor do I intend to publish another book:—ever, I was going to say, but ever and never are vain words in a man's mouth. Yet I think I can say that I'll be a different character, before I publish anything else. Look how you are turned inside out daily in every paper, at the pleasure of any worm. God deliver me

from the folly of ever returning to that game. You
can only keep the press within bounds by assuming
always the offensive . . . by chucking to them, as it
were, the less intimate details of your equipage. It's
a tight-rope game, which only a very cool-headed
person dare play. Not for me. You say *'the slightest
reticence or self-consciousness would be unpardon-
able'* . . . that from the old fox (pardon the metaphor)
who throws a red herring in the pack's face at every
twist of the chase! You are all reticences. When I met
you I discovered that the public Shaw wasn't even a
caricature, much less a likeness, of the private one.
Do you think an ordinary fellow could get away with
it? Your advice would sink my ship: would sink any
ship which had less than your speed and power of
manœuvre, and hitting power.

    *'If you have contracted to give Cape the refusal of
your next book you must fulfill your obligation in the
customary sense without . . . unusual conditions.'* I
do not see why. Cape is told he may publish it, if he
prints it textually: my terms (to him and to every
other publisher) being a million down in advance of
royalties. He refuses. Nobody else takes his place:
the book is not published. I am free to accept (for
instance) an offer I have from an American printer to
translate (anonymously) some Homer into English
for him, at a high fee. That surely isn't poppycock?
I warned Cape, when he put in that clause, that I
would, if I was strong enough, not publish another
book. I do not think it even sharp practice. I am not
proposing to change publishers: merely to exist, in
future, without a publisher.

    That is the end of your page 5 and the business half
of your letter. Don't you agree that my position is at
least a possible one? You might as legitimately take
hold of a bunch of letters that I had written, week by
week, to someone and say that they should be either,

(a) printed, uncensored, for record

or

(b) revised into an autobiography of general interest. *The Mint* is a private diary, interesting the world only in so far as the world might desire to dissect my personality. And, like my betters, I disapprove of vivisection. Things so discovered aren't worth the *cost* of finding.

Your literary criticisms are much more exciting. You put your finger on two of the three or four inventions in the book: first the purple night-scape in the story of the dead infant. What Corporal Williams said was: 'Christ, it was as black as hell.' I found that in my notes, and copied it. When I read it, stark on paper, here in Karachi, the whole story felt true. So I pulled out his too-likely phrase, and piled black Pelion on Ossa, to shake the scene out of fact into Dunsanity. Overdid it, of course, as usual. Now I'll write and tell Garnett to cross out the purple lines, and restore the bald reality.

The other passage about Queen Alexandra, shows that I've wholly missed my target with you. As I worked on it I was trying to feel intensely sorry for the poor old creature who had been artfully kept alive too long. I was trying to make myself (and anyone else who read it) shake at the horrible onset of age. And you find a touch of the grinning street-arab. Mrs. Shaw found it cruel. I was saying to myself '*You*'ll be like that, too, unless you die sooner than the Queen . . .' but it wasn't personal. There were all the hundreds of younger fellows round me in the church, and I was smelling instead the decay of Marlborough House. It only shows how aims miscarry. I didn't want to take it out of the parson even.*

---

* Shaw had suggested that T.E. take his anger out on the chaplain, if he had to take it out on somebody.

That's the sort of thing that pulls me up with a jerk when I let the comment of other people influence me to think myself a writer. Perhaps I have a punch in each hand: I know I feel things passionately; but you wouldn't call a punch-owner a boxer, if his aim in the ring was such that he knocked out the referee, and downed the four posts. And if you'd tried to paint a Japanese sunset, and the best critics of art in England gasped and said 'Sheer genius, that portrait of Mr. Lloyd George': what would you judge yourself then? I'm like a hen who lays a clutch of Mills' bombs in a flurry of ambition to play tennis.

As for Graves' book . . . I think it makes me *do* far less, and seem to *be* something far greater, than the truth. As pieces of virtuosity, my settlement of 1921 (the harder thing) and my campaign were subtle and successful. He misses the sublety, and does not attempt to set out the success: nor does he give me credit enough for my realism. I've always accepted the half-loaf as better than nothing:—for the other people, my clients.

This doesn't sound [like] a grateful letter. You have sent me seven pages. That is a great honour, and pleasure: and I'd like just to say so, and have done with it: but somehow you provoke argument. There is a waywardness in me, which would like to make me prove myself not a Shavian character, nor fully captured by your pen. If you were here in the flesh (or, better, me there) you would persuade me that you had really set out my motives and course. As it is, we are 18 months and 5,000 miles apart. Yet it is very good of you.

Yours
T.E.S.
[*Letters*, No. 357]

The same day Lawrence mailed a long letter to Edward Garnett, acknowledging that much of it was an extract from a letter to G.B.S., and suggesting that Garnett line out the purple passages in the chapter on Queen Alexandra. Much of the Cranwell section, he admitted, came from private letters (to Mrs. Shaw) he had borrowed. Further, he added in a postscript, G.B.S. and Mrs. Shaw had seen the text of *The Mint* before it was mailed to him. Now Garnett understood the "official by-pass."

Later Lawrence wrote to E. M. Forster to thank him for a letter in praise of *The Mint* (a letter he confessed having read eight times and was going to read again), and admitted that *The Mint*'s private reception had not all been of the encomium variety. The chapter he made out of letters on Queen Alexandra's funeral had had a mixed reception: "Garnett praises that. Shaw says it's the meanness of a guttersnipe laughing at old age. I was so sorry and sad at the poor old queen." Forster had pressed him as to why he "shouldn't write all sorts of books," and T.E. candidly estimated that he had a "cherry-stone talent," and besides, felt "as dry as a squeezed orange." [*Letters*, No. 364, August 6, 1928]

Although G.B.S. wanted twenty copies of an unexpurgated version of *The Mint* printed for the record, all that Lawrence would agree to eventually was the production of a few extra typescripts for safekeeping. Later Doubleday printed a few copies to safeguard the American copyright, but prohibitively priced the copies to keep it (in effect) private. In 1955 editions were published for the general public, who, expecting gross titillation after nearly three decades of rumor and secrecy had exaggerated the book's improprieties, were disappointed; and *The Mint* still awaits a time of appropriate perspective for judgment. In G.B.S.'s last years (in conversation with Stephen Winsten) he made what may still be the best comment about *The Mint*'s meaning and significance. It showed, he thought, the tragedy of sensitive men in our time: "If like T. E. Lawrence, a sensitive man if ever there was one, they find themselves overwhelmed by the callousness and treachery of the machine, then they can lose their identity in the crowd and not think of themselves as separate egos."[19]

On May 23, Lawrence left Karachi for the more northern air base at Peshawar (made famous in 1960 as the jumping-off spot for American U-2 aircraft on reconnaissance across Russia). His eventual destination was Miranshah Fort in Waziristan, a tiny R.A.F. station near the Afghan border. Within the small barbed-wire enclosure was a storehouse, brick-and-earth fort, and small airfield. Seven hundred Indian scouts, and a flight of two dozen airmen and five officers garrisoned Miranshah. One of these airmen, he reported delightedly to the Shaws, was an A/C Ross.

He was the only aircraft hand who could type, and inevitably was a clerk. It was a lonely place for any kind of employment, for the Indian troops were compartmented apart from the airmen, and they were never together. It was so unearthly quiet—the most remote station in India—that it was dreamlike in its stillness and timelessness. Now and then he would rub his ears, wondering if he were going deaf. Flights generally served only two months at this base, but Lawrence intended, if permitted, to serve out the rest of his Indian time there.

A publisher, following up Lawrence's provocative poem ("To S. A.") prefacing *Seven Pillars*, wrote to ask him if he had any more poetry that might be collected in a high-priced limited edition. Since he had a reputation of not caring for money, the imaginative publisher offered instead "the latest model Brough Superior every year for the next five years." The bait failed. Lawrence, apprehensive about attempting a work of original creativity but looking about for a new writing project, had begun thinking of a translation of Homer. In the solitude of Miranshah he began working on *The Odyssey*. The first fifty lines came to him easily, but he worried over four drafts of the first book for a month, as Homer effectively occupied his surplus of leisure. Bruce Rogers, in America, had agreed to commission a full translation if he liked a sample chapter, and Lawrence, anxious to start another book, wanted the commission to come off.

G.B.S. could not fathom Lawrence's new position, nor could he understand why T.E. ran both from and toward a literary career, while at the same time (anticipating his eventual discharge from the service) seeking a future civilian job equivalent in its lowliness to the ranks. It was abhorrent to Shaw that T.E. was striving to maintain a pattern of self-humiliation while at the same time safely testing within the pattern the literary abilities he mistrusted but loved exercising. "I should offer you a partnership," G.B.S. offered, "you to do all the business and I the writing, if I were not afraid that it would end in my having to do all the business and you the writing. Not that there is not a great deal to be said for that. But I cannot go on like this for ever. I want to retire; and ought to retire; but I cant. I shall be pressed to death under my reputation and my royalties. What is your game *really*?"[20]

To Shaw, Lawrence's talents were unquestionable, but in need of a different kind of discipline than he could find in the safety of petty employment. And Lawrence, Shaw felt, should have had enough of self-immolation by then.

It was no surprise to G.B.S., on querying him about his plans on discharge, to learn that he still intended to stay in the ranks as long as he would be allowed—1935 at the latest,

1930 at the earliest. Then, on a secured income of a pound
a day, he would settle at Clouds Hill—or if he had to work
for a living, he would work as a night watchman in a bank
—a job which often fell to ex-servicemen. He had even
asked about that kind of employment with the Bank of
England, whose new building was being constructed under
the supervision of his friend, the architect Sir Herbert Baker.
Sir Herbert spoke to the bank's governing council, and a
minute was entered that if Lawrence should apply for a
night watchman's job, his application be considered as fa-
vorably as possible. It was not really laughable, he wrote
Shaw, and, as an afterthought, added a postscript perhaps
more significant than the letter:

> I haven't answered your last line 'What is your
> game *really?*' Do you never do things because you
> know you must? Without wishing or daring to ask
> too deeply of yourself why you must? I just can't
> help it. You see, I'm all smash, inside: and I don't
> want to look prosperous or be prosperous, while I
> know that. And on the easy level of the other fellows
> in the R.A.F. I feel safe: and often I forget that I've
> ever been different. As time passes that war and post-
> war grows less and less probable, in my judgment. If
> I'd been as accomplished as they say, surely I wouldn't
> be in the ranks now? Only please don't think it is a
> game, just because I laugh at myself and everybody
> else. That's Irish, or an attempt to keep sane. It would
> be so easy and so restful just to let sanity go and
> drop into the dark: but that can't happen while I
> work and meet simple-hearted people all day long.
> However, if you don't see it, I can't explain it. You
> could write a good play, over a room-full of Sydney
> Webbs and Cockerells asking me 'why'.
>
>                                         T.E.S.
>                                 [*Letters*, No. 363]

Although exasperated, G.B.S. sent Lawrence one of the two specially bound presentation copies of the *Intelligent Woman's Guide*. Each had an unique titlepage, with printed inscription in place of the usual handwritten platitudes inscribed in such volumes. He had spoiled other copies by writing in them, G.B.S. told Lawrence, but not forgetting Lawrence's views about the defacing of books, he had made T.E.'s copy unique. "This, I trust, will meet your views," he wrote T.E. With the enthusiasm of a new convert he added, "It meets mine entirely."[21] The first unique copy was for the dedicatee, Charlotte's sister Mary Stewart Cholmondeley ("The intelligent woman to whose question this book is the best answer I can make."); the second, to T.E., bore the titlepage inscription: "*The intelligent woman's guide to socialism and capitalism. The foundation of the seven pillars, being the word of a western prophet to the deliverer of Damascus: Shaw born Shaw to Shaw that took that name upon him.*" Originally G.B.S. had prepared a special titlepage that read "*Shaw born to Shaw that took that name upon him,*" but Charlotte pointed out to him that "*Shaw born to Shaw*" could be interpreted as "*Shaw the son of Shaw.*" Rather than abet more tales about his relationship to T.E., or appear to corroborate the more wild ones, G.B.S. corrected the proof of the page for the printer by adding an extra "Shaw."[22]

When the book was published, G.B.S. told Winston Churchill that he was going to give Churchill a copy, for it was the only way to prevent him from reading it. Of course Churchill then *had* to read it.

Shaw was obsessed at the time with the idea of strong leadership. He had spent much of his time during his 1927 summer holiday at Stresa accepting flattery from Fascist officials, and had come back full of praise for Mussolini and government of the Strong Man variety. He jumped into controversies in the press in which he impugned democracy, and continued to make himself unpopular by delivering, in his Fabian Autumn Lecture, the opinion that democracy had proved itself incompatible with socialism, and that a society organized according to Fabian principles could only be brought about by a dictator. The public Shavian approval of Fascism embarrassed leading lights of the Fabian Society, and probably helped to heap upon Shaw, from quarters where he might have anticipated praise, contemptuous reviews of *The Intelligent Woman's Guide*, particularly from Harold Laski and S. K. Ratcliffe. In February, 1928, after Shaw saw the reviews, he stormed into a Fabian meeting (according to Beatrice Webb's *Diaries*) in "the devil of a temper" and denounced the membership as "dull dogs" whose factual knowledge was even more limited than their literary competence.

Resentful as Shaw was, nothing could part him from the Fabian Society, though it paid less and less attention to the extravagances of his politics, particularly in the thirties. In the middle of 1928, though he had not forgotten his outrage at the reception given his *Guide*, he came forward when the Fabian headquarters at 25 Tothill Street was condemned for demolition and lent the Society a large sum toward the purchase of a new home in Dartmouth Street. He later forgave the loan: his range of interests and associations was too multifarious to make it worthwhile for him to bear a grudge; and even his most wrongheaded notions about how mankind's course should be steered came from humane motives.

There are implications in the *Guide* that Shaw considered Lawrence a pathological exception to some of the rules he formulated on leadership and ability, for his name or exploits are never mentioned, although many other contemporaries are; and the inverse of some of Shaw's examples

clearly applied to Lawrence: the chapter on incentive, for
example:

> No external incentive is needed to make first-rate
> workers do the best work they can: First-rate work
> is done at present under the greatest discouragement.
> There is the impossibility of getting paid as much for
> it as for second-rate work. When it is not paid for at
> all, there is the difficulty of finding leisure for it
> whilst earning a living at common work. People sel-
> dom refuse a higher employment which they feel
> capable of undertaking. When they do, it is because
> the higher employment is so much worse paid or so
> unsuitable to their social position that they cannot
> afford to take it. A typical case is that of a non-
> commissioned officer in the army refusing a commis-
> sion. If the quartermaster-sergeant's earnings and ex-
> penses came to no more than those of the officer, and
> both men were of the same class, no inducement in
> the way of extra money would be needed to make
> any soldier accept promotion to the highest rank in
> which he felt he could do himself credit. When he
> refuses, as he sometimes does, it is because he would
> be poorer and less at home than in the lower rank.[23]

In a later chapter on "Rent of Ability" we again find the
inverse of Lawrence's situation described as a general rule:

> I have not the smallest doubt, nor probably have
> you, that if Napoleon and Nelson had been forced to
> choose between being respectively a drummer boy
> and a cabin boy and being a general and an admiral
> for the same money, they would have chosen the job
> in which their genius had full scope. They would
> even have accepted less money if they could not have
> secured their proper job in no other way. . . .
> Let us therefore dismiss the fear that persons of

exceptional ability need special inducements to exercise their ability to the utmost. Experience proves that
even the most severe discouragements and punish-
ments cannot restrain them from trying to do so. . . .[24]

Eventually Shaw seems to have rationalized Lawrence
into the latter mold, particularly after observing his work
at the Cattewater R.A.F. station, which seemed beyond
limitations of rank; and several years later Shaw was to
create in the character of Private Napoleon Alexander
Trotsky Meek a man who unobtrusively performed his
leadership from below.

G.B.S. and Charlotte (separately) were also sending Lawrence records as well as books: Berlioz' *Symphonie Fan-
tastique*, Tschaikowsky's *1812 Overture*, Elgar's *Cockaigne
Overture*, and art songs arrived during the summer to create
some sound in the lonely outpost. He had written sadly on
leaving Karachi that his one regret was leaving the old
music box by going upcountry, and to store up what he
could, he was spending his last days there in surfeiting himself with Elgar and others. In August he wrote Robert
Graves from Miranshah, "G.B.S., whose wings are sprout-
ing with every year he lives, has sent me off a gramophone."

By this time, though, the idyll at Miranshah was rapidly
coming to an end. One of the reasons was that Miranshah
itself was nearing the end of its history as a base, the British
government in India deciding that it was unnecessary to
keep it open when the same operations could be handled
more efficiently at Peshawar. The closing down of the base
was scheduled for February, 1929. Lawrence, hearing the
news in the summer of 1928, had no idea that he would not
be in India long enough to see the deactivation of Miranshah.

American journalism was helping curtail his tour of duty

in India, which was supposed to continue through 1930. Rumors circulated around New York, based on his transfer upcountry, and possible leakage of some correspondence he had had with Trenchard, that he had disappeared from sight at Peshawar, disguised as an Arab sheikh, on a confidential series of missions. Evading Soviet diplomatic observers, he (rumors went) effected a British agreement with the Shah of Persia (later Iran) and had gone on to Arabia to dislodge Yemen from Italian influence and—in Saudi Arabia—to pacify the irascible Ibn Saud, who had been making incursions northward into Iraq.

The only basis in fact of the rumors—other than that Lawrence had actually passed through Peshawar on his way to Miranshah—was that in April Air Marshal Trenchard had written him a private letter regretting the R.A.F.'s necessary involvement in action against raids into Iraq by Ibn Saud's tribesmen. An accommodation between Feisal of Iraq and Saud of Arabia was practicable, Lawrence replied, but added that it would solve nothing, because Arab nationalistic feeling had not actually emerged from the tribal rivalry stage, and raiding parties could not be effectively controlled from a distant capital city by the force of a proclamation.

On July 16 the British government was forced to deny the stories circulating in America, but all the denials did was to increase the publicity the rumors received. "Lawrence Still a Private," the *New York Times* reported; "British Government Denies Using Hero of Arabia in Near East." "Colonel Lawrence," went the report datelined from London, "about whose purported movements interesting stories have been printed in New York recently, is not acting as confidential or diplomatic agent for Britain either in the Near or Middle East, it was stated emphatically at [the] Foreign Office. As far as the Government knows, he is still

simply Private T. E. Shaw, attached to the Indian Army
Air Force, and the British government has not been employ-
ing him in any capacity whatever in its dealings in that part
of the world." The treaty with Persia, it explained further,
was signed without Lawrence's assistance, nor did he have
authority to act in the negotiations then going on in Arabia
with Ibn Saud. A wild new report, however, had Lawrence
in Amritsar (in the Punjab) posing as a Mohammedan saint.

A week later the Air Ministry in London concerned itself
with the reports about Lawrence, but did nothing to excite
suspicion, hoping the rumors would die of malnutrition.
Meanwhile, he reported to the Shaws that he had landed
the contract for *The Odyssey* translation, and already had
several books roughed out. He said nothing to acknowledge
that he had heard of the newspaper storm blowing up about
him. G.B.S. ignored it, too. Most of it occurred while he
and Charlotte were on the Riviera that summer, and when
he returned, his attentions had been taken up by Sir Barry
Jackson's suggestion that a summer festival of Shaw plays
be staged at Malvern. Sir Barry had suggested several of
the best-known older plays, but G.B.S. suggested a new one
as well. He had not written one for five years, but his work
on the *Guide* had stimulated his interest in leadership again.
Late in the fall *The Apple Cart* was underway, with Shaw's
continued correspondence with Mrs. Patrick Campbell reminding him of an incident out of which he fashioned the
"Interlude" scene.[25]

The Bank of England proposal still rankled Shaw, though,
and he wrote to "Luruns" (sometimes G.B.S. wrote instead
to "Auranshaw") to warn him to be realistic about accepting a night watchman's job. It would not be (as the romantic
might picture it) sitting among bags of gold in leisured creation of literary masterpieces, he cautioned; it was more likely
to be very exacting rounds-making, record-signing and

clock-punching, a week of which would drive him meekly back to the Colonial Office looking for work. Casting about for a colorful parallel, Shaw cautioned, "When a Sultan becomes a beggar for seven years to cure himself of paranoia (or whatever is the scientific name for swelled head) the cure will be so complete at the end of five years that he will find it necessary, in order to avoid going mad in the opposite direction, to throw off his rags and become, if not a sultan again, at least a Cadi or a fig merchant."[26]

While T.E. was occupying his off-hours at Miranshah trying to get the right words for the heightened style he wanted for his translation, a news item appeared in the London *Daily News* (December 5, 1928) reporting that Lawrence was busy learning Pushtu (the Afghan language). "It is inferred he intends to move into Afghanistan." David Garnett, in his edition of Lawrence's *Letters*, guessed that the report "may have arisen from a fellow airman's looking into Lawrence's Greek Lexicon." His companions at Miranshah knew his past, but his activities in India made it seem too remote for it to figure in their relationship to him. They were as remote from Greek as they were from Pushtu.

Amanullah, King of Afghanistan, had been faced with an uprising of standpat elements who opposed his forcible westernizing of the country, and both British and Soviet attempts to stake out spheres of influence in the border nation were in the balance. The British Labour Party, in Opposition, brought newspaper reports about Lawrence's activities into Parliament to charge that the government, through its arm in India, was fomenting a rebellion to extend British imperialism. It is interesting to note in the *New York Times*'s comment on the situation—while Shaw was writing his play—a reference to apple carts:

LAWRENCE THE UBIQUITOUS   Russia, always the victim
of odious conspiracies, has discovered that someone
has upset the apple cart in Afghanistan, and trembles
lest it be an act of Lawrence of Arabia.

The tale is almost like an incident from "Kim,"
reversed. Instead of the Russian agent working down
from the north into India, the British agent is working northward into Russia's sphere. In this instance he
is invested with the mystery and charm that have followed the name of Lawrence in the East, regardless of
his actual whereabouts.

If Colonel Lawrence were to write the memoirs of
adventures which he has not been through, he could
produce a volume even more enthralling than "Revolt in the Desert." ("Topics of the Times," December 11, 1928)

December 11th was the day Lawrence quietly reached
the one-third point in his translation of Homer, and received
his annual anonymous Christmas box from the Shaws: boxes
of China tea (he disliked the local Indian variety) which
had traveled halfway around the world and back again. An
even more welcome Christmas gift—surprising under the
circumstances—came from the Air Ministry at about the
time he was preparing the first portion of his *Odyssey*
translation to mail to G.B.S.'s friend (and English publisher
for Bruce Rogers), Sir Emery Walker. An extension of
service to March, 1935—actually permission to serve the
mandatory reserve time on active duty—was granted to
Aircraftman Shaw, ironically in the midst of the noisiest
newspaper controversy about "Lawrence of Arabia" since
the last days in the R.A.F. of Aircraftman "Ross."

On Christmas Day, though he had more copy on hand,
he sent only the first three books of *The Odyssey* to Sir
Emery, with the comment that it was the best that he could

do. Several paragraphs later the modesty temporarily disappeared as he concluded that his version was, for the most part, richer than Homer's original. He had spent five hundred hours, he estimated, on the first fourteen thousand words, and had reached the point of diminishing returns, for in the cycle of improvement by substituting a better word for a lesser alternative he had discovered himself returning to his original choice.

Working in the austere solitude of the isolated aerodrome ten miles from the Afghan border, surrounded by his books, records and writing materials, oblivious to the Afghan guerillas just outside the barbed-wire perimeter, and the raucous world so far away as to barely exist, Lawrence was happy as seldom before in his life. In a New Year's letter to the Shaws, his last to them from India, he made no mention of any possibility of his returning to England. Undoubtedly he did not yet know.

The news about him in England was reaching a sensational new pitch as the new year began. Afghan authorities, it was reported in London, had ordered the arrest of Lawrence on sight, and the Soviet news agency was calling him "the arch-spy of the world." At Lahore, an infuriated crowd mobbed and beat the unfortunate Syed Pir Karam Shah, convinced that he was Lawrence of Arabia in disguise. British Leftists assumed that the smoke concealed a fire, and abetted public demonstrations against Lawrence in the streets of London, in one of which—on Tower Hill—he was burned in effigy. The government had little alternative but to pull Aircraftman Shaw out of India and give him obviously innocuous duty at home. On January 8, 1929, he was—without explanation—flown from Miranshah to Lahore, and on the next day to Karachi, where an R.A.F. officer explained the matter and handed him the orders transferring him to England.

Lawrence was indignant that he had been handled so summarily, for he had to leave most of his more bulky possessions behind, including his library of books and records, and the G.B.S. gift record-player. As Aircraftman Shaw, however, he had none of the stylish attentions due Colonel Lawrence, and in the Air Ministry's current predicament it had to be rigidly observed that he did not get them. On January 12 he left India from Bombay, aboard the Peninsular and Oriental liner S.S. *Rajputana*, with orders to debark at Tilbury on the Thames before the ship reached London and report immediately to the Air Ministry. There, he felt sure, the death sentence for Aircraftman Shaw would be carried out, just as it had been for Aircraftman Ross almost six years to the day earlier.

*"He rose to his feet and stood staring at what was his own land, then sighed and clapped his two palms downward upon his thighs, crying mournfully, 'Alas! and now where on earth am I? Shall I be spurned and savaged by the people of this place, or find them pious, hospitable creatures? . . . Come to that, what do I here myself?'"*
—Odysseus, on returning to Ithaca
(T. E. Shaw translation)

# SIX

———

## *1929-1930*

The voyage home for Aircraftman Shaw had its mixed blessings. He had left the womblike security of Miranshah —and probably all future prospect of foreign service—for good, but he had a second-class cabin for himself, instead of the sardine-tin quarters of a trooper. He seldom left his cabin, spending his time flat in his berth translating Homer. In the first two weeks on board he produced as much copy as he had in the previous two months in India. The *Rajputana* was partly empty, which meant that he had less need to dodge recognition; still, he wore a civilian suit lent to him by an airman in Karachi. Even the prospect of facing reporters, or merely the lay curious, when the ship docked at Port Said after passage through Suez, was denied him. There the quay was guarded to prevent his slipping away to visit friends, and insure that the press did not board.

Aboard on the voyage home was Sir Ronald Storrs, his friend of Arabian days. Sir Ronald and his wife found T.E. in his berth quietly occupied with his translation. "He did not dissent," Storrs recalled in 1945, in *Orientations*, "when I thought that his *Odyssey* sacrificed overmuch to the desire of differing with predecessors: for instance in rendering . . . rosy fingered dawn . . . in nineteen different ways. It is therefore an arresting rather than a satisfying version. . . . Nevertheless, Lawrence's *Odyssey* possesses two outstanding merits. It represents Lawrence as well as Homer, and it has by hero-worship or the silken thread of snobbishness led to Homer thousands that could never have faced the original, or even the renderings of Pope, Chapman, or Butcher and Lang. . . ."

Plymouth was the *Rajputana*'s first port of call in England. There Wing Commander Sydney Smith waited, with orders from Air Marshal Trenchard to meet the ship in a fast R.A.F. launch and remove Lawrence unnoticed, instead of letting him go on to Tilbury, or even as far as Southampton. Before dawn on January 29, 1929, the ship anchored in Plymouth Sound. A kindly government had even prepared his formidable backlog of mail in a large bundle for him, and he clambered down the rope ladder to the small craft to receive it, opening some letters and throwing others unopened into the sea as they traveled shoreward. "Why are you doing that?" asked Smith.

"Well, it is mostly rubbish, and when it is addressed to Colonel Lawrence, I know it's from complete strangers, or from people who won't respect my change of name."

Eventually they docked at the jetty of the Cattewater

(later Mount Batten) R.A.F. station near Plymouth, and at breakfast Lawrence and the wing commander (who was commanding officer at Cattewater) gloated at the thought of the throng of reporters waiting at the wrong dock. Still, the R.A.F. had to get him to London, where he intended to spend his month's leave "underground" at Sir Herbert Baker's office in Barton Street, long one of his permanent addresses. To make certain that they had evaded the press, Smith drove him inland to Newton Abbot to avoid the boat train and get an ordinary train to London. They slipped into a coach going to Paddington Station, but did not know that it was coupled to the boat train. Even so, they dodged reporters and thought they had got off cleanly, not knowing that a *Daily Mirror* photographer had managed a shot of Lawrence climbing down the *Rajputana*'s side on a rope ladder.

To further evade reporters (apparently they were both enjoying the game) they went first to the flat of Mrs. Smith's sister on Cromwell Road, and (while a crowd gathered outside) slipped out the back entrance to Baker's office in Westminster. For days afterward, Clare Smith wrote (in *The Golden Reign*, London, 1940), letters addressed to Colonel Lawrence arrived at her sister's home.

The bungled secrecy of the R.A.F.'s handling of Lawrence's return only inflamed again the publicity about *why* he had been brought home, for the government's handling of the case only created more grounds for suspicion. The Labour Opposition had been using him as a convenient means of embarrassing the Conservative government ever since Labourites realized the political value of Lawrence as a liability to the government. While the *Rajputana* was bringing him home, questions were raised in Parliament, concentrating upon his using the name of *Shaw*. Although he had legally changed his name, he had not advertised the fact, and few other than Mr. and Mrs. G.B.S. knew of the deed poll. On January 20, Labour M.P. Ernest Thurtle asked the Secretary of State for Air, Sir Samuel Hoare, whether it was known at the time Aircraftman Shaw enlisted in the R.A.F. that he was really Colonel Lawrence; and if so, why his enlistment under a false name was permitted. The Air Minister admitted that Shaw's identity was known, but insisted that since Lawrence preferred to be known under another name, there was no reason to deny enlistment to him on those grounds.

Thurtle was not finished, for a few days later the London *Daily News* headlined a column:

GREAT MYSTERY OF COLONEL LAWRENCE
SIMPLE AIRCRAFTMAN OR WHAT?
TIME THE TRUTH WAS KNOWN
THE ARCH-SPY

Although the *Daily News* admitted that it had been informed that Lawrence would be assigned to ordinary airman's duty at Cattewater, and that the R.A.F. contended that he had performed only routine duties throughout his service career, it nevertheless editorialized that he should not be allowed to continue his masquerade. Thurtle arose again (February 6) to inquire of Hoare whether it was the usual practice for the Air Force to accept recruits when it was known that they were enlisting under assumed names. The Air Minister pointed out that there were a variety of reasons why men assumed names other than their legal ones; and when Thurtle refused to accept the hedging as an answer, Hoare admitted that the R.A.F. did accept such enlistments.

It was against such a background that Trenchard summoned Lawrence and Wing Commander Smith to his offices shortly after the *Rajputana* incident. All he could do was regret the publicity, and admit that the man involved had not done anything to cause it. Lawrence was then placed on his month's leave, and ordered to report to Cattewater at the beginning of March. Fearful that Thurtle's persistence would result in embarrassing the government sufficiently to force his ouster from the R.A.F., Lawrence brazenly visited the House of Commons to talk to Thurtle and other hostile M.P.'s, and succeeded in talking them out of their persecution and into friendship with him.

Whether G.B.S., who had some influence within Labour, had intervened in any way is unknown, but the affair resulted in the first of a series of reprimands from the Air Ministry. Lawrence was instructed to engage in no political activity without permission of the Ministry. This resulted in his having G.B.S. act as political intermediary later in the year.

While London newspapers were speculating about the whereabouts of "Lawrence of Arabia," T.E. ventured by rail to Ayot, and was seen walking past the Welwyn Station baker's shop with G.B.S. Harry Rayner, who delivered bread to Ayot St. Lawrence in his horse-and-cart, recognized Aircraftman Shaw from the newspaper photographs, and told interviewer Allan Chappelow years later of his surprise that no one else seemed to recognize the pair, especially since the younger man, wearing his puttees, was obviously making no effort to disguise his identity.

Shaw, who was rehearsing a revival of *Major Barbara* scheduled to open at Wyndham's early in March and completing his new play, *The Apple Cart*, may have been more than entertained by the parliamentary squabbling—in serious times—over the innocuous activities of a man in the ranks. *The Apple Cart*, a comedy about government, concerned itself in part with the aptitudes and ineptitudes of Cabinet ministers.

Early in February, as Lawrence was settling down for a

month in Barton Street and wondering how he was going to get free of curiosity seekers long enough to visit his friends, a new anonymous gift arrived for him—one he did not expect to be able to purchase for himself until *The Odyssey* was delivered to the publisher. In a letter to E. M. Forster he described the gift as "a very large and new and apolaustic Brough." [*Letters*, No. 369] Although used to anonymous presents from the Shaws as well as identified ones (the Miranshah phonograph from G.B.S.), the motorcycle took him by surprise. It was an open secret that the Shaws were the donors, as his letters later showed.

*Boanerges* enabled him to outdistance the autograph and souvenir hunters (and reporters), and made his leave in London tolerable. It seems no coincidence that Shaw named a character in *The Apple Cart* Boanerges. The name was familiar enough to the playwright, who in caricaturing his old friend, Labour politician John Burns, probably thought of Lawrence's reason for naming his clattering vehicle *Boanerges* (a loudmouthed preacher or orator: literally "Sons of Thunder"—the name Jesus gave to John and James).

Lawrence professed to hate the publicity he was getting and worried over its effect in the Air Ministry, yet he spent part of his leave doing such contrary things as lending M.P.'s Thurtle and Maxton a typescript of *The Mint*, and writing a politically insubordinate note to R. D. Blumenfeld, editor of *The Daily Express*, in which he told him that he had been threatened with expulsion if he saw any more newspaper people. In London he did not attempt to travel about incognito, although he did wear his borrowed civilian suit when the weather was mild. Since he had no overcoat, he changed into uniform when the weather turned cold. G.B.S. solicitously lent him his own spare overcoat, which was gigantic on the airman's small frame and nearly a foot too long; but late at night, or when it rained, he used it. It is doubtful if even the most imaginative of inquiring newspapermen could picture Colonel Lawrence underneath that huge Shavian garment.

G.B.S. had little use for any overcoat just then. Rumors were spreading about London that he was seriously ill, and even on the verge of death. Actually all he did have was a severe case of influenza, and he was annoyed at the leakage of the news and the exaggerated turn it took. Finally, on February 28, he released to the newspapers a communiqué about his condition in an interview with himself. Mr. Bernard Shaw was recovering satisfactorily, Mr. Bernard Shaw announced from Whitehall Court. The alleged serious illness, Mr. Shaw told his interviewer, was a fiction concocted by "brazen liars who might at least have stopped short of attempting to assassinate me by ringing me up in the dead of the frozen night to announce the news of my own illness to me. . . ." His mortal illness, he concluded hotly, was "blundering twaddle" invented by "needy and desperate men to extract money from editors too heavily preoccupied to be critical."

Though Lawrence visited the Shaws during his London leave, it did not become public knowledge that there was any possibility of connection between the playwright Shaw and the "other" Shaw until opening night of the *Major Barbara* revival. Dismissing caution on one of his last nights in London before returning to duty, Lawrence went to the opening with the Shaws. Of course the press located him there, as a report in the *New York Times* showed the next day:

> Col. T. E. Lawrence Sits with Author at "Major Barbara" Revival
>
> London, March 5.—Col. T. E. Lawrence, otherwise known as Aircraftman Shaw, England's man of mys-

tery, obtained some publicity tonight for the other
Shaw, namely George Bernard, by sitting in the same
box with him at Wyndham's theatre to witness a performance of "Major Barbara". . . .

Having named the occupants of his box, Shaw said:
"As it is impossible for Colonel Lawrence to go anywhere without the press gossiping about it and getting
it wrong, you may as well give it to them straight."

Lawrence reported at the Cattewater R.A.F. station on
his motorcycle, having roared in from London on it, clad in
peaked cap, goggles, gauntlet gloves and a suit of Air Force
blue. It had been a glorious ride on the heavenly new machine, he wrote Charlotte. The seaside weather, as spring
approached, exhilarated him, with its mixture of sunshine
and mist. His reception at the base was as subdued as he
could want. Since reports had circulated for a month that he
had been assigned there, any excitement the news had
caused had dissipated. Cattewater had many of the advan-
tages of Miranshah (remoteness and a sympathetic commanding officer) without the compensating disadvantages.
Though it was near Plymouth, it was a tiny self-contained
unit, on a rocky peninsula jutting out into the sound. About
a hundred airmen occupied six huts barely thirty yards from
the rocky coastline, at high tide.

It was G.B.S. who introduced Lawrence to the M.P. for
the Plymouth area, Lady Astor. Shaw had gone to Lady
Astor's Cliveden estate for the Christmas holidays, and composed much of *The Apple Cart* there, reading aloud scenes,
as he wrote them, after dinner each day. One day he took
time out to play Santa Claus at a party for the Cliveden staff
and their families. He needed no make-up. Late in March he
planned a return to Cliveden to read his completed play to
a distinguished assemblage, and had Lady Astor invite Law-

rence. The reading was a huge success: the Cliveden guests warmed to Shaw's unexpected praise of England and of the institution of a strong but benevolent constitutional monarchy. Lawrence had not expected to make the Cliveden reading, but he had a friendly commanding officer, his partner in the *Rajputana* fiasco. The play for him was no surprise; he was one of the few who already knew it. But he was most pleased at having the opportunity for a long talk with another guest: one of the heroes of the Irish literary renaissance, James Stephens.

Now that he considered the text of the new play satisfactory, G.B.S. planned to get away from it all by taking a vacation on the Italian Adriatic coast, while England worked itself into a month of frenzy preliminary to a national election. Just before departure date, Charlotte's sister, Mrs. Cholmondeley—to whom Shaw had dedicated his *Intelligent Woman's Guide*—died, casting a shadow over the holiday. The day before they left, Lawrence came up to London to offer his condolences and wish the Shaws a good journey. He promised to go to Malvern with them in August for the first festival. The English premiere of *The Apple Cart* (it was scheduled for Warsaw in June) was to be held then, and his favorite Shaw play, *Heartbreak House* ("a marvelous work of art") was to be revived. T.E. cycled back to Plymouth, pushing his machine over ninety at times, accomplishing the two-hundred-and-thirty-five-mile trip in four hours, forty-four minutes.

Lawrence now saw much of Lady Astor when she was in Plymouth. While on his motorcycle, he heard someone shriek "Aircraftman!" from a car, and he recognized his Cliveden hostess. The next day she telephoned Wing Commander Smith for permission to visit the air station—something that, as a Member of Parliament, she had no difficulty in securing. She roamed about the station until she found Aircraftman Shaw, and insisted that he allow her to ride on his motorcycle, not only within the base but out into Plymouth. They visited a workmen's housing development she had initiated in 1924, and then went to supper at her house on the River Hoe. It made the newspapers in England and America, and provided entertainment for the Shaws in Istria.

Obviously Lawrence's new unmonastic life brought his *Odyssey* project to a standstill. G.B.S. had sent him the page proof of his long preface to *Immaturity*. It was Shaw's first (1879) and never-before-published novel, now being prepared as Volume One of the Collected Works—a major Shavian project underway to mark the author's approaching seventy-fifth year. And Edward Marsh had sent Lawrence a copy of *Lady Chatterley's Lover*, which Lawrence was rereading. Books also came from David Garnett, and two packages of books came from the Shaws in Italy. His new service duties took more time than he was used to after the slow pace of Indian service. Working as clerk to the commanding officer, he was busy with details for the forthcoming Schneider Cup race for military seaplanes, and soon became involved with work on motorboats used to speed to the scene of a crack-up on the water. A vital, but then inefficient, part of R.A.F. regular equipment, they were used both for rescue and repair work. To the speed-intoxicated Lawrence, they were plodding creatures.

To the Shaws in Venice he wrote of an unexpected Whitsuntide holiday, which he used to visit Mrs. Hardy at Max Gate, F. L. Lucas and E. M. Forster at Cambridge (where they chatted like characters out of an Aldous Huxley novel), and Granville Barker and his G.B.S.-hating wife, both of whom he admitted to the Shaws liking better than before. Still, he had no reluctance in returning to Cattewater, where he was obviously happy. He loved splashing about the bay in the "duty boat" patrol, and was invited on rides on a private Moth seaplane co-owned by Wing Commander Smith and Major A. A. Nathan, who often explored the inlets and bays, and later took him on flights to the Scilly Isles and the Channel Islands.

There seemed no end to interest in biographies of Lawrence, whose return to England spurred the preparation of another one, this time by the writer on military affairs, Captain (Ret.) Basil H. Liddell Hart. As usual, T.E. helped write the book with the extravagant assistance denied most biographers by their living subjects—a response which often overwhelms the writer's critical faculties, like that benevolent deception practiced on writers by G.B.S. A decade later both Graves and Liddell Hart published (in annotated form) their long exchanges of letters with Lawrence, and interviews with him—still one of the most fascinating portraits of him in print.

In one of the exchanges with Liddell Hart in May, 1929, as T.E. was settling down into work at Plymouth, Lawrence made one comment that might have made G.B.S. turn on the political heat again had he known, for May was General Election month, and at Cliveden Shaw had openly predicted a Labour victory. Lawrence wrote to Liddell Hart that he expected to remain in the R.A.F until 1935, but if not, one of the possibilities that occurred to him was that "a compassionate Government" might place him on the Civil List. He was not being flippant, he assured his biographer.

The Shaws had to be back home at the end of June for the first rehearsals of *The Apple Cart,* and Lawrence worried aloud that he would not be able to make it, as he was to be one of the groundsmen for the Schneider Cup Competition. His taste of flying (he had even been allowed to handle the controls) had inspired a new thought, and when he visited the Shaws in mid-July, he talked over his proposition

with G.B.S. Unfortunately it was ill-timed, for the newspapers then had him again rumored as instigating trouble in
the Middle East. He had just written to Air Marshal Trenchard about an idea he had for use of one of two huge diri-
gibles (*R. 100* and *R. 101*) nearing completion, about which
he had heard rumors that trial runs were being considered to
either (or both) America and India. A flight to Karachi via
Ismailia, he suggested, could cross the *Ruba el Khali,* the
"Empty Quarter" of Arabia which no European had yet
traversed. No other kind of aircraft could do the job of exploration, and the resulting solution of one of geography's
great unsolved problems would redound to the world-wide
credit of the R.A.F. He shrunk modestly from applying to
go on the flight himself, although he admitted that he would
love to go along. [*Letters,* No. 389] It was not his first
suggestion along these lines to Trenchard, who knew that
Lawrence while in India had been eager to be in the crew
of a Cave-Browne-Cave R.A.F. flying boat on a round-the-
world flight.

At Whitehall Court, only a short walk from the Air Ministry, he urged G.B.S. to press the *R. 101* suggestion upon
his Fabian colleague Lord Thomson, who, since Labour's
victory in the May General Election (and Ramsay Mac-
Donald's return to Downing Street), had been Secretary of
State for Air. He wanted personal contact, but G.B.S.,
busy with *Apple Cart* rehearsals, wrote a letter instead,
adding his personal conviction that Lawrence would be a
good man to have along on the *R. 101*'s flight. He received a
reply almost as empty of promise as the Empty Desert:

> AIR MINISTRY
> Gwydyr House
> Whitehall, S. W. 1
> 24th July, 1929

My dear Shaw
    Yours of the 19th July. I do not think it will be

possible to act on your suggestion during the first trial flight of the airship to India, but I will certainly bear the suggestion in mind when subsequent experimental flights are being made. I am especially keen on this aspect of aviation and regard surveys of this sort as one of the principal uses of airships.

As regards including Lawrence, or Private Shaw, as you have yourself described him, I will consider the matter. His passion for obscurity makes him an awkward man to place and would not improve his relations with less subtle members of the crew. However, as a friend of yours he will be remembered.

Yours,

(*signed*) Thomson[1]

When G.B.S. mailed Lawrence a proof of his preface to the forthcoming collection of his correspondence with Ellen Terry, he enclosed the reply from the Air Ministry. Lawrence was apparently furious with Shaw, for when he saw the author Henry Williamson just after receiving the letter (July 28) he gave way to one of his few recorded outbursts against G.B.S., who he felt had failed him with the inept diplomacy born of too-easy assurance. He certainly must have seen over the years, in his many visits to Ayot, Adelphi Terrace and Whitehall Court, what Shavian authorized biographer Archibald Henderson called Charlotte's keeping G.B.S. "in a cotton-wool paradise of adulation, which was unhealthy for him and amusing to the visitor." Lawrence had been guilty of some of it himself. Now he fumed to Williamson (who had little sympathy for G.B.S. anyway): "If you don't ['keep a sense of self-criticism'], you'll become like Bernard Shaw, believing only the nice things said about you: and then you'll have to imitate yourself in order to do anything at all and the critics will say you're a classic."[2]

To G.B.S., he wrote the next day in his usual friendly

deferential manner, and thanked him for tackling Lord
Thomson, but requested that his next intervention with
Thomson be *viva voce*. It was a pity, he mourned politely,
that he had not been left out of it because it was obvious that
if he were aboard such a flight the scientific value of it would
be obscured by the press's interest in exploiting personalities.[3] The same day he wrote again to Sir Hugh Trenchard,
who had shown some interest, and complained that G.B.S.
had upset the apple cart by mentioning him for the crew,
which probably had caused the proposal to be vetoed on
personality grounds instead of being considered on scientific
grounds. To Trenchard he bowed out of consideration for
the project and hoped the R.A.F. would do the job and get
the credit. [*Letters*, No. 392]

   Lawrence, luckily, was never invited to become involved
with projects for the *R. 101*'s maiden flight. Shortly after he
returned from his Malvern Festival visit with the Shaws he
discovered that he was being reported by the press as back
(in disguise again) in the Middle East, stirring up trouble
among the Arabs. Authorities in Jerusalem officially denied
that Colonel Lawrence was there, but reports emanating
from Cairo placed him in other countries in the area. The
stories began when there were riots in Jerusalem over Jewish
worship at the Wailing Wall. Lawrence, went the dispatch
from Cairo, "disguised as an Arab, having grown a beard,
left Egypt for Transjordania a fortnight before the first
outbreak in Jerusalem." Though his present whereabouts
were not known, the report went on, "He is said to have
spent a week in Amman . . . where he was entertained by
Emir Abdullah. . . ." The *New York Times* editorialized on
September 6: "Established procedure demands that no up-
heaval of consequence in any part of the Moslem world shall
take place without (1) an immediate report that the famous
scholar-soldier and 'uncrowned King of Arabia' is the

hidden force behind the event, and (2) an authoritative announcement that 'Private Shaw' of the Royal Air Force is still on duty somewhere in India." Actually his most daring feat at the time had been riding his motorcycle spectacularly and noisily up the steep incline out of the hotel basement at Malvern after the *Apple Cart* performance.

The Schneider Cup races, in September, added to his difficulties with Lord Thomson. The race attracted many well-known people, some of whom knew Aircraftman Shaw from his days as Lawrence, and chatted familiarly with him. He was seen talking with General Italo Balbo, the Italian Air Minister, who had come to England with his country's seaplane team. The R.A.F. authorities, he later told Liddell Hart, had ordered a crew to clean the slippery green scum from its own slipway, but had ignored the Italian one; and Balbo had asked him to see that a similar job was done for the Italians. David Garnett comments that "the spectacle of an aircraftman so employed exasperated and scandalized the sense of fitness" of Lord Thomson. (In addition, Robert Graves writes of a row with Lawrence at the Paris Peace Conference in 1919 that Thomson had not forgotten.) Whatever the reason, Thomson ordered him not only permanently grounded as long he remained in the Air Force but expelled from the R.A.F. Since his terms of enlistment were that his service could be terminated at any time by either party, the *R. 101* disappointment rapidly faded when he received orders to appear before Air Marshal Trenchard on September 27.

Lawrence had a good idea what was in store for him. By appealing to his influential friends to help him get a stay of execution, he managed to get the interview delayed over the week-end to September 30. That Monday, Sir Hugh, undoubtedly on instructions from Lord Thomson, granted a conditional reprieve. Henceforth Lawrence was to perform no duties not part of the ordinary routine of an aircraft hand. He was not to fly in government aircraft. He was not to leave the country, not even to go to Ireland. And he was not to visit or speak to any "great men." He asked just who were the "great men," and had a list read to him that included most of the leading political figures of the Conservative Opposition: Winston Churchill, Austen Chamberlain, Lord Birkenhead, Sir Philip Sassoon (the former Air Minister) and Lady Astor. He inquired if Bernard Shaw was included among the forbidden great, and was told that there was no ban on G.B.S. Delighted to be saved at any price, he reported the news to Bernard Shaw, who seemed slightly hurt at his exclusion—and deflation.

Grounded as long as Thomson remained in office, Lawrence could only read about the preparations for the Indian flight of the great dirigible, which, just two weeks after his interview with Trenchard was brought out of its shed, ostensibly completed. Delays were to occur as structural changes were made to increase its lift capacity, and it was nearly a year before it left the ground, headed toward mooring towers at Ismailia and Karachi in which the Government had invested £105,000. Even then the *R. 101* was not quite ready, but Thomson had insisted on a flight by the last week of September, 1930, because he intended to go along, and further delays would interfere with his other plans. With Lord Thomson aboard, the *R. 101* took off on Saturday evening, October 4, 1930. Shortly after 2:00 a.m. on Sunday morning it crashed in flames at Beauvais, France, setting off, after the first grief, a great reaction against airships in England. Lawrence was to fly again, but never in a dirigible; and the Empty Quarter remained to be traversed the hard way—on the ground.

Sooner than he imagined, the Empty Quarter was traversed—and by an Englishman. Barely six months had passed since the *R. 101* tragedy when Bertram Thomas, Foreign Office Agent at Muscat, crossed the great southern desert of Arabia by camel. Lawrence crossed it vicariously —after first shying away from the idea—by writing a foreword to Thomas's book. *Arabia Felix: across the empty quarter of Arabia* appeared in 1932.

Lawrence, until Lord Thomson's death, honored his restrictions more in the observance than in the breach, for some months not even visiting Lady Astor. His visits to the Shaws remained frequent—usually about once a month— and alternated between Ayot St. Lawrence and Whitehall Court. Just before his visit to Trenchard, at the end of September, 1929, the Shaws had sent him a bushel of peaches and nectarines, which he divided among the entire complement within call at Cattewater. Many of the men had never tasted one before, and he efficiently remedied the gap in their experience by the Solomon-like device of cutting the fruit into halves, and giving each "irk" a sample of both. On October 25, he was back again at Whitehall Court, where G.B.S. had Laurence Housman (who suffered from being regularly identified as "brother of *The Shropshire Lad*") as an additional luncheon guest. Housman described the scene in his autobiography, *The Unexpected Years* (1936):

> [An] Irish compliment, which I did not take . . . seriously even though it greatly delighted me, was paid me by Bernard Shaw at his own luncheon-table. He was talking to Lawrence of Arabia who sat next [to] him, and presently, from further away, I heard the shrill voice of the oracle stating: "What Housman suffers from is the British public's dislike of intellect."
>
> With joy in my spine I sat up and said, "What's that, Shaw?"
>
> "Well," he replied, "don't you know it yourself?

You've got all Barrie's qualities, but unfortunately you've got intellect as well."

With that stroke of his two-edged sword Shaw was merely enjoying himself; and was no more serious about Barrie than he was serious about me. But it told me quite plainly—and that surely was a great compliment—that of the two authors I was the one he preferred.

Half an hour later, I was paid a much more genuine compliment, followed by a disappointment which I still remember as one of the most unkind strokes fate ever dealt me. When luncheon was over, Lawrence said to me, "Have you an hour to spare?" I certainly had, for the wish so indicated.

"I want to talk to you about your poems," he said. My spirits fell.

"You mean my brother's," I said.

"No, I don't; I want to talk to you about your first book, *Green Arras*."

And then, just as we were about to go off together, our hostess intervened and said to him, "Have you forgotten that you've promised to come and help us choose a new car?" He had—quite; and so I never knew what Lawrence of Arabia wanted to say to me about *Green Arras;* for we did not meet again.

G.B.S. had an elderly Vauxhall, victim of many turns into ditches, and was then hesitating between a Lanchester and a Bentley. Lawrence went with the Shaws to the Motor Show as their automotive expert, and from there met Liddell Hart to talk over the biography-in-progress. At the end of the winter the Shaws accepted delivery of a Lanchester 8—the vehicle Lawrence liked.

On Armistice Day he was back again, this time at Ayot. A storm kept them indoors, and he and G.B.S. spent the day discussing their favorite subjects of music and books (this time *Great Expectations*). They rarely discussed politics now, and it sometimes quietly infuriated G.B.S. that he could never get Lawrence to follow a political cue very far (although his correspondence with others is full of politics). One semipolitical wisecrack Lawrence passed along to the Shaws a fortnight later was his meeting a member of the peerage who sighed that it was a waste that "such a man" buried himself in the ranks. He annoyed the peer by sneering, "Ah yes, it's more useful being in the House of Lords, I suppose."⁴ Before he left Ayot, he inscribed a copy of *Revolt in the Desert* for Charlotte—the only copy he had signed, as he disliked thinking of the truncated work as a literary achievement with which to be identified. Later in the evening, after the storm had passed, he left on *Boanerges,* carrying with him some of G.B.S.'s letters which he had agreed to mail en route "home."⁵ On one of his hundred-mile-an-hour dashes to Ayot, Lawrence and his motorcycle had arrived caked with mud. T.E. asked the men on Shaw's household staff to clean up the cycle before he started back. Later he and G.B.S. went out to oversee the operation, and found Fred Drury, the gardener, and Fred Day, the chauffeur, removing the grease and grime. Shaw looked at the slight figure of his guest, clad in aircraft-hand's apparel, and then at the expensive-looking Brough Superior. Turning to Day and Drury in mock apprehension, G.B.S. warned them, "Don't clean it up too much, or we shall have the police pinching him."⁶

Back at Cattewater, T.E. guiltily returned to his *Odyssey* translation after having spent almost no time on it since his long days on the *Rajputana.* A year after he had roughed out a translation as far as Book IX he returned to polishing Book VIII. He did about five lines an hour, revising each line later an average of fourteen times, trying not only to find the best marriage of archaism and modernity but to hasten the pace of Homer's narrative, which became bogged down in descriptive detail that made (he said, remembering Sidney Webb's remark to G.B.S. about *Seven Pillars*) Borrow's style seem rapid. He worked at his clerk's desk in Cattewater, where he kept displayed a photograph of G.B.S., taken in Shaw's favorite room (the dining room) at Ayot. It attracted unexpected attention from the aircraft hands who worked regularly with R.A.F. photography, aerial and otherwise. They were not interested in who the bearded gentleman was, but rather in the kind of camera used, the proportion of enlargement, the method of developing and printing.

Christmas week T.E. spent on duty at Cattewater, ostensibly to release family men—also, no doubt, to prevent his enjoying himself too much. While G.B.S. was spending the winter months on preparing the Collected Edition for the printer, he worked through the holiday period and beyond on *The Odyssey*, reaching the surfeit point at his third revision of Book XI. With G.B.S. busy, Charlotte looked over the manuscript, noted places that seemed to her amateur eye to need mending, and mailed the copy back, or waited for his next visit to discuss it.

On a January visit he scanned an advance copy of *Immaturity*, the first of the Collected volumes. Returning to Cattewater he wrote to Charlotte to wheedle a copy for him out of G.B.S. After rereading it he reported that it was very good but weirdly unlike G.B.S. to such an extent that no one could have independently identified it as his work. He waited then for proofs of the rest of the "feast," particularly the volumes of music criticism, short stories and reviews. A wise suggestion he made for the "Ayot St. Lawrence Edition" was unfortunately not carried out. Shaw had told him that all thirty volumes would be bound in jade green. Lawrence's counter-proposal was that the bindings ought not create a row of dull-looking books. He wanted the jade green only for the five volumes of novels, with white for plays, red for polemical works and black for criticism.[7]

Throughout the first part of 1930 he acted as though Lord Thomson were constantly looking over his shoulder. He sat tight in Cattewater, performed his duties, and worked his way through Book XIV. Suddenly, at the beginning of March, he received an invitation from the Scottish University of St. Andrews to receive an honorary Doctor of Laws degree in May. Not looking for trouble—and assuming as well that it was a student prank—he declined. Then he discovered that Baldwin, Buchan and Barrie had all been behind the invitation and were embarrassed by his gay refusal. Lawrence would have been even more embarrassed by his acceptance, for regulations at the time forbade airmen from wearing civilian clothes, and he would have had to accept his doctorate in "irk" garb! Undoubtedly the Labour government would have been embarrassed by the publicity, too, and he might possibly have been sacked from the R.A.F. Even though Lawrence admitted to a morbid love of seeing his name in the papers, it is difficult to see how Buchan—who with Shaw had persuaded Baldwin to let Lawrence back into the Air Force—was performing an act of friendship by abetting the gesture.

In April, while the Shaws were holidaying in Derbyshire, Charlotte became very ill, and G.B.S. concealed the news from the press and almost all their friends. Only Beatrice Webb, Lady Astor and Lawrence were told. When, in mid-May, Charlotte was well enough to return to Ayot, Lawrence invited himself there for the week-end. They planned to go to London to see Paul Robeson in *Othello*, and T.E. worried over his being seen in uniform in London.

When conversation turned to the Liddell Hart biography in progress, the Shaws asked him if he had read *The Real War*, Liddell Hart's new book on the First World War. Its character studies of the war's generals were particularly good, the Shaws thought. But although he had received the book weeks before, he had not yet opened it. Spring and *The Odyssey* and general malaise had intervened.

Another distraction was the setting in once more of the newspapers' nearly annual silly season on Lawrence, which occurred coincident with his planning to go to the Malvern Festival again with the Shaws. He had no desire to see *The Barretts of Wimpole Street*, but did want to see Shaw's *Getting Married* and *The Dark Lady of the Sonnets*. Meanwhile, the Associated Press had reported that he was in Kurdistan, and by the time of the second Malvern season in August, 1930, the German press had become confident of his presence in the Middle East. "Turkey Astir at News that Lawrence is in Region," went the American report:

> Mardin, Turkey, April 30 (AP)—A report that Col. T. E. Lawrence, famous British Asiatic expert, is at Revandua, a town near the Turkish frontier in the desert region between Iraq and Persia, is stirring Turkish public opinion and the Turkish press.
>
> "Is he planning an uprising in Persia or Turkey?" newspaper headlines ask. Then the press goes on to assert that the Turkish government is carefully watching the Colonel's actions.
>
> The proximity of Revandua to Turkey's Kurdish provinces, seat of Sheik Said's revolt and home of still unruly tribes, explains the Turkish nervousness as to the reported presence of the author of "Revolt in the Desert," who according to Turkish opinion, is the author of his subject in more than the literary sense.
> [*New York Times*, May 1, 1930]

In August (while at Cattewater, and then at Malvern with the Shaws) T.E. was "caught" while escaping from Kurdish territory into Persia. Clad in Bedouin headdress and long cloak, and armed with an apparently jeweled dagger in his belt, he crossed the border and took refuge at the American Mission just inside the Persian frontier at Lake Urmiah. There Persian gendarmes seized "Colonel Lawrence," who turned out to be Wolfgang von Weisl, correspondent for the Berlin newspaper *Vossische Zeitung*, who had been in the area looking for traces of the elusive "El Orens." After ten days in custody Herr Weisl was established not to be Lawrence, and released with apologies and the material for a story.

Toward the close of the year Lawrence began to worry less about his restrictions. One day Lady Astor rang up the wife of the commanding officer at Cattewater and asked if she could bring Bernard Shaw over for lunch at the station. Since Lady Astor had survived the last election and was still M.P. for Plymouth, Clare Smith readily assented. When Aircraftman Shaw was not on duty, Wing Commander and Mrs. Smith treated him as distinguished friend. Of course he was on hand for lunch, which Mrs. Smith was still preparing when "Tes" (as the Smiths called him) walked in. It was to be a vegetarian lunch, Clare Smith explained. "Tes" laughed, "Oh, just make it of old bits of wood and string—he won't know as long as there's no meat in it!" After lunch they went on a tour of the station, going down to the slipway where aircraft hands were working on one of the flying boats. G.B.S.'s hat blew away when he bent down to look at one of the engines; and Lady Astor playfully—but unsuccessfully—tried to get one of the airmen to drop black paint on Shaw's head. Then Commander Smith took G.B.S. out in an R.A.F. launch to one of the flying boats, and they clambered aboard. Undeterred by his seventy-five years, Shaw was anxious to go aloft in the craft, but Smith politely blamed regulations and offered instead to start up the engines and taxi across the Cattewater. They chopped up spray across the sound, and then back, to G.B.S.'s delight.[8]

After the visit, the aircraft hands in Lawrence's hut were eager to hear a recording of a talk by Shaw announced by the B.B.C. late in October. Lawrence and the other airmen listened as the Shavian brogue came through, and the airmen swore they heard Lawrence in the background, chuckling into the microphone. It was at the same time that Charlotte had broken her arm in a fall, and Nancy Astor sent T.E. a telegram to say all was well, knowing that G.B.S. was mailing a letter with all the details. Although Lord Thomson had perished in the *R. 101* disaster, Lawrence had continued to stay away from the Astors' home overlooking the harbor at Plymouth, but now assumed the issue of his hobnobbing with the great was dead as well. Cycling over to the Astor home, he offered Lady Astor a ride on *Boanerges*. Viscount Astor warned his wife to be careful (she was past fifty), and saw them off, Lady Astor riding pillion for over an hour as they careened more than seventy miles through the narrow, twisting lanes of Devonshire, while the Viscount assumed they had just gone for a spin around the block. "Really, Lawrence," the newspapers reported Lord Astor as saying, "my wife should not be encouraged to find new ways of breaking her neck."[9] T.E. began dropping in often after dinner.

Again it was a bad time to acquire publicity, for Lawrence had cropped up in a strange new place—a treason trial in the Soviet Union. Dispatches from Moscow headlined a plot in which he was alleged to be chief British agent. The incident charged eight Russians with a counterrevolutionary plot, aided by the French and British, to overthrow the

Soviet government. An attack on Russia was supposedly to have been made the previous summer, but had been delayed until 1931 when conditions proved unfavorable. Thirty Moscow newspaper columns detailed the charges, number eight of which declared that in London and in Moscow the conspirators met representatives of the British General Staff, and "that nothing might be lacking, met the celebrated Colonel Lawrence at the Savoy Hotel in September, 1928, and he said cautiously that British military circles 'had a positive attitude toward intervention' and 'were working out definite plans.' "

The dramatic treason trial had magnificent stage props: Stalin did not improve on the system in a quarter-century of further one-man rule, although there were some additional refinements in the thirties. Prominent in the courtroom were vacant chairs for Winston Churchill, Raymond Poincaré (incumbent Premier of France)—and Colonel Lawrence. Since he was demonstrably in India at the time of the alleged plot, the "confessions" Russian prosecutor N. V. Krilenko efficiently elicited to connect the conspirators with Lawrence were ridiculous. Nevertheless, there were questions raised in Commons. A Labourite M.P. asked where Lawrence was on the date alleged, and was told that he had been in India. Lady Astor defended T.E. with the rhetorical question: "Is it not true that Aircraftman Shaw is leading a quiet, respectable and useful life?" No one answered, but there were shouts of "Hear, hear," and the House proceeded to other business.

*The Odyssey* translation dragged on; and though he wrote the Shaws that he had finished Book XX and was four books from the end, Lawrence was clearly tired of the job. Bruce Rogers and Emery Walker were anxious to get the limited subscribers' edition underway so that the price could be fixed for solicitation of subscribers and booksellers

(Charlotte ordered two copies), but even to Rogers Lawrence's enthusiasm for the project had grown noticeably weak. To Garnett Lawrence complained that the book took all his free time, including parts of his nights, and hoped it would be finished by the end of March, a year late. It would be a relief, he admitted: "I am tired of all Homer's namby-pamby men and women." [*Letters*, No. 429] An added indignity diminished his enthusiasm even more: Rogers had sent his translation (as far as it went) to an expert in the field, who had suggested a series of corrections. Rogers insisted on them, and Lawrence gave in to most of them, while defending himself strenuously:

> You may have thought me cavalier in preferring my own way. . . . Yet, actually, I'm in as strong a position vis-a-vis Homer as most of his translators. For years we were digging up a city of roughly the Odysseus period. I have handled the weapons, armour, utensils of those times, explored their houses, planned their cities. I have hunted wild boars and watched wild lions, sailed the Aegean (and sailed ships), bent bows, lived with pastoral peoples, woven textiles, built boats and killed many men. So I have odd knowledges that qualify me to understand the *Odyssey*, and odd experiences that interpret it to me. Therefore a certain headiness in rejecting help. [*Letters*, No. 431]

Lawrence loved fine printing and binding, dreaming often of setting up his own small press after mandatory R.A.F. retirement. Events often made that day seem closer than it turned out to be, but the dream only became a reality once, after a fashion, with his Subscribers' *Seven Pillars*. Often he operated his private press vicariously, by suggesting items for publication by the Nonesuch Press, the Gregynog Press and similar ones run by friends and acquaintances. In one case, toward the close of 1930, he recommended that the the proprietors of the Gregynog Press reprint Lord Robert Vansittart's *The Singing Caravan*, and was supported by both Bernard and Charlotte Shaw, Charlotte even sending a copy for the Press's consideration. A handsome edition ensued, and Vansittart (who despised self-advertising people) temporarily smothered his dislike for all three Shaws. The luxury edition of *The Odyssey*, however, seemed to get farther from completion. An *Iris III* flying boat crashed into the sea near Plymouth. Lawrence was in the party that rushed out to the rescue in a motor launch, resulting in a month's red tape and his testifying at the inquest in the middle of February. Eventually he had to take his month's leave so that he could hole up and finish the translation job.

For some reason—perhaps G.B.S.'s opinion of his own legal prowess—T.E. wrote to Shaw after the crash of the flying boat and the announcement of the paneling of a board of inquiry, asking him how to act on the stand. Shaw's response was a warning that he had to remember that he was merely a man in the ranks and could do no more than report what he saw; and that if he were tempted to usurp his commanding officer's role in the inquiry (as G.B.S. guessed was the case), the status of the inquiry—and his future in the R.A.F.—would be in jeopardy. The thought of a simple private soldier conducting affairs for his ambitious but unimaginative officer may have helped inspire a play long gestating in G.B.S.'s imagination. At any rate, the idea began developing into Shaw's new work for the stage a few weeks later. Meanwhile, he ended his epistle of advice with the heartfelt words, "Pray heaven they sack you!"

*"I never was anything higher than a colonel. . . . Not a real colonel, sir. Mostly a brevet, sir, to save appearances when I had to take command."*
—Private Meek, in *Too True to Be Good*

# SEVEN

## *1931-1932*

On shipboard somewhere between Corsica and Sardinia, early in March, 1931, Bernard Shaw began a new play, *Too True to Be Good*. The Shaws had decided that they had had enough of—and were too old for—holidays amid the artificialities of resort areas. As G.B.S. wrote several years later,

> Brioni is all very well if you play polo and golf, and swim, or if you like playing water polo in a hot swimming bath before dinner and then sitting up all night gambling and drinking; but you soon get tired of being confined in a private park, however lovely, and dash over to the mainland just to be in a street again among common crowds. I shall not revisit it. I now take my holidays on ships going as far around the world as possible, as I find that in this way alone

can I work continuously and rest at the same time.
[*Letters to Molly Tompkins*, 25th July, 1935]

Shaw told Hesketh Pearson for his book, *G.B.S.*, that
though it seemed impossible, he could work as efficiently
on a ship's crowded promenade deck as he could at home,
because he had a foolproof way of gaining freedom from
interruption while he worked: "I have an unerring eye for
the type of old dear who is flattered to death at the idea of
meeting a celebrity—and G.B.S. is not to be met by everyone. Having selected my old dear, I ask her to come and
join me one morning, fetch her a chair and a rug, tell her
I am setting to work on a new play, and she is so delighted
at being given the role of protector of G.B.S. that whenever anyone comes near she makes agitated signs to warn
him off, whispering that *Mr. Shaw is at work on a new
play*. So for the price of a rug and a chair I get perfect
peace during the entire voyage."

In such fashion the Shaws began a working pilgrimage to
the lands of the eastern Mediterranean, accompanied by
Dean Inge of St. Paul's. The "Gloomy Dean," along with
the unforgotten Aircraftman Shaw, was to figure as a
character in the play G.B.S. had begun to sketch out before
the voyage was over. Many times in the past, Lawrence had
literally or in effect challenged the playwright to "do" him
in a play, but to have done it earlier might have jeopardized
his existence in the ranks. "I do what I am told to do, and
rewrite the drafts [of routine orders] given to me, meekly,"
he had written G.B.S. in 1928. On an earlier occasion he
had insisted, "I can't do the meek touch." Also in 1928 he
had explained himself to Shaw in almost deliberatively
provocative words: "There is a waywardness in me, which
would like to make me prove myself not a Shavian character, nor fully captured by your pen. If you were here [in

India] in the flesh (or better, me there) you would persuade me that you had really set out my motives and
course." From almost the first contact between Lawrence
(then still "Ross") and G.B.S., the dramatist had been
prophesying to him, "I shall put you into a play, if my
playwriting days are not over." He had, perhaps, already
done so, by incorporating much of Lawrence's personality
into his *Saint Joan;* but the figure of the "born boss" leading
men from below, which Shaw may have seen in him, had
the elements of serious farce Shaw had yet to exploit.

Shaw regularly developed characters for the stage or for
the printed page out of facets of himself and his friends,
and had done so as early as his novel-writing days, when
Sidney Webb was caricatured into Sidney Trefusis in *An
Unsocial Socialist* (1883). Hardly any close friend escaped;
nor did any major political figure in England feel safe
from theatrical mirroring or distortion at Shaw's hand, as
academic source studies of the G.B.S. canon will continue
to demonstrate for generations. It is partly this flesh-and-
blood basis of Shavian characterization that provides the
theatre with its broadest and most memorable gallery of
*personae* since Shakespeare, making nonsense of the clichés
about Shaw's "animated ideas," "puppets" and "charlatans."

In addition to Italy and Greece, the Shaws visited the
holy places in the British Palestine Mandate, and Egypt and
Syria. It was almost inevitable that G.B.S. would find the
experience useful for his play, as he frugally put the back-
grounds of his travels into many of his plays, sometimes—as
with *Buoyant Billions* (1946)—saving the memories or the
preliminary notes for a dozen years before reworking them
for dramatic use. The result was that though the play began
in a suburban English setting, it transferred locale in later
acts to "A sea beach in a mountainous country"—an anonymous Middle Eastern location, somewhere between Syria

and the Sudan. On his return he spent two additional months working on the play, completing it at the end of June at Ayot St. Lawrence.

Shortly after the Shaws's return, they invited Lawrence's mother to lunch with them and Lady Astor on May 15. Mrs. Lawrence had heard much about them from her son. She spent many of her later years at remote missions in China, and was probably as interested in seeing the people who were acting as family for her son as her son was in having her meet them. The Shaws had not seen him since January, for even after they returned he was preoccupied with a new service project, one of which was to occupy usefully his R.A.F. career until its close. The crash of the Moth at Mount Batten (as Cattewater station had been renamed) had created interest in developing patrol motorboats for efficient, rapid rescue work—something that he had been insisting were needed since his arrival at the seaplane base. The average aircraft hand was not a policymaker but the disaster focused attention on the inadequacy of the slow naval-type launches, and Lawrence's private campaign resulted in Air Ministry action. Various contractors were asked to offer sample craft which could better attend seaplanes, and Lawrence became part of the team which tested them on runs off the southwest coast of England, often between Mount Batten and the R.A.F. base at Southampton. Becoming a marine expert engrossed him through the usual Easter and Whitsun holidays and on into June, stalling his *Odyssey* at Book XXI. Although he had laid aside his marine epic, he had not laid aside marine writing projects completely, for he was now working on what would eventually be an R.A.F. manual on the care and handling of the new "200 class" seaplane tender craft. On June 18, in sending his advance notes for the monograph to Flight Lieutenant Beauforte-Greenwood, of the team testing the boats, he commented that he had written him "almost a book upon the boat and her engines." It was no exaggeration, as the notes ran to eighty pages.

He then had the time for a trip to Ayot, cycling there just after mailing his manuscript for the boat manual. It was his last chance to see G.B.S. before Shaw left with Lord and Lady Astor and Philip Kerr (Lord Lothian) on a trip to the Soviet Union. When Nancy Astor had first mentioned the trip to T.E., he wrote to Charlotte asking her not to go, as the journey might be too much for her frail health. For that matter, he thought that G.B.S. himself would only profit by the trip in his disillusionment with the Communist means to their praiseworthy, but unrealistic, ends.[1]

At Ayot, G.B.S. and Lawrence discussed the play, which was not quite finished. The entire section in which he figured—as Private Meek—was completed, however, and he made hasty notes on this section of the play (Acts II and III) to mull over at his leisure in order to provide Shaw with more precise language and action for his military scenes and his portrait of Meek.

*Too True to Be Good* was far ahead of its time as a piece of dramaturgy—one of the reasons that it was (and still is) imperfectly understood. Its style is one Shaw pioneered: serious farce. It shows a close relationship between structure and theme, Shaw trying to mirror the chaos of the years that followed the First World War in part through the apparent chaos of the play's structural lines. Missing this point, St. John Ervine saw in this Shaw's "indifference to form," and declared that the play was "loose and incoherent," with each of its three acts irrelevant to the other.

The play uses the anti-illusionary devices considered to be the epitome of modernity thirty years later. Martin Esslin, for example, in his *Brecht* (New York, 1959), points out that the theatre which rejects illusion, "by abandoning the pretense that the audience is eavesdropping on actual events, by openly admitting that the theatre is a theatre and not the world itself, . . . approximates the lecture hall, to which audiences come in the expectation that they will be informed, and also the circus arena, where an audience, without identification or illusion, watches performers exhibit their special skills." Esslin adds, "What distinguishes the theatre from the lecture room or circus, however, is the fact that it [in Brecht's words] 'produces living illustrations of historical or imaginary happenings among human beings.' " The playwright, by destroying stage illusion and by inhibiting the possibilities of emphatic identification between audience and characters, creates a distance that forces the spectator to look at the action onstage in a detached and critical spirit.

In this spirit, after the improbable incidents of the first act of *Too True to Be Good,* the act ends with the announcement by one of the cast, "The play is now virtually over; but the characters will discuss it at great length for two acts more. The exit doors are all in order. Goodnight." And the play ends with the impassioned (but interminable) oration of a young man that goes on while the other characters exit, leaving him to preach in solitude; while at last he is enveloped in fog and darkness, and—in the opening words of Shaw's last stage direction—"The audience disperses. . . ."

The first act opens at the bedside of "The Patient" (Miss Mopply), who is ill with German measles. By her bed sits "The Monster," a microbe of human size who claims he is ill with the measles The Patient has given him. Mrs. Mopply comes in to wring her hands about her daughter's condition, while The Microbe (whom neither can see) comments on their conversation. A doctor comes and goes, and Mrs. Mopply goes out to get the night nurse, while The Monster hides behind a screen. The nurse turns out to be Sweetie, accomplice to a burglar who intends to visit the Mopply house that night. Sweetie signals her friend by switching the lights on and off twice. When he arrives and tries to steal The Patient's pearl necklace, she leaps from bed and subdues both burglar and fraudulent nurse, but, exhausted by her efforts, crawls back into bed and falls asleep.* Sweetie and Aubrey (the burglar) mull over their next move. Sweetie suggests that they take the pearls before The Patient awakes. Aubrey is more imaginative: he rouses Miss Mopply and offers her two choices. She can call the police (and remain a "miserable invalid" for the rest of her life) or "change her entire destiny" by helping to steal her own necklace and enjoy a spree on the proceeds of its sale. As an added inducement they will stage a kidnaping and take Miss Mopply (who has obviously become smitten with the suave Aubrey) to an "earthly paradise." Forgetting her measles, she agrees. (The Monster, simultaneously, becomes well.) Inspired, Aubrey comes forward to the foot of the bed and orates, half to the audience, half to his onstage accomplices, until Sweetie and The Patient (who remembers to take the jewels) lead him out.

The second act takes place in a British military enclosure somewhere in the Middle East. Colonel Tallboys, V.C., D.S.O., sitting in a deck chair reading the weekly edition of *The Times*, "is disturbed by a shattering series of explosions announcing the approach of a powerful and very imperfectly silenced motor bicycle" from which an unseen rider dismounts after "racing his engine with a hideous clatter." It is Private Napoleon Alexander Trotsky Meek, delivering a dispatch in the local dialect from the local tribal chieftain. Meek is insignificant-looking and dusty, but correct in dress and "ready and rapid" in speech. "His figure is that of a boy of seventeen; but he seems to have borrowed a long head and Wellingtonian nose and chin from somebody else for the express purpose of annoying

* What follows may be interpreted as her dream.

the colonel." Ordered by the irritated colonel to fetch an interpreter, he replies that *he* is the interpreter. With all his accomplishments, asks the colonel, why isn't Meek at least a corporal?

"Not educationally qualified, sir."
"Illiterate! Are you not ashamed?"
"No, sir."
"Proud of it, eh?"
"Cant help it, sir."
"Where did you pick up your knowledge of the country?"
"I was mostly a sort of tramp before I enlisted, sir."

Tallboys discovers that Meek wrote the letter for the chieftain and complains that the private must have misrepresented himself as a responsible officer. Meek points out that title distinctions would have meant nothing, since the chieftain addressed him as "Lord of the Western Isles." Tallboys asks who drafted the original letter to the chieftain, and is told the quartermaster's clerk—who is Meek. The letter dealt with the mission of the British force—to suppress the supposed brigands who kidnaped Miss Mopply and who are believed to be in the area. Meek insists that brigandage no longer exists there, but the colonel points out that there must be if they were officially ordered to the area to suppress it. As Meek turns to go, the "countess" and her native maid (Sweetie and a very healthy, sunbronzed Patient) enter. Meek has done a number of friendly errands for the pair, such as cashing letters of credit, but the colonel warns them of familiarities with private soldiers, who should not be treated as human beings. The "countess" apologizes, but points out that if she asks anyone else in camp about anything, they only reply, "You had better see Meek about it."

The three adventurers, awaiting Mrs. Mopply's ransom money, are bored with the place. Sweetie seeks fresh male interests, in particular a Sergeant Fielding; The Patient feels vigorous but (her rebellion over) purposeless; Aubrey is bored with both women but stuck with them. Colonel Tallboys, investigating a sudden shortage of maroons (signal flares) from quartermaster stores, suspects the countess's native servant, after discovering through Meek that her native speech is "Mary had a little lamb" spoken backwards. When the colonel tells the countess that he suspects her maid is a spy, Aubrey recalls seeing Meek cycle about with a sack full of maroons and a lot of wire. Tallboys confronts the fraudulent native maid, and elicits an admission that she is a native—but of Somerset County. One has more control of one's house as servant than as mistress, The Patient points out. Sarcastically the colonel retorts, "You will next tell me that one controls a regiment much more effectively as a private than as a colonel. . . ." But the klaxon, which warns of approaching hostile tribesmen, sounds, and Meek, shouting orders, takes control of the situation before the colonel can do anything: "Rifles at the ready. Cut-offs open. Sights up to eighteen hundred, right over their heads: no hitting. Ten rounds rapid: fire." As the riflemen go into action the maroons are fired off, frightening the raiding party into a disorderly retreat.

Coming down from the sandhill, Meek again relapses into the character of an insignificant private, and reports to the colonel, congratulating him on his victory:

> "Shall I draw up the report, sir? Important engagement: enemy routed: no British casualties. D.S.O. for you, perhaps, sir."
>
> "Private Meek: may I ask—if you pardon the presumption—who is in command of this expedition, you or I?"
>
> "You, sir."
>
> "You flatter me. Thank you. May I ask, further,

who the devil gave you leave to plant the entire regimental stock of maroons all over the hills and explode them in the face of the enemy?"

"It was the duty of the intelligence orderly, sir. I'm the intelligence orderly. I had to make the enemy believe that the hills are bristling with British cannon. They think that now, sir. No more trouble from them."

"Indeed! Quartermaster's clerk, interpreter, intelligence orderly. Any further rank of which I have not been informed?"

"No, sir."

"Quite sure youre not a field-marshal, eh?"

"Quite sure, sir. I never was anything higher than a colonel."

"You a colonel? What do you mean?"

"Not a real colonel, sir. Mostly a brevet, sir, to save appearances when I had to take command."

"And how do you come to be a private now?"

"I prefer the ranks, sir. I have a freer hand. And the conversation in the officers' mess doesnt suit me. I always resign a commission and enlist again."

"Always! How many commissions have you held?"

"I dont quite remember, sir. Three, I think."

After Private Meek salutes and steps smartly from the colonel's hut, Tallboys confides to Aubrey and The Patient that he intends to devote himself to his passion for sketching in watercolors, leaving the expedition to Meek, for "the secret of command, in the army and elsewhere, is never to waste a moment doing anything that can be delegated to a subordinate." Since they are on more intimate terms with Private Meek than he can be, he asks them to inform Meek casually that since he has a D.S.O. he would prefer instead (or, rather, his wife would) a K.C.B. To the countess, who cannot understand why he wastes his time painting pictures, he says that the occupation keeps him sane: "Dealing with men and women makes me feel mad. Humanity always fails me: Nature never."

Act Three takes place nearby before some sandstone grottoes near the beach. The soldiers call one Gothic-looking site St. Paul's and the other the Abode of Love. Sweetie tries unsuccessfully to interest the sergeant in her, but fails until she admits being fed up with her aristocratic pretenses. The tables are turned when Fielding then admits that his ideas about the relations between men and women have been mixed up since he began reading *The Pilgrim's Progress* and the Bible. He once "used to believe every word of them because they seemed to have nothing to do with real life. But war brought these old stories home quite real, and then one starts asking questions." Such predictions about cities being "burned with fire from heaven," he thinks, will become only too real in the next war. When, after his long discussion of religion leads her to shrug, "I dont call you a man," he is prompted to embrace her, to prove otherwise. The elder—a caricature of Dean Inge—arises from within the St. Paul's grotto to admonish them. He proves to be a melancholy atheist, and father to Aubrey. Newton's deterministic universe, the basis of his unbelief, has been shattered by the findings of Einstein, and there is nothing for him but "a solid footing of dogma"—but there is no trustworthy dogma. Even his son has been a disappointment, having been brought up to be "an incorruptible Godfearing atheist." Secretly ordained at college, he became an Air Force chaplain during the war. Switching from "sky piloting" to actual flying, he "won a very poorly designed silver medal for committing atrocities which were irreconcilable with the profession of a Christian clergyman." After he was wounded he lost his nerve for flying. Later, after meeting Sweetie, who cared for him in a nursing home, he turned to theft for a living, which by then he thought hardly worse than his wartime activities.

The Patient finds she cannot shake off her mother. Mrs. Mopply has arrived to see why her daughter has not been recovered, and berates the colonel, who thumps her on the head with his umbrella. When she runs off screaming, her daughter—stilll in slave-girl attire—runs after her. The shattering din of a motorcycle is heard, and Private Meek reappears with a dispatch—Tallboys has been awarded his knighthood for his activities (reported by Meek) in suppressing brigandage, rescuing a British lady and winning the battle of the maroons. "The Government is preparing for a general election, and has had to make the most of the modest achievements." The elder is incredulous that Meek should remain a humble soldier while Tallboys struts with his K.C.B., but the colonel admits to envying Meek's opportunities to soil his hands in doing "life's daily useful business" while he has to resort to brandy-and-water and watercolors to keep from going mad. Private Meek interjects helpfully that Tallboys can exchange his pay, rank and K.C.B. for the ranks if he wishes:

> "Nothing easier: I have done it again and again. You resign your commission; take a new and very common name by deed poll; dye your hair and give your age to the recruiting sergeant as twenty-two; and there you are! You can select your own regiment."
>
> "Meek: you should not tantalize your commanding officer. No doubt you are an extraordinary soldier. But have you ever passed the extreme and final test of manly courage?"
>
> "Which one is that, sir?"
>
> "Have you ever married?"
>
> "No, sir."

"Then do not ask me why I do not resign my commission and become a free and happy private. My
wife would not let me."

Sweetie asks for a month's leave for Sergeant Fielding so
that they can get married. Mrs. Mopply returns with her
daughter. The clout by the colonel's umbrella has cleared
her brain in all but one particular: she now realizes that she
has killed two of her children and almost reduced the other
to a helpless invalid by overprotective care, but she will not
recognize the native servant as her daughter. Still she has
taken a fancy to the former Patient, asks her to come with
her as companion. As Meek disappears to undertake the
repatriation of the expedition, Aubrey begins an interminable sermon. He is a soldier who has lost his nerve as well
as his creed, but he must go on looking for both again. The
characters disperse, but his gift has possession of him, and he
preaches on in solitude until he disappears in darkness, while
claiming, "I must preach and preach and preach no matter
how late the hour and how short the day. . . ."

Whether G.B.S. recalled (or consulted) *Seven Pillars*
for any of the raw material from which he molded his
caricature of Lawrence is now only a matter for conjecture
and the pleasant academic game of parallel passage-hunting.
Rather than the echo of particular lines and incidents, we
find an evocation of some of the many sides of the younger
Lawrence, who could make a game of war and military
customs and proprieties, who could enrage helpless superiors—and who could get his job done. An example from
*Seven Pillars* is Lawrence's recounting of a partial victory
over the Turks, after which his men were prevented by
heavy snow from following up their achievement by a pur-
suit of the enemy:

> Next day and the next it snowed yet harder. We
> were weather-bound, and as the days passed in mo-

notony we lost hope of doing. We should have
pushed past Kerak on the heels of victory, frighting
the Turks to Amman with our rumour: as it was,
nothing came of all the loss and effort, except a report
which I sent over to the British headquarters in
Palestine for the Staff's consumption. It was meanly
written for effect, full of quaint smiles and mock
simplicities; and made them think me a modest
amateur, doing his best after the great models; not a
clown, leering after them where they with Foch,
bandmaster, at their head went drumming down the
old road of effusion of blood into the house of Clause-
witz. Like the battle, it was a nearly-proof parody of
regulation use. Headquarters loved it, and innocently,
to crown the jest, offered me a decoration on the
strength of it. We should have more bright breasts in
the Army if each man was able without witnesses, to
write his own despatch.

When Lawrence was invited to Ayot so that Shaw could
read an act of the new play to him, T.E. listened partly
with anxiety and partly with relief, not knowing how he
would come out of it; but soon he discovered that Meek
was a thorough but affectionate caricature. The real suspense under which he listened left him unable to discuss
many of the points of the play with Shaw right away, but
after he returned to duty he mailed Shaw some notes and
suggestions. Some were taken verbatim into the play, others
substantially adopted, as Shaw tried to marry farce to military reality. Lawrence's letter from Mount Batten was dated
June 26, four days before Shaw gave the play to Miss Patch
for typing.

A point about Pte Meek occurred to me last night,
driving back from Torquay as guide to an R.A.F. car
(or is it Meake?): He wouldn't have told the Colonel
that he was his *Intelligence Officer*. He might have

said, "I do the Intelligence work" or more likely "I am also your Intelligence Staff, Sir," . . . to which the Colonel would have responded by dwelling on the Staff, probably, and forgetting the Intelligence. The Meeks of the world are shy of describing themselves as officers.

It is so hard to judge by just one act of a play. Who could deduce the Apple Cart from its 2nd Act? [The Magnus-Orinthia "Interlude"] But I liked this new thing. It should get home.

Rifles at the ready: stand by with the maroons: sights up to 2000, over their heads, no hitting: contact. Charge your magazines (or cut-outs open; if magazines were already charged). Ten rounds rapid fire. . . . Something like that.

Meek wouldn't have said illiterate. . . . at least he doesn't. His difficulty is having not passed the educational exam. for promotion. He would probably have said that he hadn't got his educational certificate. "Not educationally qualified" is written on my half-yearly return for promotion!

These squalid inaccuracies should not affect G.B.S. He must write so that audiences will comprehend.[2]

The third act had been hastily put together, and gave G.B.S. difficulties he could not cope with before he left for Russia in midsummer. It was the first play Lawrence had worried over with Shaw, and he wondered whether there would be a second draft to improve the play, after G.B.S. returned.

Shaw spent his seventy-fifth birthday in the Soviet Union, with the Astors (including son David) and Lord Lothian. Charlotte remained home. The five traveled by rail via Brussels, Berlin and Warsaw, and found conditions both promising and deplorable during the nine days' tour (which included an interview with Stalin). On Shaw's return he wrote a number of magazine articles stressing the promising aspects of the Soviet social revolution, and (for the most part) evading the political aspects. In October, he broadcast a talk about his visit over the B.B.C., in which he declared that "God is well-pleased" with the Soviet situation, while western capitalism, for all its pretensions to moral and material superiority, was mired in depression. In an article on the Russian tour he spoke of the "sensible arrangements" by which the Communists imposed their reorganization of society. The aftermath of the Russian tour, followed closely by the "In Praise of Guy Fawkes" speech to the Fabian Society, in which G.B.S. (his enthusiasm was short-lived) held up British Fascist Sir Oswald Mosley as an example of the kind of leadership he thought should supplant inefficient parliamentary government, was the nadir of Shavian political insight.

The low political ebb inspired a weak sally in *Too True to Be Good,* the dialogue unfortunately given to the Lawrence figure, Private Meek. In the last pages of the play he is discovered making passport arrangements for The Patient and others to go to the paradisiacal country of Beotia (pronounced, no doubt, as in *Russia*). "The Union of Federated Sensible Societies," Private Meek explains to Colonel Tallboys. "The U.F.S.S. Everybody wants to go there now. . . ." It is a place, we learn, where culture and leisure are respected but private property is not. Fortunately for the play, the political passage is only a brief lapse, its pertinence much clouded over by time.

While Shaw was in Russia, Lawrence took his twenty-eight days' leave to finish *The Odyssey,* and holed up at Sir Herbert Baker's office, where he seemed to find the optimum in solitude. Just before his leave ended, he finished the twenty-fourth and last book of the translation begun so long before, it seemed, in Karachi. When his fair copy was

returned by Emery Walker, he gave it to Charlotte Shaw.
For Charlotte he penned a special title page:[3]

*The Odyssey of Homer*
*Translated from the Oxford Greek Text, by*
*T. E. Shaw*
*at*
*Karachi,*
*Miramshah,*
*On the S. S. Rajputana, in the Indian and Arabian*
*Seas, the Red Sea, the Mediterranean & the Atlantic,*
*at*
*Plymouth*
*and in*
*London*

| *1927* | *1928* | | *1929* | *1931* |
|---|---|---|---|---|
| | | *1930* | | |

*This is the fair and final copy, sent to Emery Walker*
*the Publisher, and afterwards given by TES to*
*C.F.S., not to read, but because she knew Samuel*
*Butler, who translated the Odyssey greatly.*

. *5* .    *viii*    . *31* .
*"I feel that virtue has gone out of me."*

Lawrence missed Malvern in 1931, having just returned
to duty after his leave. It was an unsettling time, for he had
begun that part of his marine craft work that required
moving about R.A.F. seaplane bases a great deal, and his
friend and commanding officer at Plymouth, Wing Commander Smith, had been transferred to another station.
Completion of *The Odyssey* was also unsettling, as it left
him without a writing project; and while he was writing
Charlotte Shaw to press G.B.S. to improve *Too True*, and
to begin another play, John Buchan was suggesting that he
do a life of Alexander, since he had lived and worked in the
lands in which Alexandrian legions marched, and had the

military background for the task as well. To Buchan he claimed contentment, out of which no useful literature could arise, and projected a small literary career of occasional translations.

Through the fall and winter of 1931 Aircraftman Shaw worked in literature vicariously through the continuing revision of *Too True*, and the surveying of the G.B.S. *Collected Edition*, volume by volume, as it came through the Shaws to him. He was spending a great deal of time at Hythe, near Southampton, testing boats, and lived with a few others in the unmilitary atmosphere of Myrtle Cottage, a rooming house. It was closer to London than Plymouth, which enabled him to cycle to the city often: so often, that letters between him and the Shaws show the marked decrease of close contact, and letters to others at this time evidence his trips to Welwyn (Ayot St. Lawrence) and Whitehall Court.

He was still alternating domiciles between Hythe and Mount Batten in the cold, rough weather of January, 1932, when the Shaws on the Royal Mail Motorship *Carnarvon Castle* left Southampton on a vacation to South Africa. From the ship, as it moved out through the bay, Shaw wrote a note dated January 4 to Blanche Patch, asking her to send a copy of the first *Too True* rehearsal copy (1931 proof) to "Colonel Lawrence" (G.B.S. always referred to him thus) at his Plymouth station, addressed to "338,171 A.C. Shaw R.A.F." Lawrence registered his comments— as was so often his practice when he wanted to get something to G.B.S.—in a letter addressed to Charlotte. As usual the letter[4] bore no salutation:

> Miss Patch has sent me the proof of "Too True" and I have read it three times. It makes a superb impression on me. . . . "Too True" by virtue of its last act ranges with Heartbreak House and is magnificent.

. . . I know you do not think of Heartbreak House
as I do: it fits my mind and moods as nothing else . . .
until this "Too True."

It varies more than Heartbreak House, and gains
by the contrast between its movements. The first act
is Mozart-Shaw, by which I mean that he has written
it, and its themes, before. The doctor—the mother:
they are nearly extinct creatures. He has laughed
them to death. When the existing species have gone
there will be no successors. Also the fresh air school is
triumphant over them, and the present women are not
hypochondriac. The microbe is good: and the curtain
to the act brought me down in a heap ["The play is
now virtually over; but the characters will discuss it
at great length for two acts more. The exit doors are
all in order. Goodnight."] Only I can't imagine any
voice but Thesiger's able to say that "goodnight" and
the part is too short for him: so it will not be fully
played. It is a wonderful curtain, and the act does its
bit in making these impossible three young people
possible. Only ramping lunacy, of this sort, could have
achieved it. I did really feel, after it, as if the play was
over, now.

The second act is priceless. I haven't any comment
to make upon it. . . . its reality makes the perfect foil
to the classicism of Act I. At the end of Act II, I felt
that no conceivable third act could be any other than
an anti-climax. The play had been keyed too high for
any final movement.

Not true: for the IIIrd act swept me off my feet, as
it ended. That final speech of Aubrey's beats the
Tempest into fits. I do not know if it will play: but
as reading it transcends the great [Lilith?] speech
of Methuselah. The whole long act leads up to it
splendidly, too: and gives us time to admire the stage-
work: the way the figures enter and (especially)
leave. G.B.S. told me once that plays do not end with

a big bang, climaxes being put in Act 3 and softened by Act IV. Only this time the bang really comes, and is devastating. The play is terrific, when you look back on it. No single part of it is, but the collocation of three such diverse movements overwhelmed me.

Of course I know nothing about the theatre: but I think that "Too True" is probably the finest acting thing G.B.S. has ever made. I'm afraid, only, that Hardwicke will let my conception of Aubrey frantically down. He will never understand what he represents. I shall dread seeing the play acted, for fear it does not come up to what it is. . . .

Only at one point did my nature want to say "no" to G.B.S.: where he said that the war had spoiled the Services. It did alter them profoundly, for the time. After troops had left England for one of the fronts there was no brotherhood remaining. It was fighting spoilt it. But after real peace came, the pre-war mood returned. Relative to civil life the service today is more serene than it was of old. I cannot clearly tell you why this is. People dare not analyze this contentment. Partly we feel eternal. The army is always aged about 20. . . . the peacetime soldiering is still the best lay brotherhood. Look at my life.

Here enclosed is a sheet of unimportant details for G.B.S. to consider if he has time. . . . I have not so enjoyed a printed thing since "Her privates we" of years ago. It is much more important than the Apple Cart. . . .

Though *Too True* has not weathered as well as *Apple Cart*, the fault may lie in our viewing it from the wrong perspectives. If so, its day may yet come, and Lawrence's judgment be upheld. His comment about Aubrey is a case in point. The actor playing Aubrey, T.E. feared, "will never understand what he represents." The implication is

that Lawrence did. Although it was always an open secret that Private Meek, complete to the long head adorned
with Wellingtonian nose, was a portrait of Private Shaw, it
has not been realized that Aubrey Bagot, ex-R.A.F. combat
officer, represents another side of the same complex man—
the "Colonel Lawrence of Arabia" side. Here is the young
officer thrust into the horrors of military necessity so
graphically described in *The Seven Pillars*, from the murder
of prisoners to the massacre of civilians in mined railroad
cars. Aubrey, who had left behind his university education,
and his ordination in the Church of England, to join a
combat service, is warped by his wartime experience to such
an extent that he cannot resume his life at the point war interrupted it and relapses into irrational behavior. "I was
hardly more than a boy," Aubrey recalls, "when I first
dropped a bomb on a sleeping village. I cried all night after
doing that. Later on I swooped into a street and sent machine gun bullets into a crowd of civilians: women, children, and all. I was past crying by that time. And now you
preach to me about stealing a pearl necklace!" He had been
awarded, we recall, "a very poorly designed silver medal"
for the wartime deeds for which his conscience tormented
him. "What am I?" he asks: "A soldier who has lost his
nerve, a thief who at his first great theft has found honesty
the best policy. . . . Nature never intended me for soldiering or thieving: I am by nature and destiny a preacher. . . .
But I have no Bible, no creed: the war has shot both out of
my hands. . . ."

Lawrence's page of details, attached to his letter of January 9, 1932, showed extremely close attention to the text,
and proved very useful to Shaw, who amended his play
accordingly. A copy of the published text will show how
G.B.S. utilized this advice from his "Private Meek." Its page
references were to the 1931 proof of *Too True*:

p. 14. Actually, to have had them once is no defence against *German* measles.

p. 21. "Hell I will" is usually "Will I hell!"

p. 25. Ignition switches on motor bikes are almost unheard of. I race my engine on stopping as I pull out the clutch or put her into neutral—not to fill the cylinders (two!) but because I take off the lead suddenly.

p. 27. "The fact is, Colonel." It would outrage the Colonel to be called Colonel by an "other rank." It is a style reserved for fellow-officers—or civilians.

p. 28. Last line. Ditto. (It is all right later where Meek gets Tallboys educated up to him!)

p. 31.32. We only half-salute ladies. Just raise the hand to the front (not the side) of the forehead. The Col. does the right thing on p. 35.

p. 38. "the same old priest . . . for centuries."* I expect this is intentional?

p. 42. "influenza" Perhaps malaria in that climate?

p. 43. Is hanging "bumps off"? I fancied it was a term for murder or illegal execution.

p. 81. "Ten rounds rapid—go." Last word should be "fire." Orders are never ambiguous. "Go" might mean charge or run.

p. 89. "Subalterns" An officer's word. The Sergeant would sat "lootenants."

p. 81. "Nuder than unshorn lambs." I fail to see this very clearly. Lambs would be nuder shorn: but seldom are worth shearing!

G.B.S. incorporated all the suggested changes and excisions, rewriting where necessary to make his point more

---

* Here G.B.S. took Lawrence's hint, and altered Aubrey's lines to the more realistic "I could be happy as a Buddha in a temple, eternally contemplating my own middle and having the same old priest to polish me up every day."

clear or to fill in around the alteration. Hardly had he finished when another letter arrived from Hythe. Lawrence apparently was returning to *Too True* with the same hypnotic fascination Lowell Thomas's Albert Hall illustrated lectures had engendered in him. This time, though, the return visits were to a loving caricature of himself, and were made more with delight than with morbid awe. He wrote of continued testing of boats being constructed at a yard in Southampton and a writing project of his own—approval had been given for his doing an official manual for the model 200 motorboat. Winter work in Channel waters was unpleasant, and though he enjoyed his work, the hours were long and the tasks on repetition were monotonous: by daylight he worked on the boats; at night in off-hours he worked on the handbook. Still, he had been drawn to further close reading of his proof copy of *Too True* and incorporated new observations and criticism in a letter dated January 27, 1932:

> . . . what excellent reading "Too True" is. I have read it again and again, for pure enjoyment. . . . Until the last speech the play is all loose threads. That speech knits it all together and makes it [the impact] terrible. . . . The people will not like it so well as the Apple Cart, I think, but it is far finer.
>
> I regret to see that, probably by my fault in being too exclusively an engine-monger these days, on page 51 the rifles here have "cut-outs." These should be "cut-offs," of course. I am also not sure if Meek should twice "double" or "trot" out (pp. 32 and 53). In the R.A.F. and Navy other ranks double *to* an order. In the Army progress is always at the march. Perhaps I pettifog? I suppose, too, that Articles of War is correct for the Army Act? We always called it the Army Act, officially.
>
> "Too True" is the only bright spot in my existence

this winter. It gave me inexpressible pleasure. I went about for days with a feeling that some great unknown benefit to me had happened. And that does *not* mean Pte. Meek!

Again G.B.S. made all the suggested changes, rewriting around them. He was following his friend's editorial advice as closely as Lawrence, in revising *Seven Pillars*, had followed G.B.S.'s. It is likely that there were yet other alterations suggested on visits made to Ayot on a new Brough motorcycle Lawrence had acquired early in the year. Some of the changes from the 1931 proof that appear in the 1932 proof of the play affect the portrait of Meek in a way that seems to suggest that Lawrence felt the earlier references could have been construed as personally derogatory. We discover, for example, this exchange between Meek and the "countess" in the earlier version, when the private tells Sweetie that hauling her boxes of new clothes from Paris will require the hiring of a camel. She had also asked him to get a letter of credit cashed:

> THE COUNTESS. Oh, strings of camels if necessary. Expense is no object. And the letter of credit?
> MEEK. That will involve a Jew. I will do my best.
> COUNTESS. Thanks. So good of you.
> *Meek comes to attention, salutes, left-turns, and goes out on the double.*

On the equivalent page in the 1932 proof there is a significant alteration in the exchange:

> THE COUNTESS. Oh, strings of camels if necessary. Expense is no object. And the letter of credit?
> MEEK. Sorry, Countess: I have only two hundred on me. You shall have the other two hundred tomorrow. [*He hands her a roll of notes; and she gives him the letter of credit*].

THE COUNTESS. You are never at a loss. Thanks.
So good of you.

It is possible that Lawrence was unhappy about the possibility that Meek's line smacked of anti-Semitism, which even in his most pro-Arab days had been repellent to him. The line, which may have been automatic in the conversation of many, slipped past Shaw only in the first version, and was then excised.

Another line representative of textual changes to better match Meek to Lawrence occurred in Tallboys' reference to Meek as "only half-witted, and apt to forget himself." The passage, which followed Meek's cashing personally Sweetie's letter of credit, was qualified to, "He is only half-witted: he carries all his money about with him."

The final portrait of Meek appears in the second proof, titled *Too True to Be Good: A Collection of Stage Sermons by a Fellow of the Royal Society of Literature;* and the published version, subtitled more briefly as *A Political Extravaganza.* Here appear definitive details of Colonel Lawrence-Aircraftman Shaw: his appearance, insignificant and authentic in physical particulars; his pseudo-meek quick-wittedness, combined with modest omniscience; his voluntary shifting down the ladder of rank from colonel to private; his knowledge of dialects and tribal psychology (as in his suggestion that Tallboys keep an offered bribe, because the chieftain "wont believe you have any authority unless you take presents"); his charismatic leadership qualities; his technical facility with mines, in blowing up bridges and trains (the mines replaced farcically by colored flares in the play); his unseen but ear-shattering motorcycle.

The stage Private Meek's first meeting with Shaw came when G.B.S. was casting *Too True*, and Walter Hudd had been recommended to him as fitting the Lawrence description. The exchange was brief. Shaw examined Hudd shrewdly and quizzically, and told him that the role involved was a stage likeness of Colonel Lawrence of Arabia. "You look like him!" said Shaw, pleased. "Can you act?"

"I think so, Mr. Shaw," said Hudd modestly.

"In that case," said Shaw, after a chuckle, "we should have a satisfactory combination."[5]

As usual, Shaw oversaw the rehearsals with Sir Barry Jackson, the director. The single hitch that developed was that there was a delay of eight days between dress rehearsal and the first Malvern performance, which was to be a Saturday matinee on August 6, 1932. Seats were at a premium for both the matinee and evening performances, one journalist reporting that "a wild-eyed lady" who had been unable to buy a seat had offered £20 for his. The earlier plays in the Malvern season had, almost without exception, been of historical interest only—*Ralph Roister Doister, The Alchemist, Oroonoko, Tom Thumb the Great* and *London Assurance;* the Festival pilgrims were looking forward to a new play by the Malvern *"Genius Loci"* (as the official program dubbed G.B.S.).

Unfortunately, Saturday, August 6, 1932 was an unfortunate day—even in a global sense. In America (which had seen the play earlier in the year, and had not liked it), the ill-starred "Bonus Army" of World War veterans, having been evicted from Washington by General Douglas MacArthur, was gradually scattering from the encampment to which they had retreated at Johnstown, Pennsylvania. Their destinations were uncertain, as it was estimated that about four-fifths of the nine thousand marchers had no homes to go to. In England, unemployment was reaching a new high. In Germany, post-election Nazi terrorism was increasing, while Adolf Hitler negotiated with the government as to what decisive place his party would assume in it.

At Malvern, plans to fly a contingent of London drama critics to Malvern on a chartered plane went awry. First, some were reluctant to take to the air, even at the Festival management's expense. Then the plane was late in getting off the ground, and, after battling a strong head wind, was late in arriving. The two o'clock curtain was held up forty minutes, while the audience squirmed and fussed. Finally, the play began even though the critics had not arrived, because any further delay would have caused a conflict with the evening performance.

The London drama critics staggered in during the first act, rumpled, exhausted and airsick. One of them on alighting from the plane vowed, "I am going to bash Shaw." Accounts of the opening have become part of the Shavian apocrypha, for some accounts report the opening curtain delayed over an hour, and put the arrival of the Londoners even later. St. John Ervine writes in his *Bernard Shaw* that the critics from London "turned up in the middle of the second act, some of them in a dilapidated condition as they had been ill on the way, and almost immediately after they had entered the auditorium, one of them collapsed." Ervine adds wryly, "Their experience did not put them in a fit state to witness any play, especially one demanding some exercise of the mind, although one might pardonably have thought that men who were accustomed to seeing four plays in a week in a theatrical season, many of which were nauseating, could have soared through the heavens without the slightest discomfort."

After watching the ill-fated *première*, Shaw expressed surprise to the press that so few English and American critics had identified one of the play's chief characters. Private Meek, he announced, was a portrait, complete in every detail, of his very good friend, Colonel Lawrence of Arabia, now Aircraftman Shaw. Even Shaw's friend, critic Des-

mond MacCarthy, confessed that though observing the play
left him with no coherent idea of what it was about, "I can,
however, report what Mr Shaw intended the play to be
about, because while we critics were being carried, as the
guests of Sir Barry Jackson, to the scene of the action in a
sumptuous aeroplane, a printed letter from Mr Shaw was
distributed among us." The letter was Shaw's piece for the
*Malvern Festival Book*, which later was adapted into his
preface to the play. In his review, MacCarthy complained:

> . . . Here am I, an attentive playgoer, yet I can't tell
> you what the play I have just seen at the Malvern
> Festival is about. I could have told you what *Major
> Barbara* was about. I could have told you what *Get-
> ting Married* was about, because, though there was no
> story in which the theme was embodied, the charac-
> ters at any rate discussed one theme—marriage; and
> their various slants upon that problem were most illu-
> minating. But in *Too True to Be Good* there are
> dozens of subjects. I have forgotten nine-tenths of the
> best things, because there was no focus to group them
> around. As I sat in the stalls I kept exclaiming to my-
> self, "Ah, that goes deep; that's worth thinking
> about." But afterwards I did not know what general
> conclusion I, or rather Mr Shaw, had reached. The
> play seemed to me a series of snapshots taken from
> different angles of a post-war state of mind. But it was
> not a picture of that state of mind. The play did not
> embody it. It was more like a series of notes of all the
> things that playwright would somehow have to work
> in if his picture of that state of mind were to be any-
> thing like complete.[6]

After the eight scheduled performances at Malvern, the
play moved to Birmingham for three weeks. Lawrence
came up from Hythe to see the play there at a matinee, and

then visited with the Shaws at Malvern. In Birmingham, he and G.B.S. were joined for lunch at the Queen's Hotel by Cedric Hardwicke (the King Magnus of *The Apple Cart*), who played Aubrey. Over lunch G.B.S. did all the talking, expounding upon what was wrong with modern Arabia, while Lawrence tried to make a dialogue of it, and failed.

After two nights at Malvern, the Shaws took him to Worcester to meet Sir Edward Elgar, his favorite English composer (and Shaw's), to whom Lawrence later wrote of "the kindness of the Shaws in bringing me with them that afternoon. The chance of meeting you is just another of the benefits that have accrued to me from knowing G.B.S., who is a great adventure." [*Letters*, No. 465, December 12, 1932]

While at Birmingham T.E. shrank from the adventure of meeting Private Meek backstage, and waited until he was in London en route back to his base to write Walter Hudd.

> Union Jack Club
> 91, Waterloo Road,
> London, S.E. 1.
> 3. IX. 32.

Dear Mr Hudd,

Ayliff [who played The Elder] told me you knew I had been with G.B.S. to see "Too Good" last Thursday, and that must be my excuse for writing.

As you can imagine, the first seeing was rather an occasion for me. The part you play is obviously a hit at me, and I felt very nervous, until all was over, lest something in it should hurt.

Actually I thoroughly enjoyed it—or rather I should say that I hope to come one night in London and see it again, for enjoyment's sake. That first time my stomach felt a bit hollow all through.

I thought you did the part admirably. You looked decent (I am always as correct as I can be, regimen-

tally speaking) and I only wish nature had let me look
half as smart and efficient as yourself. Only I get more
gaiety out of my position. It's comic really, and I
often see that, whereas you looked grim.

I hope you find the part a comfortable one. Acting
and plays aren't much in my line—but I thought
G.B.S. had really given you some pretty good
chances, which you fully took. The house wriggled
with delight over some of your quips and business.

If you want a long run in the part I hope you get
it: or are long runs long boredoms? Don't answer this:
in fact you can't, for I'm off from here tonight: I
have written only to thank you for a very rare and
peculiar kindness you are doing my reputation,
nightly.

Yours ever<br>
T. E. Shaw. [*Letters*, No. 462]

*Too True* moved to London, where it opened on September 13 at the New Theatre. The newspapers were full
of the play's bad earlier reception at Malvern, although at
Birmingham afterward it played to packed, enthusiastic
houses for three weeks. Opening night, nevertheless, was a
brilliant occasion. Shaw had mended some of the play's most
feeble lines, and the production had been improved. He and
Charlotte presided in a box, with Siegfried Trebitsch, the
German translator of the play, as special guest. It was
well-acted, Cedric Hardwicke speaking the "stage sermons"
magnificently, and Leonora Corbett and Ellen Pollock
making the most of their opportunities as The Patient and
The Nurse. It was a superior cast throughout: Ernest Thesiger as The Monster, Barrie Livesey as The Doctor, Margaret Halstan as The Elderly Lady, Scott Sunderland as
Colonel Tallboys, Ralph Richardson as Sergeant Fielding,
and Walter Hudd as Meek. The reviewer for *The Times*,
kinder than at Malvern, reported that the play had been

tightened and improved, but remained "what it was—a string of fiery islands in an ocean of farce." Meek and Tallboys, he thought "were always the best of the fun," and now were better than they were at Malvern. "The play is to be seen," recommended *The Times*, "because now and then discussion of a great theme—no less a theme than the struggle of the world to proceed beyond the terror of spiritual nakedness—emerges from it; and it is, if you can regard the jokes as anything but interruptions, to be laughed at on the principle that nowadays Mr. Shaw 'can 'ave 'is pick.' "[7]

The derogatory reviews made *The Times*'s look almost laudatory. In *The Spectator* Derek Verschoyle complained that by the end of the first act "the apprehensive playgoer may begin to suspect that Mr. Shaw is sheltering under the widely accepted and benevolent tradition, which British tolerance habitually makes as a concession to genius, that great men must be allowed their little joke." The rest of the play, it went on, was only "slightly less a strain on our credulity" with its "nit-wit Colonel" and "ingenious private." There was no mention of Lawrence—something which was strangely true of most press comment on the play. It was almost as if the press were afraid that mention of Meek as a caricature of Lawrence would give the play a notorious appeal inconsistent with its lack of merit.

Lawrence's friend H. S. Ede angled for an authoritative comment on Meek after seeing the play, and wrote to ask him what he thought of "The Pte. Shaw part." Lawrence answered from Plymouth on October 18 that he had seen the play a second time in London:

> Yes, I saw Too True: and I went round the back afterwards to see Pte. Meek, who turned out to be Walter Hudd, and very charming. Thin armed, thin legged, taller than me, not made up at all, lovely-voiced. Very shy, we both were. I thanked him for

making the part neither impudent nor servile (its
dangers), and tried to hide my regret that the coun-
terfeit was so much nicer than my original reading of
the part.

For the play, I felt that it was a statement of the
fact of three or four years ago: and that we had already agreed that no answers to general questions of
life or death are desired or desirable or possible: and
so we carry on. What an impertinence, this frenzy to
know! [*T. E. Lawrence's Letters to H. S. Ede*, London, 1942]

Walter Hudd recalls that when Lawrence went backstage to meet him, he—as a professional actor—wanted to
see what he could learn from the man whom his role caricatured, in order to act him better. But "his most striking
characteristic appeared to be his *repose*. This aspect of him
I had already used, however. He spoke briefly & quietly,
examined me curiously, & then shyly withdrew."[8]

Soon afterward the "Last Weeks" notices were posted, to
G.B.S.'s dismay. It was an expensive play to produce and
maintain, and box-office receipts had begun to fall off after
the first two weeks. When the announcement came from
Sir Barry, a representative of *The Observer* visited the
New Theatre dressing room of Cedric Hardwicke, and
came away with an interview on the situation for the issue
of Sunday, October 9.

"Of course," said Mr. Hardwicke, "it is by no
means certain that it has been a failure yet. Many
people imagine that because the play is by Shaw it will
run a year, and take their time about coming to see it.
Since the 'last weeks' were mentioned, the booking
has gone up enormously. We may have to extend our
time at the New Theatre beyond Saturday week after
all.

"But assume it has been a failure—why should we

have run only six weeks, and Mr. Shaw's last play,
'The Apple Cart,' have run ten months? Well, there
are various possible reasons.

"There is the reason of the construction of the play.
The old man can turn out streams of dialogue—and
of eloquence—these days; but he is always getting engaged in controversies, and giving interviews, and
writing articles, and there is no doubt that he does
not take the time to think out the plot and the balance
and the intricacies, the *design* of a play as he used to.

"Do you remember 'The Apple Cart'?—How he
got nearly all his serious doctrine into the immensely
long first act, which played an hour and a half—but
which was played when the audience was fresh? Then
he went on to the light interlude with the King's
friend, Miss Edith Evans; and then finished up with a
short last act, which had the quite good 'dramatic
surprise' in it of the King offering to abdicate his
throne, and all the comedy that went with it. The
audience went away feeling that it had been at a light
entertainment.

"In 'Too True to Be Good,' he has reversed the
process. The first act is light comedy in the bedroom,
and then the second act is the brilliant comedy between the Private and the General [*sic*] in the desert;
and in the meantime he has kept all his preaching—his
possibly justified preaching of the despair and in-
sufficiency of the age—for his last act, when the
audience is tired. There is a second character in the
last act, that of the Preacher [The Elder], who has
speeches at least as long and important as mine, the
Burglar.

"Again, there is the question of 'Does the West End
of London want to be preached at, however relevant
the sermon is to the existing situation?' What is
exactly the West End of London? The square mile
that lies round Piccadilly-circus is always substantially

the same. It has not changed in the fourteen years since the middle of the war—except that the lights are up! It represents a class of people apart from the rest of England, a population out in search of pleasure; and when it is swollen by visitors from other parts of England, by visitors, for instance, who have come down to London from the North, it is again swollen by people who have come here for pleasure, and who want to forget, for the moment, about the North.

"It must not be forgotten that the play was written as much as a year ago. If it had been produced then it would have corresponded with the pessimism of the times. But now (at least as regards the limited circle of London) there has been a minor revival of optimism, and people don't want to be told that we are going to wrack and ruin. It was noticeable that when we played in Birmingham just before coming to London—Birmingham, a Midland industrial city close up against present industrial reality—the play was a prodigious success. There were people standing at every performance."

The closing notice was posted for October 22. After six weeks receipts had dropped to £1000 a week, not enough to sustain a play in the still-prevalent theatrical economy which allows only hits to survive. Shaw thought it proved the need for state-subsidized theatre. The day before the play closed Lawrence wrote to the Shaws to thank them for seeing his mother and brother before they left again for a mission in China. To help rationalize G.B.S.'s disappointment he theorized that there was an idea about London that he had pressed Shaw to write a play about him, and that the play's failure would be an implied rebuke to Lawrence, who had then been getting some unsolicited and exaggerated newspaper publicity about the R.A.F. speed boats

which offended the Air Ministry. "You will find Too
Good," he commiserated, "always a little like Heartbreak
House: much liked by some people: not popular with
crowds. It leaves you to go off down the street with a question mark in your stomach."[9]

To his friend Wing Commander Marson he wrote ap-
proximately the same thing several days later, deploring the
failure of a good play. One month afterward, in *The Spectator* of November 25, 1932, buried among the book reviews in the rear, was a critique of Archibald Henderson's
newest biography of Shaw, the title of which—*Playboy and
Prophet*—sounded like an echo of the play of recent
demise. In his review H. W. Nevinson mentioned some of
G.B.S.'s most recent dramatic efforts: "*Too True to Be
Good*, one of his greatest and most unpopular plays. . . .
*The Apple Cart*, his worst and almost the most popular."
"Too Good" was Lawrence's significant abbreviation of
the play in his letter of consolation to the Shaws. Both remarks seem in the nature of epitaphs; yet the play does
spring to life on the rare occasions when it is disinterred,
and it may yet find its theatrical place as more than documentary evidence of the friendship between Public Shaw
and Private Shaw.

*"I admire your courage and practical sagacity" said the conjurer; but I am not built that way."*

*"Do not admire such qualities" said the Arab. "I am somewhat ashamed of them. Every desert chieftain displays them abundantly. It is on the superiority of my mind, which has made me the vehicle of divine inspiration, that I value myself. Have you ever written a book?"*

—Jesus and Mohammed, in G.B.S.'s *The Adventures of the Black Girl in Her Search for God*

# EIGHT

---

## *1932-1933*

G.B.S. had left for South Africa in the first days of 1932. Leaving behind his apparently completed (but for Lawrence's intervention) *Too True to Be Good,* he took with him the beginning of a new play. It was to be a companion piece to *Too True,* and dealt with some of the themes touched on by the just-completed play. One was the problem of what to do with the "born boss," for, as Shaw wrote later in his preface to the play (in August, 1935), it is undeniable "that individuals here and there possess a power of domination which others are unable to resist. . . . It is

the final reality of unequality." Again his play was to take
the shape of serious farce, with a parallel, it seems, to *Too
True*'s Private Meek, whose prototype, "fully conscious of
his gifts and mental rank" once told Shaw, "No matter
where I am I always rise to the top."[1] The companion play,
however, was to have a female "boss"—and Shaw, who
never mentally discarded anything he wrote, put the heroine of what was to become *The Millionairess* together from
fragments of Lydia Carew (the domineering millionairess
heroine of his 1882 novel *Cashel Byron's Profession*),
Beatrice Webb, and Lady Astor. The play did not go
smoothly, and Shaw toyed with it for the next three years.

Meanwhile, he had found more congenial occupation on
his trip to South Africa. Ironically it was the outgrowth
of a near-tragedy. Shaw had learned to drive in 1908 on
an automobile that had its accelerator pedal placed between
the brake and the clutch, rather than to the right, as became more common. In South Africa, because the old
system had become dangerously automatic for him, Shaw
caused a mishap that would have been ludicrous had the
three aboard Shaw's vehicle escaped injury. Charlotte, frail
and past seventy, was the lone victim. Commander Newton
of the British Navy had been guiding Shaw along the route
between the seaside resort of Wilderness and Port Eliza-
beth when the car hit a bump and veered to the left. Shaw
twisted the wheel of his rented vehicle as far as he could
to the right and applied what he thought was the brake.
As he wrote Lawrence from the town of Knysna, where
Charlotte was to be laid up for a month, the result surpassed
all his previous exploits as a motorist. He had driven the
car at full speed over a ditch and a hedge and into a fence
made up of five strands of barbed wire. Finally Commander
Newton asked Shaw, "Will you take your foot off the accelerator and put it on the brake?" The car came to a stop

with one strand of the barbed wire still holding. Meanwhile, Charlotte had been bounced around in the back seat with the luggage.

All their further itinerary had been canceled, Shaw wrote Lawrence, and their earliest possible arrival at Southampton would be April 11. He had sent Lady Astor a more detailed account the same day, and suggested that T.E. consult it for additional information about the consequences to Charlotte, as G.B.S. hoped the accident would escape the press. Up to February 10, the day of the catastrophe, the press had covered Shaw nobly. He had spoken for nearly two hours for the Fabian local group at Capetown (enriching their treasury), made a country-wide radio broadcast in which he attacked South Africa's colored near-slavery, and allowed himself to be feted and lionized.

One low point in the visit to the Cape was what St. John Ervine described as a "maladroit meeting" with General Jan Christian Smuts, South African war hero and Prime Minister. It was at a luncheon party given in Shaw's honor by the novelist Sarah Gertrude Millin. Ervine tells the story, based on Mrs. Millin's account of it published in *The Spectator* shortly after Shaw's death in 1950:

> The conversation at the party was uneasy. Smuts and G.B.S. had not much in common, apart from high intellectual quality, and their interests seemed not to touch anywhere. The fact that they were absorbed in politics might have been thought likely to set their tongues wagging, but it was a political remark which ruined any hope of agreeable discourse between them. Smuts, making conversation, had talked about guerrilla warfare, without awaking G.B.S.'s interest, another odd fact, considering that Colonel T. E. Lawrence, a brilliant guerrilla warrior, was now an inti-

mate friend of G.B.S. and Charlotte. It would have
seemed simple to mingle the memories of Smuts with
the experience of Lawrence.

Instead of talking of the Lawrence Smuts knew,
G.B.S diverted the conversation to the Lawrence of
whom Smuts had scarcely heard: D.H.; and insisted
on talking about *Lady Chatterley's Lover*, a work of
which Smuts, who was not a novel reader, was totally
ignorant. "Every schoolgirl of sixteen should read
*Lady Chatterley's Lover*," said G.B.S. oracularly, and
Smuts, wondering what the work was, politely murmured, "Of course, of course!"[2]

When Shaw turned the flagging conversation to the Gold
Standard, and took a side contrary to South Africa's interest, the party hastened rapidly to an end.

Possibly another aspect of his first weeks in South Africa
came home to him as he awaited Charlotte's slow recovery:
several "well-wishers," he had reported in his radio address,
had written to ask "very earnestly where I will spend
Eternity." He may have given the question additional
thought at the time of the accident, for while he sat out
the mending of Charlotte's lacerations and bruises at the
Royal Hotel in Knysna, and later back again in Wilderness,
he felt no urge to continue *The Millionairess* or begin a new
play. Instead, the idea for a modern religious fable took
hold of him and did not let go until he had composed, in
the spirit of Voltaire's *Candide*, his prose tale, *The Adventures of the Black Girl in Her Search for God*. Shaw
claimed an "inspiring force" beyond himself circumvented
his intention "to write a play in the ordinary course of my
business as a playwright; but I found myself writing the
story of the black girl instead." *The Black Girl* analyzed
via Shaw's favorite means—parable—how humanity developed and sophisticated the concept of God. Shaw's deity

in *The Black Girl* is an evolving one. The simple native girl, after adventures among the unsatisfactory concepts of *Old Testament, New Testament, Koran* and modern science, learns from an auburn-bearded young Irishman who is busy spading Voltaire's garden that God is "not properly made and finished yet." Pleased with himself, Shaw had the tale rushed into proof stage when he and Charlotte returned in April.

Lawrence saw the Shaws in April, and felt relieved that Charlotte had come through her ordeal well. G.B.S. took the opportunity to invite him to what Lawrence called a "feast of giants"—Shaw hosting a dinner party which included Yeats and Elgar. But though Lawrence was in London on Air Ministry business, it was that business which directed him back to Hythe instead of to Whitehall Court. There were other luncheons and dinners, however, one of them recalled by another guest—Sir Osbert Sitwell—to have occurred in 1932:

> I never grew to know Lawrence well, though I often met him, especially in these years: but, for all his parade of ordinariness, for all his vanity, which led him to believe that he possessed such powers as would make the world safe only if he were not in a position to exert them, for all the perky banality of the mask he wore, it would have been impossible not to like him, or not to realize, even though you did not understand, the qualities he possessed. But most of all I liked him . . . at a luncheon in Whitehall Court with G.B.S. and Mrs. Bernard Shaw. Perhaps he was always at his best in their company, for they loved and comprehended him; and there was, I noticed, a sort of audacity of mischief about his attitude and conversation when they were present, that was enchanting.[8]

It was not until early in July, when Lawrence visited the Shaws, that he was given a proof copy of *The Black Girl*. Having known about it, he had been wanting to read it, but hesitated to ask. On the cycle riding back to Hythe, he mulled it over. Unquestionably it did recall *Candide*, he thought, but ended more weakly. He liked the restraint in Shaw's humor, and the terseness of the prose.

The businesslike notion to give value for money and eke out his seventeen thousand words with enough additional pages to make a commercially respectable volume may have caused G.B.S. to have the slim *Black Girl* volume illustrated. He may also have become interested in book illustration from his work with Lawrence on *Seven Pillars* —as his attempt to commission Lawrence's artist-in-chief, Eric Kennington, to work on *The Intelligent Woman's Guide* suggests. Whatever the reasons, after he returned from South Africa, G.B.S. set out to find an illustrator, and in May had commissioned John Farleigh to do a series of woodcuts according to ideas which he himself had literally sketched out. By September the job had weathered a long correspondence and several alterations in the woodcuts. On the twenty-fourth, Shaw sent Farleigh a check in full payment for the job. Though the work was completed, he admitted in the letter accompanying the check that one flaw had been found in Farleigh's witty, happy treatment of the tale:

> One fearful mistake has been discovered.
> Aircraftman Shaw, alias Colonel Lawrence, Prince of Damascus, etc., etc., who is among other things a keen book fancier, saw yesterday the set of proofs you sent me (many thanks) and highly approved of them, but made the devastating remark that no Arab ever sat with his legs crossed. We shall have to assume that Mahomet was an exception to all rules.[4]

Farleigh had mentioned the error himself at a luncheon meeting with G.B.S., but Shaw either had forgotten or had not taken it seriously until Lawrence noticed it independently. At the time Farleigh first pointed it out, Shaw shrugged it off, saying that it was a pity to alter a good design merely because of an academic error, and that they were justified in pleasing themselves. No move was made by either party to alter the sketch, for Farleigh considered the check as evidence that the job was satisfactorily completed. The engraving was published with Mohammed crossing one leg over the other. Lawrence thought the book was a "triumph of production."

Charlotte sent him an advance copy of the first edition, warning him to keep it a secret until publication date, December 5. The book, paradoxically, became a great pre-Christmas best seller because of the publicity it received from religious groups who attacked it as blasphemy. There were editorials, paid anti-*Black Girl* advertisements, news items about bannings of the book by public libraries, and a resolution (which failed to carry) that G.B.S. be expelled from the County Wexford Bee-Keepers' Association, in which he was a life member. *The Black Girl* survived it all, and eventually reached its present status of a minor classic.

Lawrence reread *The Black Girl*, and confessed that the book improved on rereading. His first thought had been that it was merely a handsome job of bookmaking, but he found that the final effect upon him was a recognition of the subtlety of its humor. In a letter to Charlotte, T.E. regretted that G.B.S. had done so little prose.

One of G.B.S.'s concurrent projects had been the founding of an Irish Academy of Letters. With W. B. Yeats, he planned an Academy of twenty-five members who were not only Irish, but had done creative work of an Irish nature; and ten Associates of Irish ancestry who neither resided in Ireland nor based their work upon Irish themes. In a letter dispatched to prospective Academicians early in September, Yeats and Shaw described the value of having an authoritative instrument to represent and act for *belles lettres* in Ireland, where official censorship stifled the vigor of literary activity, yet where the people themselves had "a deep respect for intellectual and poetic quality." Their jointly signed invitation ended with a humble note: "In making this claim upon you we have no authority or mandate beyond the fact that the initiative has to be taken by somebody, and our age and the publicity which attaches to our names makes it easier for us than for younger writers."[5]

James Joyce declined to be a Founder Member, feeling, probably, that he had no right as a voluntary exile to accept the role of spokesman—even in a collective way—for Irish Letters. Among those proposed by Shaw and Yeats for Associate Members—the latter almost certainly by G.B.S.—were Eugene O'Neill and T. E. Shaw (son of an Irishman). Both accepted. Rather than send his reply (as requested) to the Academy's Provisional Honorary Secretary, George Russell (AE), T.E. forwarded his assent to the Shaws. Charlotte passed on the information to Yeats, then in Dublin. Yeats responded with gracious notes to T.E. and to Charlotte, telling T.E. (whom he had never met) that he admired his gallantry, charm and intellect; and telling Charlotte that there was no nominee whose acceptance he so coveted as Aircraftman Shaw. Charlotte sent the letter she received to T.E.[6]

Aircraftman Shaw soon fulfilled his new dignity as an Academician. Toward the close of 1932 Lawrence's *Odyssey*, with typography and decoration by Bruce Rogers and translation by "T. E. Shaw," was published. The translator had insisted that his "Lawrence" name was not to appear on the book, for he did not want people buying it on the strength of "Lawrence of Arabia's" reputation. Nevertheless, it is unlikely that many people who bought the book then did not know through the publicity and the reviews that the "T. E. Shaw" on the title page was Lawrence. Today, reprint editions of the translation bear both names.

Although many reviews of the translation appeared, he was less interested in the reaction of others to it than to his "personal" books, the *Seven Pillars* (and its abridgement) and *The Mint*. It was partly that the literary way of life was fading from him as he became absorbed in work on R.A.F. watercraft, and partly that he had (or circumstances had forced him to) let the work of translation drag on until he felt sated with Homer. Also, where previously he had welcomed editorial help first from Edward Garnett and later from Bernard Shaw, G.B.S. (busy with new work and the Collected Edition) had shown little interest in *The Odyssey*. All the suggestions from Ayot had come from Charlotte, a literary amateur; and worst of all, there had been unwanted literary advice—and pressure to accept it —from those who had commissioned the translation and then hesitated to trust the translator's scholarly authority in the matter. Still, he had collected £600 for the effort, and was reasonably satisfied with his part of the book, though disappointed with Bruce Rogers's decoration.

*The Odyssey* translation received favorable reviews both in the United States and in England. The *Sunday Times* (November 5, 1932) called it a "wonderful performance. . . . The greatest of all romantic tales has been rendered into English as rich and as rhythmically subtle as the original." The *New York Times* called it a "ruggedly and roughly masculine" translation, with a use of adjectives and adverbs that gave it "distinctive ornament and color." *The*

*Book-of-the-Month Club News* recognized it as "one of the notable books of our time." None of the praise cheered Lawrence, who described it as "manufactured writing," and felt that its chief value lay in providing him with funds for the refurbishing of Clouds Hill for permanent occupancy.

Clouds Hill, to which he drifted back regularly through the years since he had left Bovington Camp for the Air Force, was not habitable all year round. When the R.A.F. relieved him of his boat work at Southampton and returned him to routine duties at Plymouth, Lawrence suddenly felt the necessity to get the repairs done. If every newspaper story about him could cow the Air Ministry into taking him out of the work he loved (he was no longer content with simple enlisted man's duties), it was time, he thought, to consider becoming a civilian.

At the end of the year, when *The Black Girl* was ready for publication, the Shaws went off on their longest working vacation, a cruise around the world on the *Empress of Britain*. They left Lawrence a detailed itinerary so that he would know where to send his letters, and he stowed it in his letter-box for safekeeping. He was amused by G.B.S.'s plans to stop in the United States—a place he had avoided for so long, in spite of entreaties by lecture-booking offices. "It would be like the old man," he wrote Mrs. Sydney Smith, "to take a boat home from Panama to miss the States." There was no respite from news about the Shaws' travels, for London newspapers gave them coverage that almost made the regular letters he received unnecessary.

The Shaws' disappearance from the scene made Lawrence's world considerably emptier. It was a reason why, he wrote Mrs. Smith on January 27, "time does not press." On returning on February 20 a reproduction of a portrait of him she wanted autographed, he lamented to G.B.S.'s secretary, Miss Patch, "I can't write to those wanderers of yours! Somehow the feeling that they are nowhere in particular breaks in—"

The Shaws circumnavigated the globe from west to east, making some of the usual tourist tours into the interior when the *Empress of Britain* anchored somewhere. They looked into Vesuvius, viewed the Pyramids, saw temples in India and Ceylon, flew over the Great Wall of China, went to a Chinese theatre, stopped in Japan, and crossed the Pacific to San Francisco. There G.B.S. visited the untypical American home of William Randolph Hearst at San Simeon, rejoined his ship at Los Angeles, and sailed through the Panama Canal to New York. On April 11 he left the *Empress of Britain* just long enough to make an unflattering speech about the United States to a large, curious audience at the Metropolitan Opera House. Lawrence, curious about the reports in the English press concerning the speech, cycled into London, when he knew American newspapers would be arriving, and bought a *New York Times* in order to read the full text of the talk,[7] which was later published as a pamphlet, "The Political Madhouse in America and Nearer Home."

Aboard ship between stops, G.B.S. dutifully performed his vocation as playwright, producing *On the Rocks* while going through the Indian Ocean, and writing a playlet he labeled a "comediettina for two voices" (*Village Wooing*) "in the Sunda Straits," according to the published play.

*On the Rocks* was a political play born out of Shaw's disillusionment with Ramsay MacDonald, Prime Minister of the primarily Conservative coalition "National Government" that was navigating England through the depression years without attempting to press for any of the legislation his Fabian and Labour background promised. It was uninspired writing, about the problems of a leftist Prime Minister, Sir Arthur Chavender, in enlisting support for his program to combat business depression and unemployment. Neither Labour nor the Conservatives back the Prime Minister's strong measures, leaving him with no alternative but to fight for a dictatorship. This he has not the will to do, and the play ends with confused noises heard from his window, as rioting begins in the streets and England heads toward "the rocks."

Though the play has political interest, in that many of the characters are parodies of people then in public life, on the stage the play had no life. When it opened in London in November, 1933, it was a flop, lasting forty-one performances. Lawrence had little to say about it, politely wishing Shaw luck at the opening, and diplomatically saying no more. Later, when Shaw sent him a new volume of plays which sandwiched the little "comediettina," *Village Wooing*, between *Too True to Be Good* and *On the Rocks*, he praised the "one in the middle" and again ignored *On the Rocks*.[8]

*Village Wooing*, a playlet composed of three "conversations" between "A," a writer, and "Z," a village postmistress, takes place first on the cruise ship *Empress of Patagonia*, then in the village post office, and lastly in the village store, where "A" and "Z" set up shop and agree to marry. The play, subtly infused with many of Shaw's preoccupations from the Life Force to minor crotchets, is one of his most charming and actable pieces, and in the first scene conveys much of his working habits aboard ship.

When the *Empress of Britain* docked in England late in April, 1933, the Shaws expected to find Lawrence in civilian clothes, for he had written them six weeks before that he had applied for discharge effective one month from the date of his application, which he made March 6, the same day that he wrote the Shaws to inform them of his decision.

Routine R.A.F. station duty was too dull, and he fretted at the inactivity after the pace of Schneider Cup preparation and the challenge of improving R.A.F. watercraft. Rumors flew rapidly that he had been kicked out of the R.A.F.; but that was only because, in the routine of handling his release earlier than his contract called for, it was necessary for his commanding officer to attest that Lawrence's discharge would "cause no manning difficulty." [*Letters,* p. 763]

In the middle of March T.E. received permission to see Sir Geoffrey Salmond, who was due to become Chief of Air Staff a few weeks later. On the surface he was inquiring about the status of his application; actually he wanted to make it clear that he did not want to leave the Air Force, but instead wanted more challenging duty. Then he followed up his interview with two letters to Sir Philip Sassoon, Under Secretary of State for Air. He had served for eleven years, he wrote, and had "learned every square inch of the R.A.F." His present duties were the kind any aircraft hand could perform. "It seems a pity to leave so much knowledge unused," he added, as if unaware that the duties he expected were performed by ranks he had in the past refused to accept, and which were awkward when given to an ordinary enlisted man, whatever his past glories. He would be willing to return to experimenting with boats, he wrote, but would, "best of all [like] to do a long flying-boat voyage and write a log of it." [*Letters,* No. 486]

Nothing happened as April 6 approached. On the Saturday before the Thursday he was due to depart the R.A.F., he returned all of his uniforms and equipment except what he wore, and took a load of books, records, personal tools and clothes to Clouds Hill, which was still being worked on. Since no word came from the Air Ministry, he was forced to remain at Mount Batten; but the silence meant to him that his request for other duties was being taken seriously. On April 21, the Air Ministry decided to shift Aircraftman Shaw to the marine craft section of the R.A.F. station at Felixstowe, in Suffolk, which specialized in experimental work on seaplanes. It was a vindication for Lawrence, and he wrote delightedly to Mrs. Shaw and Mrs. Smith when he received the news several days later that his retirement had been postponed.

David Garnett's edition of Lawrence's *Letters* quotes an Air Ministry confidential report of April 26:

> I think he can very advantageously be employed watching Air Ministry's interests at contractors' yards, in compilation of trial reports, and notes on running and maintenance. He has ideas on highspeed craft worth considering. I propose to send him to Mssrs. White, Cowes, thereafter to visit the Power Boat Co. where we have several experimental craft under construction. . . . Are you satisfied he can live decently on 30/-a week plus his pay if he has to go to Cowes for a month in the summer?

The new assignment took him to the Isle of Wight, where he was to wear civilian clothes and otherwise avoid publicity. It also left him without a motorcycle and without ambition to travel. He had one ambition now—to prepare Clouds Hill for occupation. He was well aware that his new start was only a reprieve, and that he had a deadline rapidly approaching from which there would be no reprieve—March, 1935.

He spent his leave at Clouds Hill, putting in running water, a boiler to heat it, and a bath. On the ground floor, bookshelves and new flooring were put in. It was being "*Odyssey*-finished," he told Edward Garnett. It was the reason he gave the Shaws for not joining them at Malvern in August. When water came in, he wrote Charlotte happily of his "house-wetting." Clearly, he was in no mood to continue an erratic literary career, or turn out more "manufactured writing." To Garnett he wrote that he was past his prime, which he placed between "digging Hittites" before the war and completing *The Mint*. The heat had gone out of him, and he could write nothing worth having. [*Letters*, No. 496] A few months later Charlotte caught him in the same state of mind when she suggested that he needed to begin a new writing project, and that the best possible one would be his autobiography. His answer, in capital letters, was bold and concise: "NIX."⁹

Liddell Hart was still working on his Lawrence book in 1933. The Shaws were about to close Ayot St. Lawrence for their annual trek to Malvern, when the biographer asked to borrow volumes of the World War I *Arab Bulletin* on which Lawrence had worked in Cairo and had given to Charlotte for safekeeping until he had a permanent place for them. She sent them to Lawrence, who sent them on to Liddell Hart, with instructions to return them to Charlotte again when he finished with them. At the time (August), Liddell Hart was probing Lawrence's political philosophy, and found him full of admiration for the Platonic philosopher-king, but discovered that T.E. had acquired his current interest not directly from Plato, but through King Magnus of *The Apple Cart*, and Andrew Undershaft of *Major Barbara*. G.B.S.'s Undershaft helped convince him that political power was most effectively exercised when it was least obtrusive, he told Liddell Hart, who noted in his biography afterward that Lawrence "welcomes, and enjoys, the opportunity of influencing the course of events, of deciding policy and directing action without the appearance."

Toward the end of 1933 he became more involved in

literary interests again, but first in someone else's behalf.
The Garnetts had asked him to enlist some support for a
Civil List pension for T. F. Powys, the great and still neg-
lected novelist, whose brooding allegorical tales of rural
England, such as *Mr. Weston's Good Wine,* had failed of
commercial success. He wrote to Charlotte to win over
G.B.S., and Charlotte broached the matter to her husband.
Neither she nor G.B.S. recalled reading a line of T. F.
Powys and knew nothing of his work. It was not cricket,
Charlotte reported back, to recommend someone on no
acquaintance of him or his work, and concluded with a
positive *no.* Smarting from the rebuff, but unwilling to admit the extent of his failure, Lawrence wrote Edward Garnett that since, in response to his inquiries, neither Charlotte
nor Bernard Shaw had heard of Powys, he hesitated asking
them to recommend anyone they did not know.

He was then living in Southampton and regularly going
out into Southampton Water in one of his experimental
boats. His home base was still Felixstowe, from which he
was sent out on temporary duty to stations where marine
craft work was underway. He was gaining weight and
getting gray, and was over forty, all of which made him
brood about where he was heading. It led to a letter to
Charlotte:

> Southampton
> 9 XII 33
>
> . . . something happened to me last night, when I lay
> awake till 5. You know I have been moody or broody
> for years, wondering what I was at in the R.A.F.,
> but unable to let go—well last night I suddenly under-
> stood that it was to write a book called "Confession
> of Faith," beginning in the cloaca at Covent Garden,
> and embodying The Mint, and much that has hap-
> pened to me before and since as regards the air. Not

the conquest of the air, but our entry into the reserved
element, "as Lords that are escheated, yet with a silent
joy in our arrival." It would include a word on Miranshah and Karachi, and the meaning of speed, on land
and water and air. I see the plan of it. It will take
long to do. Clouds Hill I think. In this next and last
R.A.F. year I can collect feelings for it. The thread of
the book will only come because it spins through my
head: there cannot be any objective continuity—but
I think I can make it whole enough to do. . . . I
wonder if it will come off. The Purpose of my generation, that's really it.

 . . . Three years hence we'll know. . . .[10]

It was Charlotte's rejected autobiography idea, reworked
into a peculiarly Lawrence frame of reference, but it never
came off.

 At the end of the year also, he and G.B.S. collaborated
in a gesture of sincere good will. In a nursing home in
Worcester, Shaw's composer friend Edward Elgar, stricken
with incurable cancer, was painfully living out his last
days. On December 5, G.B.S. sent Elgar a copy of his
newly published *On the Rocks*, and a letter expressing the
hope that Elgar would soon complete his Third Symphony,
which Shaw had already arranged with Sir John Reith of
the B.B.C. to broadcast. He looked at the new volume with
pride all day, Elgar dictated in an acknowledgment, but
could not read it through because he was "in the depths of
pain." Lawrence heard from the Shaws about the composer's hopeless condition, and, three days before Christmas, wrote to Elgar from Clouds Hill, where he was spending his holiday leave:

Dear Sir Edward,

 This is from my cottage and we have just been
playing your 2nd Symphony. Three of us, a sailor, a

Tank Corps soldier, and myself. So there are all the Services present: and we agreed that you must be written to and told (if you are well enough to be bothered) that this Symphony gets further under our skins than anything else in the record library at Clouds Hill. We have the Violin Concerto, too; so that says quite a lot. Generally we play the Symphony last of all, towards the middle of the night, because nothing comes off very well after it. One seems to stop here.

You would laugh at my cottage, which has one room upstairs (gramophone and records) and one room downstairs (books): but there is also a bath, and we sleep anywhere we feel inclined. So it suits me. A one man house, I think.

The three of us assemble there nearly every week-end I can get to the cottage, and we wanted to say "thank you" for the Symphony ever so long ago; but we were lazy first; and then you were desperately ill, and even now we are afraid you are too ill, probably, to be thinking of anything except yourself: but we are hoping that you are really getting stronger and will soon be able to deal with people again.

There is a selfish side to our concern: we want your Symphony III: if it is wiser and wider and deeper than II we shall very sadly dethrone our present friend, and play it last of the evening. Until it comes, we shall always stand in doubt if the best has really yet happened.

Imagine yourself girt about by a mob of young pelicans, asking for III; and please be generous to us, again!

Yours sincerely,<br>T. E. Shaw [*Letters*, No. 506]

Two months and a day later, Sir Edward Elgar died.

*"Life as we see it is so haphazard that it is only by pick-
ing out its key situations and arranging them in their significant order (which is never how they actually occur)
that it can be made intelligible."*          —Bernard Shaw

# NINE

*1933-1935*

Lawrence spent Christmas of 1933 at Clouds Hill. Part of
the time his Farnborough airman-friend Chambers was
there with him. Since the cottage had only two chairs, this
was as much company as he could comfortably handle at
one time. Bedding accommodations were also limited—two
sleeping bags. No dishes, no pots, no pans, but hundreds of
books and records.

In Ayot, the Shaws were planning another long voyage.
They thought that it was private information until Lawrence read about it in the gossip columns (Charlotte
claimed to have told only Lady Astor). They planned to
cross the Atlantic and (through the Panama Canal) the
Pacific to New Zealand. The choice of routes and ports of
call was based on the fewest opportunities to be hunted
down by reporters and photographers, for G.B.S. vowed

he would write three plays before the *Ranjitane* returned in May. One play would be a rewriting of *The Million-airess*, which still did not satisfy him.

Before the Shaws departed, Lawrence wrote to them of a loss at Clouds Hill he mourned—someone had taken his copy of *Saint Joan* with the "Public Shaw to Private Shaw" inscription. It was the wittiest such note, Lawrence gloated, since Whistler's "Theodore—Whatt's Dunton?" and he had found a first edition for G.B.S. to reinscribe. He posted the volume to Charlotte, and asked her to ask Shaw if he would "preserve the memory of his jest, without labouring it."[1] "To Shaw from Shaw," G.B.S. wrote in the book, "to replace many stolen copies until this, too, is stolen." Another Shaw book missing from the Clouds Hill shelves returned a few days after they sailed for New Zealand— Lawrence's proof copy of *Too True*, which he had lent to Geoffrey Keynes.

G.B.S. did get a substantial amount of writing done en route to New Zealand. When the ship touched at Jamaica the Shaws sent a postcard (with a picture of the *Ranjitane* on the back) to Lawrence, telling him how the voyage had "renewed" them. However, the first play G.B.S. worked on—*The Simpleton of the Unexpected Isles*—came to a halt during the month they spent in New Zealand, and he claimed in a letter to St. John Ervine that he had forgotten it to such an extent when he was about to embark for home —and wanted to continue it—that he had to cable Blanche Patch, to whom he had sent the early shorthand draft, to ask her to send him a list of the names of the characters.

One thing that pleased him about New Zealand was that in a frenzy of anticommunism, a law had been passed prohibiting the landing of any person who had recently visited Russia. This Shaw discovered after having been feted and lionized in the principal cities of the Commonwealth. Lawrence, meanwhile, avoided London while the Shaws were away, visiting there only twice between February and May. Then, feeling the city Shaw-less and barren, he returned to his base sooner than was necessary each time. One London trip was to see novelist Henry Williamson, whom he had not seen in five years, embark on the *Berengaria*. Hands behind his back, leaning against a bulkhead, he waited at the dock for Williamson, and finally recognizing him, called out "in a voice soft with a slight Irish brogue, 'Is it you? You've changed. You're not so tall.' "

Williamson thought he heard a change that had taken place in Lawrence's voice over the years—"it had Bernard Shaw's brogue, but clearer, less Irish. . . ."[2]

Early in 1934 a number of factors were producing a radical change in Lawrence's attitude toward the world outside his enlisted man's milieu. Since his return from India, his work had been far from the ordinary routine of the ranks, and—as G.B.S. had predicted—T.E. seemed less and less to want to lose himself in the anonymity of that routine. His threats to resign if not given special employment demonstrated that change. With his enlistment entering its final year in March of 1934, he began to think about his public future, having long contemplated its private aspect, and found that despite his disclaimers in earlier years about interest in politics, these interests could not help but be reinforced by the disparate political involvements and interests of his friends. The Astors and their Cliveden visitors; Bernard Shaw and his increasingly political plays about the breakdown of parliamentary government in a crisis; the gravitation of friends such as Henry Williamson toward Mosley's British Fascists (Shaw, too, for a brief period, as his mischievous "In Praise of Guy Fawkes" speech to the Fabians showed);[3] the interest of other friends (whose leader was Churchill) in rearming England

against a threat from Nazi Germany—all these intensified
Lawrence's confusion about whether—and how—to seek
a place in the sun again, and attempt to influence the direction of the British transition.

In the nineteen thirties, as Lord Vansittart put it, some
came to Cliveden for its view of the Thames, while others
came for its view of the world. After G.B.S. had introduced him to Lady Astor, Lawrence visited the Astor resi-
dences at Plymouth and Cliveden often, except during the
Lord Thomson-enforced hiatus. He was at ease at Cliveden—to the extent of keeping some of his books there—and
sometimes he would arrive with the incongruous (but announced) intention of reading quietly. He often kept clear
of other guests, but when he discovered the atmosphere to
be to his liking found release from his aloofness and reticence. "If, for instance," Maurice Collis wrote in his biography of Lady Astor, "Bernard Shaw was asked, there
would be great fun, a sparkling conversation, wherein he
[Lawrence] was just as brilliant as Shaw or Lady Astor."[4]

The "Cliveden Set" of Lady Astor was not an organized
group, nor was it pro-Fascist as alleged, and the guests at
Cliveden represented less a collective view than a variety
of political opinions. Yet regular visitors were often later
accused of being part of a "Cliveden Set" by opponents
of the "Let's not be beastly to the Germans" school of
thought. Some of the most frequent guests at Cliveden were
also members of an influential group of Fellows of All Souls
College, Oxford, whom Lawrence had known since his
days as a Fellow—Lord Lothian, Lionel Curtis and Tom
Jones. Forming a powerful clique at All Souls were these
and other backroom figures and headline makers in the
vanguard of appeasement, committed from the early days
of Hitler's regime in 1933 to what now seems the almost
suicidally naive course of believing that international "fair

play" existed—that they could deal with Hitler and company as decent, honorable men across the bargaining table
from other decent, honorable men. In the All Souls group
were such manipulators of Imperial strings as Lord Halifax,
Viscount Simon and Geoffrey Dawson (editor of the
Astor-owned *Times* of London). The College they belonged to (and where Lawrence, as a resident Fellow,
stretched out full-length on the floor in a room overlooking
the entrance, had written much of *Seven Pillars*) is in some
ways an institute for advanced studies, after which Abraham Flexner patterned the American equivalent at Princeton. Unlike active Fellows at Princeton, however, many of
the Fellows of All Souls concurrently were (and are)
active in public life.

The "perennial game of remaking the Cabinet" was
played at Cliveden, including the theoretical relocating of
pieces removed from the chessboard. At one point Ramsay
MacDonald (whom G.B.S. and others of widely different
political faiths considered an apostate) was theoretically
replaced as Prime Minister and shunted off to the Colonies
to be Ambassador to the United States. At Cliveden, too,
Shaw, the literary peacock of the "Set," read his political
plays as they hatched. A similar country-house location
where some of the same people were often found was
Gregynog Hall, from which Tom Jones wrote to Abraham
Flexner in August, 1933, that after dinner each evening,
G.B.S. read to his guests from a new play that seemed to
Jones a British equivalent of a recent American novel,
*Gabriel over the White House*. The Prime Minister, Jones
reported, was a combination of MacDonald and Baldwin,
and goes off to a nursing home when a lady doctor, a
"healer," diagnoses his condition as an underworked brain.
At that place Shaw had stopped. In the next act, Jones
thought, the Prime Minister emerged as a Communist and

had a Cabinet crisis to contend with. The play was *On the Rocks*.[5]

Although Lawrence, through his friends, was on the fringe of both the All Souls group and the Cliveden circle, there is no substance for the conclusion that he shared much of their political or military (disarmament-oriented) viewpoints, or contributed to their making. He was not so much living in their world as living in contact with it. The pressure on him to resume political activity may not have been all indirect, nor of his own choosing. Erik Lonnroth, a Swedish historian, writes that "From Germany Hitler's men sought to establish contact with him, and the National-Socialist foreign affairs representative Kurt von Ludecke was in touch with him in 1932, but Lawrence rejected these advances." This suggestion, that he was considered by the emergent Nazis as a possible figurehead around which an English Fascist movement could rally popular support, has no basis in available circumstantial evidence, but nevertheless seems logical enough on the face of his associations, and may have been followed by a further overture in 1935.

Lawrence, however, was already aware of a possible war with Germany: he wrote to Lionel Curtis in March (1934) that he thought the R.A.F. could do a better job preparing for the aerial rearmament of Germany, even without greater expenditure, by creating the *"capacity"* to expand the R.A.F. rather than by building aircraft that would become rapidly obsolete. He wanted more airfields and more emphasis on up-to-date aircraft design and plant. He thought that large surface warships were sitting ducks in the air age, and wanted smaller, more maneuverable craft. [*Letters*, No. 513] In June, when he talked to Liddell Hart, he mentioned that the "Fascists had been after him" but that he "wouldn't help them to power." His chance would come not under Mosley, he told his biographer, but "if somebody big took him under their wing."[6] The "somebody" he had in mind may have been Churchill. Liddell Hart then asked Lawrence whether he would want to lead a new political movement, and he retreated to his oft-repeated determination to settle down at Clouds Hill. Nevertheless, the biographer reflected in his notes of the conversation, that Lawrence's attitude was "certainly changing—more than he is conscious of."

One thing that was not changing was his attitude toward his adopted name. In May, a publisher wanted to quote him on the dust jacket of Wilfrid Ewart's *Scots Guard*, and referred to him as "Colonel Lawrence of Arabia." Soon came the answer: "This is fourteen years out of date! My only legal name is Shaw. . . . I cannot be a Colonel and an aircraftman at once. . . . Introductions aren't ever wanted on books that are worth publishing. . . . If you want to quote me, you must use my correct name. . . ." It was signed "T. E. Shaw."[7]

Although he never used "Lawrence" interchangeably with Shaw, there appeared at the time a bogus double, who introduced himself to people as "Aircraftman Shaw, formerly Colonel Lawrence." Liddell Hart discovered the impersonation, and told Lawrence, who worried over how to take legal or other action to stop the impersonation. He must have more than one impersonator, he wrote Liddell Hart, in thanking him for the disturbing information. He regularly received letters, he noted, from "women of whom I appear to have taken some advantage. Sometimes when they get too urgent, I have got the police to help me out by asking them to make the correspondence cease." [*Letters*, No. 522]

On the thirteenth of June, with Eliot, his solicitor, he interviewed the bogus Lawrence-Shaw, who had been picked up by the London police, and turned out to be a little man who was under psychiatric care under the name of T. E. Lawrence. Since he was a "little worm of a man," Lawrence wrote Liddell Hart that he was not flattered that the impersonation had been so successful. The impostor agreed (after some persuasion) that he was neither Colonel Lawrence nor Aircraftman Shaw. [*Letters*, No. 528] It was not Lawrence's last such difficulty, for his notoriety bred impostors.

When the Shaws had returned from New Zealand in mid-May, he wrote them that his cottage was renovated, inside and out, and invited them to visit it with him when he could take time off from his work on R.A.F. boats at Southampton. The Shaws did get to inspect Clouds Hill again, but apparently (from his letters) without Lawrence, who appealed to them in July to make their next visit to his cottage when he could be there.[8]

During June and July, he had managed visits to the Shaws in London. The first time he discovered Charlotte was ill, and G.B.S. was out. The second time he found no one home at Whitehall Court, and was about to leave when G.B.S. returned. They went back in and had lunch, while Shaw regaled Lawrence with tales of rehearsing the new Malvern play, and about the origin of his new short play, *The Six of Calais*.[9] Before the First World War, Shaw had seen in the market place at Calais Rodin's heroic statue of the six burghers. Then he had gone back to Jean Froissart's *Chronicles* to see what had inspired Rodin, and decided that he could twist history into a better approximation of Rodin's figures. The project remained unrealized for twenty years. On July 17, the playlet had its *première* at the Open Air Theatre in Regent's Park, as a curtain-raiser for *Androcles and the Lion*.

Eventually Lawrence, then spending most of the summer

months at Southampton, and running target boats between Southampton and Plymouth, found that he could take time off to go to Malvern with the Shaws, and wrote for a program. Charlotte sent one, and he made plans to arrive on a Monday afternoon. Instead of accompanying the Shaws, he went straight to the Malvern Hotel. He was well-known there and did not need to wait for the Shaws to check in.

Roy Limbert, then the director of the Malvern Festival, recalled, in an interview fourteen years later in the *Yorkshire Evening Post*, G.B.S.'s rehearsing the Festival company that Monday:

> At rehearsals Shaw will act every part and produce every passage. Years ago he rehearsed us in *You Never Can Tell* at Malvern. The rehearsal started at 11 o'clock. Shaw said he was far too old to have a long rehearsal.
>
> That, mark you, was more than a dozen years ago. At 1:45 some exhausted actor murmured something about lunch. Shaw hadn't noticed the time. He apologized profusely. "We'll go immediately to lunch," he said. The Company breathed relief. "And," said G.B.S., "we'll be back at 2:15 sharp."
>
> Back they were. Throughout the afternoon Shaw played every part in turn, brilliantly. About 5 o'clock Limbert was a little worried. Another show was on that night, and a dress rehearsal was needed.
>
> He gently drew Shaw's attention to the time. Shaw was shattered. Again the passage of time had escaped him. "I must go," he said. "I have an appointment at 4 o'clock with the other Mr. Shaw."[10]

Soon after he returned from Malvern, Lawrence was shifted to Bridlington, in Yorkshire, to oversee the refitting and maintenance of the ten boats that serviced the R.A.F. bombing range offshore there. The work was scheduled to occupy him through the winter months, after which his term of service would be over—"world's end," he wrote a friend. The move delayed a visit to Ayot St. Lawrence, and he wrote the Shaws in November to apologize and to query G.B.S. about the progress of the revision of *The Simpleton of the Unexpected Isles*. He suggested idiosyncracies in the characters, "like that nest of hyenas that howl through Heartbreak House." There should be, he thought, a Colonial Secretary like Edward Marsh, a colonial governor like Ronald Storrs, a governor's wife like Lady Rhondda. He wanted characters, not animated ideas.[11]

A week later he wrote Charlotte that his Clouds Hill neighbor, Mrs. Knowles, had died suddenly. It considerably saddened the prospects of his retiring there, for just a few months before, he had arranged with the widow of his Tank Corps comrade to eat breakfasts at her home, and for her care of his cottage during his absences. In return, he had agreed to take over her lease, at £12 a year, which had eased her finances.

The same day (November 23), however, he turned down an offer from Sir Montagu Norman (later Lord Norman) to become—after discharge in March—secretary of the Bank of England. Lord Vansittart thought Sir Montagu was mad to make the offer, but for a number of reasons it was not strange at all that Lawrence, who had requested a night watchman's job in Threadneedle Street, should be offered instead one of Threadneedle Street's most important positions. The job was offered, he was told, because a man who was good at one thing could be good at anything else he attempted.

Perhaps, however, Sir Montagu had seen a kindred spirit in Lawrence. In *Georgian Afternoon*, L. E. Jones writes, "Sir Montagu Norman was a tremendous, but enigmatic, figure. With his long, pale, handsome face, his dark, pointed beard, his broad-brimmed, soft black hat, his cloak and cane, he looked to be every inch not a banker. He looked like a Spanish hidalgo, and a conspiratorial hidalgo at that. It was in keeping with this outward appearance that he had a taste for travelling incognito, as Mr. Skinner. But, like Aircraftman Shaw, he took care that the world should know who Mr. Skinner was and where he was going." Lawrence seems not to have written the Shaws about the proposition, for a few months later G.B.S. was still trying to secure the elusive pension, something he might not have done had he know that Lawrence had rejected the Bank of England sinecure.

In December, 1934, G. M. W. Dunn, an airman friend and an amateur poet, visited London and stopped in Lawrence's favorite bookshop, Bumpus's, whose proprietor, J. G. Wilson, was also Lawrence's friend. Wilson had recently decided to move the shop from 350 to 477 Oxford Street, and was holding an exhibition of rare books and masterpieces of bookmaking, in conjunction with a special sale. On display was Lawrence's copy of William Morris's Kelmscott *Chaucer*, lent for the occasion. Queen Mary, visiting the exhibition, admired it, and Lawrence was pleased. What he had not known was that also on exhibition was an Oxford edition of *Seven Pillars*, which he had let Bumpus's store keep for him, knowing that specially favored customers would be shown into a private back room to gaze upon the volume that was even more rare than the Subscribers' *Seven Pillars*. Not only was the Oxford *Seven Pillars*—far from a gem of typographical skill—on display, but with it, Dunn reported, was a letter to T.E. from Bernard Shaw. Much embarrassed, Lawrence had the letter and book withdrawn, apologizing to the Shaws that he did not know how the letter had slipped away from him.¹² Possibly it had been put away—for safekeeping—in the Oxford *Seven Pillars*, and had gone with it to Bumpus's.

By Christmas the Bumpus affair was settled, and the holiday season was marked by the usual chocolates from Charlotte, sent to the Ozone Hotel, Lawrence's official R.A.F. quarters in Bridlington, a gloomy boarding house overlooking the harbor. Off on *Boanerges*, he spent part of his Christmas leave visiting old haunts in London and Southampton, and managed to fit in an overnight stay in his cottage, where he discussed with Pat Knowles (the son of his late neighbor) the possibility of setting up a small printing press at Clouds Hill. After his discharge they would run off on their own press an edition of some form of *The Mint*. To Pat he talked of expanding the book to include later Air Force experiences. They thought of building a shed to house the printing equipment, and by May of 1935, Knowles had begun to acquire materials for the project. [*Letters*, p. 844]

He spent part of his holiday quietly reading and writing Christmas letters to his friends—all but Lady Astor, with whom he had developed an annual custom of sending her a reply-paid telegram of "Merry Xmas"—to which she answered "Same to you." At the time, the only thing he had to look forward to before discharge—which he anticipated with trepidation—was that *Too True to Be Good* was scheduled for a three-night stand at Bridlington. He wondered if it would be unseemly for him to see the play, as his presence was well-known in Bridlington. When it arrived, he and Private Meek became the major subject of conversation. Everyone waited to see whether he would go to the play to see himself. He did not.

Just before the new year Charlotte had written that since G.B.S. was exhausted from writing labors and other activities that went along with being a very public figure, she would again take him away from it all to go on a cruise to South America. It was her usual way of rationalizing her own desire to get away, but since G.B.S. was approaching his eightieth year, it was reasonable enough for both of them to look for a warmer climate in which to spend the winter months. There seemed little likelihood that Lawrence could get to see them before they sailed, and it seemed likely, moreover, that by the time they returned he would be a civilian again. He could not have known how ironic his lines to Charlotte were, in a letter written on the last day of 1934: "When you come back my great change will have happened. . . . When you come back, Time will mean nothing to me."[13] The same day he wrote a letter to G. Wren Howard, of the Jonathan Cape publishing firm which published his *Revolt in the Desert* and now was publishing the Liddell Hart study of Lawrence. After some brief paragraphs of business comment, he underlined: *"And may no other blitherer ever write a book about me until I'm dead, for Heaven's sake."* [*Letters*, No. 551]

With only sixty days of Air Force time left to him, Lawrence savored them, and hoped that each time he came upon something troublesome in his work on the target boats it would be capable of solution within his narrowing span of service. Hardly noticing, in his application to the task of winding up his R.A.F. work, that no mail from the Shaws was arriving at Bridlington, he wrote to them through January as if there had been no interruption in the continuity of their correspondence. He may have thought that they had begun writing to Clouds Hill, for in anticipation of his release he had begun telling friends to write to him there, and had supplied neighbor Pat Knowles with a stock of large stamped envelopes in which to forward mail at intervals of about ten days. In his instructions to Knowles he added that he wanted forwarded letters addressed to any of his names!

To Mrs. Shaw he wrote on January 13 that he supposed she was busy packing for the South American voyage, and admonished the Shaws to be careful of themselves, remembering their South African mishap. Another letter followed two weeks later, although there had been no news from them. Finally, in the last days of January, word arrived from G.B.S. that cruise plans were off. Charlotte had been seriously ill for weeks, but the Shaws did not want to disturb him with the news, for they realized the emotional wrench he was scheduled to undergo shortly in the form of an R.A.F. discharge. Mrs. Shaw had reinjured her South African wound while packing for the voyage and had been near death from blood poisoning, G.B.S. wrote, but she had now taken a turn for the better. Three doctors had been in attendance at Whitehall Court, including a titled homeopath from Harley Street.

In spite of the breathless haste of his letter and the bad news it contained, the playwright could not help but recall that Lawrence's local theatre in Bridlington had recently played what G.B.S. hastily or deliberately mistitled "Too Good to Be True." He wondered if T.E. had seen it.

Lawrence, having imagined the Shaws off on their cruise, was shocked: he had already been checking the mails for the inevitable Shavian postcard from the dock. Although he wanted to see Charlotte when she was well enough to receive visitors, for the time being he would not write, since G.B.S. had enough to worry about. So did Lawrence himself at the time.

One of his recurrent worries, especially since *Too True to Be Good,* had been the possibility of a film version of *Seven Pillars of Wisdom,* or of the Lawrence of Arabia story even beyond that. He was news, and there was no copyright on a news story. He was history, and there was no copyright on an historical event either. Shaw's play, in spite of its commercial failure, had almost created a film star out of the actor who played Private Meek. Pleased by the vivid impression Walter Hudd had made, Alexander Korda had placed him under contract to play the cinematic Lawrence. In January of 1935, plans still hung fire because of Lawrence's objections, but Walter Hudd remained under option. This time Lawrence went to see Korda personally and got him to agree to put the film off until its subject agreed to it—or was dead; and Hudd's film career as Lawrence ended before it began. Thirty years were to go by after the demise of *Too True* before a cinematic Lawrence was added to the theatrical prototype. And then the part was played not by an actor who physically resembled the short-statured prognathous Lawrence, but by an actor who towered eight inches over the figure he was recreating.

The Air Ministry had already decided that unless it heard from Lawrence "to the contrary" it would proceed to discharge him at the proper time. On February 6, he wrote to his superiors that he would make no attempt to sign on for another hitch, as he would be too old. He was forty-six, turning chunky and greying. But he knew he would "feel like a lost dog" when turned out. In its answer, apparently, the Air Ministry warned him that the press was beginning to get curious about his activities again, suspecting his imminent discharge. [*Letters*, Nos. 560, 561] Lawrence's friends did not help matters, for the *Sunday Express* on February 17 published a letter he had written to T. W. Beaumont revealing his intention to retire.

Anticipating an even heavier volume of correspondence following news of his discharge than before, Lawrence ordered a stock of Shavian-like correspondence cards printed, reading laconically:

To tell you that in future I shall
write very few letters.


                                    T. E. S.

He planned to put them, without comment, in nearly every letter he would henceforth write. But on many he could not restrain himself from appending a *verso* note.

To evade newspaper publicity, Lawrence was discharged on Tuesday, February 26, 1935, two days ahead of schedule. He left quietly on an ordinary bicycle, intending to visit friends as he traveled slowly south toward Clouds Hill. Although he had heard that reporters and photographers were lying in wait, his reception was beyond his expectation. They wanted to take his picture as a civilian, record his future plans, vie with each other for headline-making news about the "Prince of Mecca's" retirement. He refused all entreaties, insisting that he was no longer going to make any news. One reporter came with a questionnaire beginning with the wildly improbable "Do you plan to make yourself Dictator of England?"[14] They persisted, banging on the cottage door to demand that he pose for them. He opened the door far enough to lean out and punch one newspaperman in the eye, then slammed it shut again. The photographers then set a trap for Lawrence, who was becoming more interesting as he resisted. Had he made a few concessions to journalism, much of the persecution would have ended. While he remained indoors, the photographers hid a camera in the rhododendron bushes facing the cottage door, so that they could get a picture of him when he emerged. To get him to come out, two of the gentlemen of the press climbed a hill above the cottage and tossed rocks onto its roof. The tactics broke the siege, and some roof tiles as well.

Rather than give a perfunctory news conference which might, for lack of interest, have driven the press away, he managed somehow to escape—on his bicycle—to London. While he hid away as "Mr. E. Smith" in a rooming house at 3 Belvedere Crescent, reporters continued the vigil at Clouds Hill.

On the twenty-second of March, Lawrence, in gray flannel trousers and brown tweed coat, appeared at the hotel suite of Ralph Isham, who had given T.E. his address in hope of arranging a writing project for him. Isham had arranged *The Odyssey* publication with Bruce Rogers and proposed to Lawrence that he write a biography of Mohammed for the American firm of Simon and Schuster. Lawrence thought about it on the spot, and declined, saying that he wanted to forget the East, and did not need the money enough to forego idleness. They spoke of an approaching European war, and T.E. said he was worried most of all that a Mussolini-threatened war between Italy and Ethiopia might initiate what would eventually be a spreading conflict between the arrogant white race and the darker races of the world. They changed the subject, and the book on Mohammed was forgotten.[15]

In the middle of March the Shaws were able to pack their bags for the voyage delayed by Charlotte's serious illness. Where originally the cruise had been planned by her for the sake of her husband's health, it was now neces-

sary because of her own need to recuperate. Before they
left, G.B.S. felt he had to manage at least one more effort
to accomplish for Lawrence that which he had set out to
do a dozen years before, and had never forgotten. He got
in touch with Thomas Jones, a friend to whose interests in
the Gregynog Press both G.B.S. and Lawrence were devoted, and who had helped Lawrence get Doughty a Civil
List pension a decade earlier. Jones, a confidant of eminent statesmen, had been Deputy Secretary to the Cabinet, and was Secretary of the Pilgrim Trust. His diary
entry for March 19, 1935 has the ring of Shaw's epistles to
Baldwin in 1923 and 1924:

> G.B.S. is off to Africa "to leave the middle of the
> stage clear for the King." [the Silver Jubilee of
> George V in May] He suggests a brace of knight-
> hoods for the Honours List, the return of the Lane
> pictures to Dublin, "they are good enough for a ges-
> ture;" and a pension of £800 a year for T. E. Shaw,
> *alias* Lawrence, "now a destitute discharged aircraft-
> man." "Not since Belisarius has there been such a
> scandalous ignoring of supreme literary merit. I put
> it strongly to Baldwin years ago; but Baldwin is a
> genial smoker who promises everything."

Shaw could not have anticipated that by the time he would
return from his cruise Baldwin would again have become
Prime Minister, succeeding his partner in the Coalition
government, Ramsay MacDonald. But Lawrence, by then,
would be gone to rewards beyond the Civil List.

Shaw could also not have anticipated any interest on
Lawrence's part in political activity, nor any interest in him
on the part of the government, for Lawrence, who once
had regularly talked politics to Shaw, had not done much
of this for several years. T.E., who was probably unsym-

pathetic to the political direction in which G.B.S. leaned during the thirties, wisely turned the conversation to other matters so often that when Shaw was asked to contribute to the Lawrence memorial volume published in 1937 as *T. E. Lawrence by His Friends,* he could not recall Lawrence's discussing with him "politics or religion or any other branch of sociology," although he had "talked to him on every subject on which he could be induced to talk; and they were many and various. . . ." Lawrence never mentioned seriously anything connected with the trip G.B.S. and Lady Astor made to Soviet Russia, and avoided talking with Shaw about many of the important world issues arising in the early thirties. "Any little chieftain who was putting up a fight, whether in Morocco against Spain or in Syria against France, he would talk about with keen interest, laying down the law as to his strategy and his chances of success; but he showed no consciousness of the existence of Lenin or Stalin or Mussolini or Ataturk or Hitler. . . ."

Nevertheless, one of Bernard Shaw's comments picked up by the press the previous summer (June 23, 1934) sounded as if it had come from the experience and the developing interests of Aircraftman Shaw. "Bernard Shaw," it was reported, "today reduced the next war to an absurdity. 'Any war that happens now will swiftly end in a stalemate. The means for attack are tremendous but the means for defense are none. Suppose Italy declared war on England. Mussolini would send a first-class squadron of bombing planes with Balbo in command and in a few minutes would reduce London to ashes. We would do the same with Rome, and so on.' " The speculation turned out to be wildly wrong, but it was true that English air defense was in a primitive state.

The record of Lawrence's correspondence and conversa-

tions with other people than G.B.S. does not show the
diminution of interest in world affairs that Shaw later remembered, but Shaw's pronouncements on European politics at this time were too often irresponsible, and it is easy
to see reasons for Lawrence's reticence with him. On
March 16, 1935, for example, Hitler took to the radio to
announce that henceforth the Germans themselves would
be responsible for the safety and security of the Third
Reich. France had his solemn assurance that the Saar question had been settled, and that he would not "make or raise
any further territorial claims on France." Yet Hitler added
that because the "Jewish-Bolshevik" Soviet Union had rejected disarmament, he was obliged to adopt a similar
policy in the interests of German security. There was no
need for alarm, he cautioned, for Germany was not "seeking to establish a military hegemony in Europe."

In "Bernard Shaw and Adolf Hitler" [*Shaw Review,*
January, 1961], H. M. Geduld remarks, "Hitler's broadcast
created sensational news in every European capital; but it
did not disturb Shaw's equanimity." Newspapers on March
22 reported that before sailing for an extended vacation,
Shaw announced to reporters that "It is nice to go for a
holiday and know that Hitler has settled everything so well
in Europe."

It is unlikely that Lawrence ventured near Whitehall
Court while in London incognito. Their itinerary now
changed from South America to South Africa, the Shaws
were getting ready to embark upon the postponed cruise.
G.B.S. had been with Charlotte almost constantly during
her illness, leaving her only once, to week-end with Sir
Barry Jackson early in February. Charlotte refused to have
visitors while she was ill; and, as soon as she was able to
travel, went to Bournemouth with G.B.S. from March 3 to
March 11. Since the Shaws sailed from Tilbury on March

21, after returning to London for a fortnight of cruise preparations, there was not much time in which Lawrence could have visited the Shaws' flat. But he *had* expressed the desire to visit Charlotte when she had recovered from her illness, and apparently had not done so; and G.B.S. seems to have remarked then that they had not seen him for some time. It had been an unusually long absence, commented Shaw, wondering aloud to Charlotte whether there had been any quarrel or unpleasantness he had not known about. "No," said Charlotte—who could not have imagined Lawrence's confusion of mind at the time of his separation from the ranks that had been his bulwark for a dozen years. "No unpleasantness. But he is such an INFERNAL liar."[16] It was probably temporary pique, for Shaw himself often thought of T.E. as "not a liar" nor "a monster of veracity," but a "pure, undiluted actor."[17] He could only do so with a seldom-concealed admiration. G.B.S. was made of the same ingredients, as both he and Charlotte knew.

While in hiding in London during the middle of March, Lawrence emerged intermittently from his obscurity to visit news photographic agencies and newspaper proprietors to get them to agree to declare a moratorium upon Lawrence of Arabia stories. Since what he did was legitimate news, the best he could do was get an agreement that if he did nothing, they would have nothing to print. It was, as he told John Buchan, a "precarious peace." When he returned to Clouds Hill he found newspapermen still there, and his cottage and grounds damaged by their vigil. He left the cottage again until he could persuade the local police to patrol his grounds and ward off trespassers. During daylight he kept indoors—until he found he was running out of firewood.

Early in April he found himself finally free of newspapermen. He licensed his motorcycle, and rode into the

town of Poole to buy things he needed for the cottage. One
item on his shopping list proved difficult to obtain. Possibly
his fealty to G.B.S.'s *Heartbreak House* had created in him
a little of the retired seafarer in the character of Captain
Shotover, whose house was fitted out to resemble the after
part of a ship. Having left watercraft, T.E. missed their atmosphere, and wrote T. B. Marson on the sixth of April
that he needed a porthole and light for his upstairs room.
It was too small for a factory-made bed, and he had built
in a bunk of ship's cabin type, complete with drawers beneath to store his clothes. Because the recess was too dark,
T.E. wanted a ship's porthole, complete with the square of
plating into which it fit, to make it easier for installation in
the wall. Marson's connections with a ship breaker's yard
enabled him to acquire, with delivery within a fortnight,
exactly what he wanted to make a nautical bunk area in
which Captain Shotover would have felt at home.

The Shaws were then passing through the Suez Canal
and into the Red Sea. As they cruised near the scenes
of Lawrence's World War adventures (Charlotte wrote
to him), she and G.B.S. thought and spoke of him.
On the back of her postcard was a picture of their ship,
the two-stacked *Llangibby Castle*.

Almost imperceptibly to Lawrence, April faded into
May. Few friends heard much from or about him. He
seemed dazed by the reality of his leisure, much as Charles
Lamb described his own retirement in "The Superannuated
Man":

> For the first day or two I felt stunned, over-
> whelmed. I could only apprehend my felicity; I was
> too confused to taste it sincerely. I wandered about,
> thinking I was happy, and knowing I was not. I was
> in the condition of a prisoner in the old Bastille,
> suddenly let loose after a forty years' confinement. I
> could scarce trust myself with myself. It was like

passing out of Time into Eternity—for it is a sort of Eternity for a man to have his Time all to himself. It seemed to me that I had more time on my hands than I could ever manage.

From a poor man, poor in Time, I was suddenly lifted in a vast revenue; I could see no end of my possessions; I wanted some steward, or judicious bailiff, to manage my estates in Time for me. . . .

Lawrence wrote Sir William Rothenstein early in May that he spent much of his time just sitting and wondering about nothing in general, finding comfortable leisure "a very poor state after busyness." To Lady Astor he described himself as going about as if "there is something broken in the works. . . . my will, I think. In this mood I would not take on any job at all." [*Letters*, No. 582] To Eric Kennington, who wondered what T.E. was doing alone at Clouds Hill, he wrote: "Well, so do I, in truth. Days seem to dawn, suns to shine, evenings to follow, and then I sleep. What I have done, what I am doing, what I am going to do, puzzle me and bewilder me. Have you ever been a leaf and fallen from your tree in autumn and been really puzzled about it? That's the feeling." [*Letters*, No. 579] To Flight Lieutenant Norrington, with whom he had worked on R.A.F. boats, he wrote that life felt queer and aimless, and that he puttered about the cottage, beginning jobs and putting them down, unfinished. He advised Norrington to hang onto his job as long as he felt it was in his power, because there was a shattering blank afterward.

Whether Lawrence was being considered at this time for an important government post, and whether (in this condition) he could have or would have accepted it, has become a question about which there will be endless speculation until official papers or authoritative documents settle the dispute. Richard Aldington, in his "Biographical Enquiry,"

comments upon Lawrence's "habit of attributing offers of
imaginary grandeur to himself," and classified his confiding
to his Clouds Hill neighbor Pat Knowles early in March,
1935, that he might be asked to take over the job of reor-
ganizing "Home Defense," as such a fantasy. In Liddell
Hart's notes of a conversation with Lawrence on March 22,
1935, we find him referring to "approaches" that he become
"successor to Hankey," who was both Secretary to the
Cabinet and Secretary of the Committee of Imperial Defense. Lawrence, rather than being considered for a Civil
List pension, as G.B.S. stubbornly insisted, may have been
thought of instead for an active role. Winston Churchill,
Lord Winterton wrote in his memoirs, held the view "just
prior to Lawrence's death" that T.E. should be appointed
Minister of Defense. Churchill, though spokesman for a
large following in his party, held no office, and had no
direct power; but those in power, Liddell Hart thought
twenty years later, had something along lesser lines in mind:

> The actual defense post for which Lawrence was
> then being considered was not on such a high level,
> though of key importance. I was then military corre-
> spondent of the *Times*, and well acquainted with the
> whole background of the matter. There was at the
> time—early in 1935—a strong urge in government
> circles to develop our defense planning organization,
> in view of the rearmament program, and in this con-
> nection it was proposed that Sir Maurice Hankey,
> who was both Secretary of the Cabinet and Secretary
> of the Committee of Imperial Defense, should be pro-
> vided with a deputy and eventual successor on the de-
> fense side. Lawrence was quite correct when he said
> that he had "received approaches" whether he would
> take the post if asked—that fact was confirmed by
> several people who were close to the Prime Minister,
> Stanley Baldwin.[18]

Tom Jones (the former Deputy Secretary of the Cabinet), who was the very influential liaison between the feuding Lloyd George and Stanley Baldwin, seems not to have known of any political overtures to Lawrence. On May 20 Jones wrote to Lady Grigg (and quoted his remarks in his diary entry for the day) that G.B.S.'s entreaties to help put Lawrence on the Civil List would have been valueless because a more difficult task would have been to get him to accept it. His own plan, he added, had been to interest Lawrence in the production of Gregynog Press books, and he had acquired his address from John Buchan so that he could negotiate with him about it. If Lawrence had been talked of—or talked to—with regard to a government position, it appears clear that the soundings had escaped two men who had their ears to the political ground— Bernard Shaw and Tom Jones. Still, if true, Lawrence's entertaining the "approaches" shows how far he had come from the days when he wrote the Shaws that he wanted to be degraded to the ranks so that no one would ever want to offer him a responsible position again.

Though the offer apparently hung in abeyance as he dazedly savored his freedom in April and early May, he had, on his last trip to London, dropped a hint to Sir Herbert Baker (who was in contact with the mighty) that he ardently desired "to do some great national work." In an after-dinner discussion about national defense strategy, he talked of wanting to serve in the guiding of it. "Hankey has too much to do," he exclaimed.[19] Sir Maurice (later Lord) Hankey was—as C. P. Snow has described him in *Science and Government* (1961)—"one of the great invisible influences in English affairs, particularly military affairs, for a generation."

On the thirteenth of May, it must have seemed to Law-

rence that his opportunity to do "great national work" had
indeed arrived. The flattering suggestion arrived from his
Rightist friend Henry Williamson that he was the man to
negotiate an English *modus vivendi* with Nazi Germany. In
1935 it was still possible to be visionary about the Nazis,
though it was becoming more and more of a strain, even
upon the visionaries. But Williamson saw Lawrence as the
potential leader of an England that lived in friendship with
Germany. "You alone are capable of negotiating with
Hitler," he wrote to Lawrence. "I must speak to you about
this immediately." Why there was such urgency has never
been explained. Whether the Nazis professed some public
admiration for Lawrence, or thought of him as close not
only to English political life as viewed from Cliveden, but
close as well (even to adopting his name) to an English
writer who openly admired dictators such as Mussolini and
Hitler (albeit with reservations), who criticized English
parliamentary democracy, and some of whose plays were
permitted to be performed in the Third Reich, may never
be known. It is only a coincidence, no doubt, that among
the English-language volumes Tom Jones noticed in Nazi
Foreign Minister von Ribbentrop's personal library in 1936
were *Revolt in the Desert* and *The Intelligent Woman's
Guide*.

Any hope the Nazis may have had that Lawrence would
have been useful or was sympathetic to them was not
merely misguided. For Lawrence, it proved tragic. He responded to Williamson's suggestion by jumping on his
motorcycle and racing to the post office at Bovington
Camp, nearby, to send a telegram inviting his friend to
Clouds Hill the next day, May 14, rain or shine, to talk
politics: "LUNCH TUESDAY WET FINE COTTAGE ONE MILE
NORTH BOVINGTON CAMP."

Racing back to his cottage he saw in his path, just over

a dip in the road, two boys on bicycles. He swerved to avoid them, but was going so fast that his motorcycle skidded out of control, throwing him over the handlebars onto the road. His skull was fractured and there was severe damage to his brain. He was taken to the hospital at Bovington Camp, where he had first enlisted as Shaw. Never regaining consciousness, he died six days later, on May 19, 1935. He was forty-six.

Two days later Lawrence was buried at Moreton Church, near Clouds Hill. Storrs and Newcombe, of Arabian days, Kennington, Pat Knowles, a Tank Corps soldier and an airman were the pallbearers, while Winston Churchill walked behind, alone. A gravestone later identified "Shaw" by the name from which he could never shake completely free: Lawrence.

The sense of mystery which followed him, and which he abetted, through his adult life, pursued Lawrence even to his death. At the inquest, a witness—a corporal from Bovington Camp—thought he remembered seeing—just before the noise of the crashing motorcycle—a black car pass Lawrence speeding in the opposite direction. The boys on bicycles, shaken by the incident, remembered no black car passing them. [*Letters*, p. 873] Later there were even unfounded rumors of suicide, based more on Lawrence's intermittent despondency—and, perhaps, a misinterpreted remark of G.B.S.—than anything else, for though the rumors continue through the years, no evidence to support them exists.

At the time of his death, Lawrence's mother, seventy-three years old, was sailing down the Yangtze River with another son, and could not receive the news until she reached Shanghai. The Shaws, Blanche Patch recalls, were cabled the news by her. "His death was Greek tragedy to them. They met it like Stoics."[20] There was good reason, as few then knew. The Shaws had provided Lawrence with the motorcycle which led to his death. Later G.B.S., discussing T.E.'s mania for drowning himself in speed, confessed wryly that the gift "was like handing a pistol to a would-be suicide."[21]

At Durban, South Africa, newspapermen converged on G.B.S. when news that Lawrence had died reached the city. Shaw voiced his deep regret, then added: "What about Westminster Abbey? His country, which refused to give him a small pension, owes him at least a stone." But G.B.S. was too far away to do more than let the press carry his futile suggestion.

Saddened, the Shaws went through the motions of completing their cruise. En route home a week later, G.B.S. wrote a preface to *The Six of Calais* while at sea. "Life as we see it," he wrote, "is so haphazard that it is only by picking out its key situations and arranging them in their significant order (which is never how they actually occur) that it can be made intelligible."

# TEN

## *Epilogue*

On June 13, 1935, exactly one month after Lawrence's fatal crash, twelve of his friends met at a location which had been familiar to him: Martins Bank, in Lombard Street, London. They were Lady Astor, Sir Herbert Baker, Robin Buxton, Lionel Curtis, Alan Dawnay, Eric Kennington, B. H. Liddell Hart, Stewart F. Newcombe, Bernard Shaw, Sir Ronald Storrs, Lord Winterton and Lawrence's brother, A. W. Lawrence. The purpose of the meeting was to discuss the possibility of a memorial to Lawrence, and a small committee from the group was chosen to consider suggestions which might come to them after a notice of the group's intentions had been made public. G.B.S. recalled the meeting in an anecdote to Stephen Winsten:

> A number of friends met at Martins Bank to consider a memorial to Lawrence. One suggested that his face be carved on the rocks of Arabia, but he had overlooked the fact, which I had to point out to him, that the Moslems object strongly to the making of graven images. Then came the suggestion that there was a

277

certain book of which he had heard privately, which could be published as a memorial to its author. He told us that Lawrence had told him about this book on the understanding that he was not to whisper a word about this to anybody else. Of course, we soon discovered that Lawrence had mentioned the book to each one of us on the same promise. I had to show my copy to convince them that I, too, was in the know. Lawrence had that habit of making each feel that he alone was in his confidence. Need I say that the book suggested was none other than *The Mint!*[1]

Through the years after Lawrence's death, the Shaws must have felt the impoverishment of his loss. They were too old for another to replace him, as he had apparently replaced Granville Barker in their lives. Both G.B.S. and Charlotte thought that death, at forty-six, was in some ways a release for the tormented Lawrence, who might have been directionless in civilian life, and who they thought dreaded the attraction-revulsion which pain and the idea of death had for him. To both he seemed the strangest person ever to have come into their lives; yet to G.B.S., whom he resembled in many ways, and who created characters embodying many of Lawrence's traits long before the two met, he was a figure familiar as Keegan, the unfrocked Irish priest of the sickly conscience in *John Bull's Other Island*, who found that the world

is very clearly a place of torment and penance, a place where the fool flourishes and the good and wise are hated and persecuted, a place where men and women torture one another in the name of love; where children are scourged and enslaved in the name of parental duty and education. . . . It is a place where the hardest toil is a welcome refuge from the horror and tedium of pleasure, and where charity and good works are done only for hire to ransom the souls of the spoiler and sybarite. Now, sir, there is only one place of horror and torment known to my religion; and that place is hell. Therefore it is plain to me that this earth of ours must be hell. . . .

A little later in the same scene, in an encounter between Broadbent and Keegan, the Englishman admits complacently: "I find the world quite good enough for me: rather a jolly place in fact."

Keegan inquires: "You feel at home in the world then?" and gets a satisfied reply: "Of course. Dont you?"

"*From the very depths of his nature*" (G.B.S.'s stage directions read) comes Keegan's answer: "No."

Bernard Shaw's recollections of Lawrence, undimmed by time, were a strangely mixed lot. He was proud of his relationship to a man who had become a legend in his own lifetime, yet was jealous of his wife's attentions to Lawrence. It proved, he told Hesketh Pearson, that "If we had children, Charlotte would certainly have quarreled with me over them and would have been jealous." Often impatient with Lawrence, G.B.S. told friends that he was annoyed at T.E.'s constant deferential praise of him, in letters and in conversation. Yet, when David Garnett's edition of Lawrence's *Letters* was published, Shaw told Lady Kennet, "His letters to me are good. He couldn't fool me."[2]

The attraction the image of Lawrence had for G.B.S. continued into his nineties, probably renewed with each disposal of property he made in his later years, as he gave much of his memorabilia to the British Museum and offered smaller items for sale at auction at Sotheby's. In this way, from Whitehall Court and Ayot St. Lawrence, books and documents belonging to him and to Charlotte (who prede-

ceased him by seven years, in 1943), and reflecting their
association with Lawrence, gradually returned to his notice,
then disappeared from his life into public and private col-
lections. In his nineties the process still continued, and
G.B.S.—when he thought about it—was even irritated to
discover that Lawrence lurked so often in the corridors of
his consciousness. For after all, in the course of a long and
active life, he had known many of the great men of the
nineteenth and twentieth centuries, and no other figure was
so tenacious. Stephen Winsten (in *Shaw's Corner*) tells of
visiting Shaw in his ninetieth year and awakening the sage
from an afternoon nap. Shaw expressed his gratitude:

> "I was in the throes of a maddening dream. I was
> talking Chinese with T. E. Lawrence and quite flu-
> ently. He made himself perfectly clear to me and, of
> course, he laughed at all my jokes."
> "How do you know it was Chinese?"
> "I took it to be Chinese. It may have been a talk in
> the world beyond the grave. Only I don't believe
> there is a world beyond the grave, and the last person
> I want to talk to is Lawrence. Oscar Wilde, yes;
> Chesterton, yes, but not Lawrence."[3]

To the last, G.B.S. kept some of the mementos that linked
Private Shaw with Public Shaw. A photograph taken at the
Mount Batten R.A.F. station, before a seaplane, is still in
his desk at Ayot St. Lawrence. In the sitting room there is
a copy (one of thirty printed) of *Two Arabic Folk Tales*
translated by Lawrence and privately printed by Carlow at
the Corvinus Press, and presented to G.B.S. These, to the
pilgrim at Ayot St. Lawrence, are some of the outward
signs of the Shaw-Lawrence years. On hundreds of thousands of public and private library shelves are the results
of the impact, each upon the other, of T.E.S. and G.B.S.—

in such works as *Saint Joan* and *Too True to Be Good,* in *Seven Pillars of Wisdom* and *The Mint.* In these volumes—and to a lesser extent, in others as well—two incorrigible actors upon the world's stage pooled their unique and strangely complementary genius.

# Appendix

[SEE PAGE 28.]

The success in London and New York of Terence Rattigan's chronicle play *Ross* carries with it an unusual price tag; for there is the hazard that, in the wake of the theatrical success, history will again be replaced with new legends about the already sufficiently legendary "Lawrence of Arabia." The play, which first opened at the Haymarket Theatre, London, on May 13, 1960 (its American *première* was December 26, 1961), is built upon the scaffold of the last twenty-four hours of Lawrence's five-month career as Aircraftman Ross.

The curtain rises on an R.A.F. depot near London in the winter of 1922. A businesslike flight lieutenant is dealing out summary sentences to recruits guilty of minor infractions. Ross, a small man, older than most recruits, is marched in, and admits to the charge that he had been eighteen minutes late in returning to camp on expiration of his pass. Interrogation reveals that he had been in a motorcycle accident and had to run the rest of the way to camp, having been left "with very little bicycle." Pressing on with the inquiry, the lieutenant learns that Ross had been away to "have a meal with some friends" at "a place in Buckinghamshire." The recruit hesitates stubbornly when

asked his friends' names. When the officer makes it clear
that the request is an order, Ross sighs out the names of
Lord and Lady Astor, Mr. and Mrs. George Bernard Shaw
and the Archbishop of Canterbury. Enraged by what he
considers a provocative answer, the lieutenant throws his
pencil down, screams something about insubordination,
and orders Ross marched out.

After Ross returns to his hut, a demobilized ex-officer—
for economic reasons now in the ranks—identifies him as
"Lawrence of Arabia," and attempts to blackmail him; but
Ross, not rising with his billfold to the threat that the story
will be sold to the press, pleads hopelessly to be allowed to
find the peace he has sought as a private soldier. The play
soon fades into flashback as Ross sleeps; troubled dreams
shape themselves about Lawrence's rise to wartime leadership in Arabia and postwar notoriety as the subject of a
lecture-circuit. Inherent in these glimpses into Ross's Law-
rence-past (the body of the drama) is Rattigan's suggestion
as to why the masks of "Ross" and later "Shaw" had to be
adopted and the episode of "Lawrence of Arabia" closed
("I sicken myself").

The final scenes take place the next morning in the lieutenant's office. The story has broken; headlines bring the
harassed commanding officer in to arrange for the immediate—and quiet—discharge of A/C 2 Ross. Naively, the
lieutenant wonders aloud whether all the fuss and secrecy
have anything to do with the insubordination charge he had
scheduled for hearing. The commanding officer is incredulous. "You know who you've charged with insubordination? Lawrence of Arabia. . . ."

"He was late on pass," the lieutenant appeals, still not
awake to the situation. "I asked him who he'd been with
that night. He said the Archbishop of Canterbury (*his voice
begins to falter*) Lord and Lady Astor, and Mr. and Mrs.
George Bernard—oh my God!"

Ross, in his last scene, is packing his kitbag. His barrack-mates, unaware of his identity, look on uncomprehend-ingly, erroneously thinking that the discharge was ordered because the authorities thought that the quiet, older man did not "fit in." An airman asks him what he intends to do, and Ross quickly answers, "I'm going to get back into the R.A.F. as soon as I can."

"Think you can do that?"

"Well, I'll have to change my name, I suppose. Ross won't do anymore. Shaw. I thought of that this morning. . . ."

So goes the new legend of Lawrence's discharge as "Ross" and incarnation as "Shaw," the name he was to keep the rest of his life. It is not history, but it is—effectively so —the "Dramatic Portrait" of Rattigan's subtitle. The Law-rence who moves through Rattigan's drama is a dramatically realized study: effective theatre rather than chronology or literal fact. Like most writers of memorable plays based upon history, Rattigan has worried more about the illusion of history than about historicity. "It might well have hap-pened," says the playwright of the invented episodes that open and close his play. And it is likely that the consider-able public educated by his play, and then (since *Ross* is eminently cinematic) by the inevitable film made from the play, will soon come to accept the incidents which provide the frame for Ross not as having the appearance of truth, but as representing history.

The summary punishment scene and the under-wraps dis-charge scene the following morning are Rattigan's telescop-ing of history. They might well have happened, but would have to have been placed much later in time than Law-rence's "Ross" period. As "Ross" he was a lonely man, his enlistment cutting him off from many of his old friends as well as his postwar acquaintances. He had met Bernard Shaw in March, 1922, and had not yet seen him again, although their correspondence began in August, just before he enlisted. He was introduced to Lady Astor by Shaw (who in 1922 did not yet know her himself) almost seven years after the invented dinner at Cliveden House, his name first appearing in the Visitor's Book there in 1929.

In *Ross* the names of the Astors and of the Shaws have, because of their associations with Lawrence, the ring of authenticity. That of the Archbishop of Canterbury, though inspired humor, does not. It is unlikely that Lawrence ever met him, though it is possible that he met another prominent churchman, the "gloomy Dean" of St. Paul's (Dean Inge) through Bernard Shaw. Whether or not the two ever knew each other, it is interesting that G.B.S. later caricatured both friends in his religious farce, *Too True to Be Good* (1932), Lawrence as Private Meek, Dean Inge as The Elder.

Time is again telescoped in the events of Lawrence's discharge. A month actually elapsed between the howling headlines (December 27, 1922) of "Lawrence of Arabia" in the ranks "seeking peace" and the quiet carrying-out of a Cabinet-level discharge order on January 23, 1923. Other facts, too, are altered for dramatic effectiveness, a technique of which Lawrence himself was a master. He claimed that an officer had recognized him (no attempt at blackmail was ever mentioned) and sold the information to a newspaper for thirty pounds—a suspiciously Judas-like number. Rattigan changes the officer to an ex-officer serving in the ranks —a brilliant improvement upon Lawrence's history—and raises the price to one hundred pounds. Also, the sympathetic barrack companions of Ross, through the last scene, give no indication that they recognize him to be any more than a recruit both unemployable in civilian life and too old to have the stamina to begin again in the ranks. But their ignorance—a Rattigan invention—adds irony as well as compassion to the close. Lawrence himself realized that his presence was an open secret, and that his fellow "irks" often sheltered him from unwanted inquiries.

Lacking historic truth, the frame of the play has instead something perhaps more appropriate to history in the theatre—the appearance of truth. *Ross* may find its way upon that thinly populated shelf of dramas which have had the power to replace history with a legend perpetrated by the playwright.

# References

Key to abbreviations used in References:
Add. Ms.—British Museum Additional Manuscript.
A.l.s.—autographed letter signed.
A.p.c.s.—autographed post card signed.
Arents Ms.—G.B.S.'s autograph notes in Charlotte's copy of
    *Seven Pillars*. Arents Collection, New York Public Library.
HRC—Humanities Research Center, University of Texas.
T.l.s.—typed letter signed.
*Letters—The Letters of T. E. Lawrence*, edited by David Garnett, London, 1938.
*Exhibition Catalogue—Catalogue of an Exhibition of Paintings, Pastels, Drawings and Woodcuts Illustrating Col. T. E. Lawrence's book "Seven Pillars of Wisdom."* Preface by George Bernard Shaw. [See Bibliography]

## Chapter One

1. Christopher Hassall, *Edward Marsh: Patron of the Arts* (New York and London, 1959), p. 499.
2. Add. Ms. 45922, 31 Dec. 1922.
3. Add. Ms. 45903,4, 29 March 1927.
4. Stephen Winsten, *Jesting Apostle* (New York, 1957), p. 171.

## Chapter Two

1. Testimony of Pte. C. M. Devers, referred to in Edward Robinson, *Lawrence the Rebel* (London, 1946), p. 218.
2. *Exhibition Catalogue.*
3. Quoted by Erik Lonnroth, *Lawrence of Arabia* (London, 1956), p. ix.
4. *Letters*, p. 535. The letter has since been printed in full, and its author identified, in *Letters to T. E. Lawrence*, ed. A. W. Lawrence (London, 1962), pp. 119-20.
5. Gene Tunney, t.l.s. to David Marshall Holtzmann, 14 April 1960.
6. Mrs. Georgina Musters, t.l.s. to Sir Sydney Cockerell, 29 Oct. 1959.
7. Winsten, *Jesting Apostle*, pp. 142-43.
8. A.l.s., T. E. Lawrence to Harley Granville Barker, 2 Dec. 1923 and 7 Feb. 1924, Houghton Library, Harvard University. Also *Letters*, No. 241.
9. Anthony West, *Principles and Persuasions* (New York, 1957), p. 43.
10. V. S. Pritchett, *Books in General* (London, 1953), p. 38.
11. From an interview in *Shaw the Villager and Human Being*, ed. Allan Chappelow (London, 1961; New York, 1962), pp. 162-63.
12. Osbert Sitwell, *Laughter in the Next Room* (Boston, 1948), p. 123.
13. A.l.s. to Edward Garnett, 30 Jan. 1923. HRC.
14. Lennox Robinson, ed., *Lady Gregory's Journals* (New York, 1946).
15. *Exhibition Catalogue.*
16. *Ibid.*
17. Richard Farr Dietrich, "Shaw and the Passionate Mind," *The Shaw Review*, IV, 2 (May, 1961), p. 9.
18. *Ibid.*
19. Ms. correspondence in HRC.
20. See Lawrence's letters of 1923 in *Letters.*
21. Quoted by Sydney Cockerell in a letter to the author.
22. Arents Ms.

23. "Confusion on the Left," in *The Baldwin Age*, ed. John Raymond (London, 1960), pp. 66-67.


## Chapter Three

1. Add. Ms. 45903,4, 13 Dec. 1923.
2. T.l.s., 14 July, 1944, HRC.
3. C. M. Devers, "With Lawrence of Arabia in the Ranks. Personal Recollections of a Private in the Tank Corps," *The World Today*, L (July, 1927), 141-44.
4. Viola Meynell, ed., *The Best of Friends* (London, 1940), p. 360.
5. Arents Ms.
6. "New Lawrence Protest on Arabs Found; But Shaw Doubts Depth of His Bitterness," Associated Press dispatch in the *Boston Transcript*, 23 May 1939.
7. Add. Ms. 45903,4, 11 May 1924.
8. Add. Ms. 45903,4, 27 Sept. 1924.
9. *Letters*, No. 257.
10. Add. Ms. 45903,4, 13 Oct. 1924.
11. Add. Ms. 45903,4, 15 Oct. 1924.
12. Memorandum of Agreement, 26 March 1925, 4pp., with holograph corrections by Shaw, Lawrence and Savage. Collection of Bayard L. Kilgour.
13. A.p.c.s., HRC.
14. Add. Ms. 45903,4, 4 July 1925.
15. Add. Ms. 45903,4, 28 Sept. 1925.
16. Add. Ms. 45903,4, 24 June 1926.
17. Add. Ms. 45903,4, 22 August 1926.
18. Florence Hardy, *The Later Years of Thomas Hardy* (New York, 1930), pp. 249-50.
19. Add. Ms. 45903,4, 2 Dec. 1926.


## Chapter Four

1. S. N. Behrman, *Portrait of Max* (New York, 1960), p. 279.
2. *Ibid*. The friend was Sir William Rothenstein, who also knew Lawrence well.
3. Pritchett, *Books in General*, p. 42.

4. Richard Aldington, *Lawrence of Arabia* (London, 1955), pp. 328-29.

5. R. A. Scott-James, *Fifty Years of English Literature* (New York and London, 1951), pp. 190-92.

6. Winston Churchill, *Great Contemporaries* (London, 1959 [first publ. 1937]), pp. 133-34.

7. Jean Beraud Villars, *T. E. Lawrence* (London, 1955), p. 296.

8. *Ibid.*, pp. 296-97.

9. Malcolm Muggeridge, "Poor Lawrence," *New Statesman* (27 Oct. 1961), p. 604.

10. A.l.s., Lawrence to E. M. Forster, 27 May 1927. Collection of Bayard L. Kilgour.

11. E. M. Forster, *Abinger Harvest* (New York, 1936), p. 146.

12. See G.B.S.'s equation of *Seven Pillars* with Milton in his *Spectator* review.

## Chapter Five

1. Add. Ms. 45903,4, 28 Jan. 1927.

2. T.l.s. to Lawrence, 7 March 1927.

3. Add. Ms. 45903,4, 19 May 1927.

4. T.l.s., G.B.S. to Lawrence, 23rd June 1928. Letter inserted in Lawrence's copy of *The Intelligent Woman's Guide*. HRC.

5. Add. Ms. 45903,4, 18 Aug. 1927.

6. Add. Ms. 45922, 17 May 1927.

7. M. R. Lawrence, ed., *Home Letters of T. E. Lawrence* (Oxford, 1954), p. 368.

8. Margaret I. Cole, ed., *Beatrice Webb, Diaries 1912-1924* (London, 1952), pp. 62-63.

9. Add. Ms. 45922, 9 Sept. 1927.

10. Add. Ms. 45903,4, 27 Dec. 1927.

11. Add. Ms. 45903,4, 4 Jan. 1928.

12. Blanche Patch, *Thirty Years with G.B.S.* (London, 1951), p. 80.

13. Add. Ms. 45922, 16 Jan. 1928.

14. W. M. M. Hurley, in *T. E. Lawrence by His Friends*, A. W. Lawrence, ed., (London, 1937), pp. 407-08.

15. T.l.s., G.B.S. to Lawrence, 23rd June 1928.

16. Add. Ms. 45903,4, 16 Feb. 1928.

17. T.l.s., 12 April 1928.

18. From the manuscript in the British Museum.
19. Stephen Winsten, *Days with Bernard Shaw* (New York, 1949), p. 267.
20. T.l.s., G.B.S. to Lawrence, 23rd June 1928.
21. *Ibid.*
22. Early proof of special Lawrence titlepage to *The Intelligent Woman's Guide*, with autograph revisions in G.B.S.'s hand. HRC.
23. Standard Edition (London, 1932), p. 74.
24. *Ibid.*, p. 339.
25. St. John Ervine, *Bernard Shaw, His Life, Work and Friends* (London, 1956), p. 516.


Chapter Six

1. T.l.s., Lord Thomson to G.B.S. Published by permission of the Air Ministry.
2. Henry Williamson, *Genius of Friendship* (London, 1941), p. 32.
3. Add. Ms. 45903,4, 29 July 1929.
4. Add. Ms. 45903,4, 23 Nov. 1929.
5. Add. Ms. 45903,4, 11 Nov. 1929.
6. From an interview with Fred Drury in *Shaw the Villager and Human Being*, ed., Chappelow, p. 53.
7. Patch, *Thirty Years with G.B.S.*, p. 85.
8. Clare Smith, *The Golden Reign* (London, 1940), pp. 109-10.
9. *New York Times*, 17 Nov. 1930, p. 1. However, Lady Astor had ridden pillion with T.E. before, in April, 1930.


Chapter Seven

1. Add. Ms. 45903,4, 29 March 1931.
2. Add. Ms. 45903,4, 26 June 1931.
3. From the manuscript of the Lawrence translation of *The Odyssey* in the British Museum.
4. Add. Ms. 45903,4, 9 Jan. 1932.
5. Letter to the author from Walter Hudd, 27 Dec. 1960.
6. Reprinted in Desmond MacCarthy, *Shaw* (London, 1951), p. 190.
7. *The Times* of London, 14 Sept. 1932, p. 8.

8. Letter to the author from Walter Hudd.
9. Add. Ms. 45903,4, 21 Oct. 1932.


Chapter Eight

1. Arents Ms.
2. Ervine, *Bernard Shaw, His Life, Work and Friends*, pp. 521-22.
3. Sitwell, *Laughter in the Next Room*, p. 211.
4. John Farleigh, *Graven Image* (London, 1940), pp. 248-49.
5. Allan Wade, ed., *The Letters of W. B. Yeats* (London, 1954), pp. 801-02.
6. A. W. Lawrence, ed., *Letters to T. E. Lawrence* (London, 1962), pp. 213-14.
7. Add. Ms. 45903,4, 24 April 1933.
8. Add. Ms. 45903,4, 5 March 1934.
9. Add. Ms. 45903,4, 12 Nov. 1933.
10. Add. Ms. 45903,4, 9 Dec. 1933.


Chapter Nine

1. Add. Ms. 45903,4, 2 Feb. 1934.
2. Williamson, *Genius of Friendship*, pp. 58-59.
3. G.B.S.'s leanings even encouraged an overly optimistic article, "G.B.S. on the Brink—Will He Ever Wear a Blackshirt?" in a 1934 issue of the British Union of Fascists' *The Fascist Week*. Hope that he would become the movement's patron faded rapidly.
4. Maurice Collis, *Nancy Astor* (London and New York, 1960), p. 151.
5. Thomas Jones, *A Diary with Letters, 1931-1950* (Oxford, 1954), entry for 27 August, 1933.
6. *T. E. Lawrence to His Biographer Liddell Hart* (London, 1938), entry for 25 June 1934.
7. G. F. Sims (Rare Books), Catalogue No. 39, item 91.
8. Add. Ms. 45903,4, 19 July 1934.
9. *Ibid.*
10. *Yorkshire Evening Post* (Leeds), August 18, 1948, quoted in Archibald Henderson, *George Bernard Shaw* (New York, 1956), p. 681.

11. Add. Ms. 45903,4, 16 Nov. 1934.
12. Add. Ms. 45903,4, 11 Dec. 1934.
13. Add. Ms. 45903,4, 31 Dec. 1934.
14. A. W. Lawrence, in *T. E. Lawrence by His Friends*, p. 595.
15. Ralph W. Isham, in *T. E. Lawrence by His Friends*, pp. 304-06.
16. Arents Ms.
17. Arents Ms.
18. B. H. Liddell Hart, "T. E. Lawrence: Man or Myth?", *Atlantic Monthly*, November, 1955, p. 71.
19. Sir Herbert Baker, in *T. E. Lawrence by His Friends*, p. 254.
20. Patch, *Thirty Years with G.B.S.*, p. 87.
21. Stephen Winsten, *Shaw's Corner* (New York [1951]), p. 82.


## Chapter Ten

1. Winsten, *Days with Bernard Shaw*, pp. 267-68.
2. Kathleen, Lady Scott (Lady Kennet), *Self-Portrait of an Artist* (London, 1949), p. 327 (entry for 25 Nov. 1938).
3. Winsten, *Shaw's Corner*, p. 21.

# Bibliography of Major Publications

*T. E. Lawrence (Shaw)*

*Seven Pillars of Wisdom: a Triumph.* London and New York, 1935.
*The Letters of T. E. Lawrence,* ed. David Garnett. London, 1938.
*T. E. Lawrence to his Biographer, Robert Graves* and *T. E. Lawrence to his Biographer, Liddell Hart.* London, 1938.
*Oriental Assembly,* ed. A. W. Lawrence. London, 1939.
*The Home Letters of T. E. Lawrence and His Brothers,* ed., M. R. Lawrence. Oxford, 1954.
*The Mint. A day-book of the R.A.F. Depot between August and December 1922 with later notes by 352087 A/C Ross.* London, 1955.


*Bernard Shaw*

*Catalogue of an Exhibition of Paintings, Pastels, Drawings and Woodcuts Illustrating Col. T. E. Lawrence's book "Seven Pillars of Wisdom."* The Leicester Galleries Exhibition No. 427, February 5th-21st, 1927. London, 1927. [Preface by Shaw]
*The Intelligent Woman's Guide to Socialism and Capitalism.* London, 1932.
*The Adventures of the Black Girl in Her Search for God.* New York and London, 1933.
*Prefaces by Bernard Shaw.* London, 1938.

*The Complete Plays of Bernard Shaw. London,* [1949].

[Letters] *To a Young Actress.* New York, 1960.

*Platform and Pulpit,* ed., Dan H. Laurence. New York and London, 1961.


*Other Sources*


Richard Aldington, *Lawrence of Arabia. A Biographical Enquiry.* London, 1955.

John Buchan, *Memory Hold the Door.* London, 1940.

Allan Chappelow, ed., *Shaw the Villager and Human Being.* London, 1961; New York, 1962.

St. John Ervine, *Bernard Shaw. His Life, Work and Friends.* London, 1956.

Archibald Henderson, *George Bernard Shaw: Man of the Century.* New York, 1956.

Thomas Jones, *A Diary with Letters, 1931-1950.* Oxford, 1954.

A. W. Lawrence, ed., *T. E. Lawrence by His Friends.* London, 1937.

——, ed., *Letters to T. E. Lawrence.* London, 1962.

B. H. Liddell Hart, '*T. E. Lawrence.*' *In Arabia and After.* London, 1934.

Erik Lonnroth, *Lawrence of Arabia.* London, 1956.

Blanche Patch, *Thirty Years with G.B.S.* London, 1951.

Hesketh Pearson, *G.B.S. A Full-Length Portrait.* New York, 1942. *G.B.S. A Postscript.* New York, 1951.

Terence Rattigan, *Ross. A Dramatic Portrait.* London, 1960.

Clare Sydney Smith, *The Golden Reign. The Story of My Friendship with 'Lawrence of Arabia.'* London, 1940.

Robert Vansittart, *The Mist Procession.* London, 1958.

Jean Beraud Villars, *T. E. Lawrence.* London, 1955.

Henry Williamson, *Genius of Friendship. 'T. E. Lawrence.'* London, 1941.

Stephen Winsten, *Days with Bernard Shaw.* New York, 1949.

——, *Shaw's Corner.* New York [1951].

——, *Jesting Apostle. The Private Life of Bernard Shaw.* New York, 1957.

# Index